Unwanted

孤兒

(Orphan)

Al Lovejoy

Mail: lovejoytrust@yahoo.co.uk
WhatsApp: +27 72 733 27 32

Printed by Tiny Little Faeries Inc., In the Land of Nod.

First printing, 2021.

Rabbithole Tie Press.
Under the Oak Tree.
The Shire.

Also by Al Lovejoy:

Acid Alex

The Smell of Tears

to

Jean, my darling Big-Sis

Eric, my Blood Brother

Joe, The Hobbit

Minkeyboy, who shares his DNA with me

(… and his loving Minkeymomma)

&

For my entire lost family … out there …

This is for you, so that we can bring you all **Home***.*

Author's Note

This is either going to make you wildly excited or … *very*, *Very Angry* – either way … you have been *Warned.*

If this book does unveil incipient balkanization, Awesome! Because that means *you* have personally discovered the first basic lesson regarding the nature of hate. And that is: *being full of hate,* is exactly like *drinking poison*, then wistfully hoping that person *you* actively despise – *will die*. Nope, this book cannot help *you* at all. *And,* it will fuel more sputtering outrage in whatever *you* have left of an independently functioning mind – So, all the very best and most gracious good luck with that! *Bon voyage …*

This tiny tome is about the deadly vanities of mortal apes and fake magic rings. Of greedy indecent kings. A map. Peering at shapes, *convening* within the misty futures we are loaning from tiny *Unwanted* miracles.
Should this provoke a sense of *Awakening …*

Then, Cousin – *You* might want to think about *Being* what the *Great Scholar* suggests … then tune in…
… turn on… *get down,* and roll on down the rocky road … *with Us.*

The true strength of this book will undoubtedly reflect in your unabashed willingness to openly share that you have read *Unwanted…*

… and …

‡§‡

This was written for the current ___ and on behalf of the future ___ *Empire.*

I accept, *Full Responsibility* – for nothing less.

Peace out Y'all …
Al

‡§‡

Acknowledgements

Top of the list is you Son.

Thank you for convincing me, *once you understood why* – That I have no choice, *I have to write this…*

Similar thanks to Eric.

You were right, I needed to inject some structure into thoughts and put the flesh into my *Mission*.

Big-Sis, if it weren't for you being a rock-solid anchor in my life – I doubt that I would have been able to give voice to this either.

Thx for just being there.

And so … to the Hobbit…

Well done!!

Dude, if it were not for your insights and feather touch, *Unwanted* would have been far more difficult to write. I think I've maybe mentioned this. Who knew you had a top-notch closet editor in you?

Let's assure ourselves we did our job well enough for the Reader, *and* ultimately … *this Idea!*

My greatest thanks go out to the folks who also convinced me that I have to write this on behalf of their communities and *Unwanted*.

The truly sad thing is most of them will never be able to read this, much less understand the text.

Neither those who urged me on … *nor the ones still to come.* Voices that will never be able to be heard – unless someone makes the choice to stand in for them.

The primary reasons why this was written in the first place. To work towards putting *an end* to that sort of thing.

Lastly, if you are returning to this book, this time as a *Pearl of Wisdom* … then, We, all bow to you in deep respect, *and* … with eternal enthusiastic gratitude and thxs … *Thank You.*

Al Lovejoy
Stellenbosch – November 2021

Table of Contents

蜘蛛蟹

Spider Crabs – 14

陰

Yin

看到

The See – 122

陽

Yang

‡§‡

蜘蛛蟹

ancient volcanic sands erupt
dark mushroom cloud blooms
billowing every violent fury.

corals blizzard
smoky Brownian dearth
tainting bright
briny azure.

yet so,
from the Deep
Our
merciless claws march onwards.

festering mindless legionairés,
crusading
lightward obscenely,

to
war and war and war
and war then even more

in endless
frantic
chattering black-masses.

hissing, scratching
chitinous demonéan.

righteous
unto the very Light.
and upon
these:
our most foul
Evil

Crustacean Brothers

‡8‡

陽

Mother's Memes
for
Fathers Only

Words exist because of meaning
Once you have the meaning,
you can forget the words.

Where can I find a man
who has forgotten words,

So … I can talk with him?

~ Chuang Tzu ~

I don't mind dying
but I sure hate to leave my children
I don't mind dying
but I sure hate to leave my children cryin'

Robert Plant – "Funny in my mind"

<u>All We Need is Love (A-side)</u>

With all the things that have been *said and done* … 20/21, is definitely and has rather curiously become the most focused 20/20 point of hindsight the human race has ever been afforded.

Or, more to wit … had enforced upon it *pandemically* – since that momentous day when Michael Collins became the first person to take a color photograph of all of mankind …

Say Cheese

Snapped, during that grand international celebration of Neil Armstrong's Giant Leap for Mankind – which looks totally cool from the high… *almost* Pink Floyd – Dark Side of the Moon's perspective.

But … then again… utterly diabolical and the pretty space-marble *photo-op* mere political meaninglessness – from inside the hellish nightmare of an underground bunker network somewhere in Vietnam,

Where …

… A young gang-rape survivor, skillfully cradling a Soviet AK-47, tries to feed two tiny terrified twins small rancid rice balls by a flickering oil-wick lamp. Listening with a highly trained ear for politically expendable adolescent Tunnel Rats, whom she knows to be a bigger threat than Uncle Sam's Air-to-surface Missiles, Agent Orange, and the Devil-infused Napalm raining down on her world from the unseen Hells above.

She holds her breath in petrified horror.
Not for herself …
One good strike, and …
… and her little ones are gone.

Buried alive – deep into a shallow political grave.

Remnant of a beautiful green world she was born into but cannot freely roam, live in, care for her children, and watch them grow up openly …
… without suffering the terror of cold evil men … she has never met.

Monsters, exactly like their brutal faceless fathers … who will kill her and her babies – with no more value assigned to her, and millions like Her – than the inevitable outcome of a vastly more important, geospatial, and three-dimensional Global Equation.

She's been here and the other lightless places of their relentless war of hate against her kind, exactly like the French, and long before the cursed Yankees started building vile war-penis rockets.

The moon is a million miles away.

Especially when you cannot see it through smoke, scorched jungle, and the stench of blind burning corpses.

And what exactly is a million miles?

Far enough … Not to hear … the delicious sounds of French champagne and fine crystal embracing. The faux smacking of painted lips … not-quite kissing-up to scarlet détente – yet feverishly celebrating Everything, and ultimately ingesting nothing more than tomorrow's dreary merde…
… with foul-mouthed morning breath.
That far?

Far enough not to be able to spit their saintly acerbic spite … at her Unwanted babies personally?

Her children may never know this.

They've never even seen the moon …
… far too dangerous for them.

So, she does what she has to do … listens through the earth-shaking crumps of the detonating bombs… listens for the creeping death whispers of equally terrified GIs … listens into the endless clawing dark inside the dusty tunnels … tries to hush her babies' whimpers. Dry their choking tears. Doggedly feeds them too little from almost nothing … keeps her finger pressed rigidly onto the cold carbine's trigger guard … and waits for Orders.

But, secretly entreaties the Sacred Mother of her grandmother's ancestors … grits her weary stained teeth …
… Curses bayoneted Hope.

‡§‡

‡§‡

The only difference between 1969 and 20/21, is way back then – We still appeared to believe *We* had everything – including all the *Right* choices.

To be, or not to be … A Believer …

… without a leaden shred of doubt in John Lennon's mind.

American … *unamerican,*
Right-Wing … *wrong-wing*
Grunt … *hippy,*
Square … *queer,*
Taxpayer … *welfarer,*
Cracker … *niggra,*
Fuzz … *felon,*
Owner … *bum,*
Heir … *bastard …*
Born-Again … *eternally Cursed.*

Menkind - and a lone century of the merciless Universal Suffrage of … A momentary Title 9 woman. Dragged barefoot from the kitchen and into WWII … to cook two glowing shiitake mushroom clouds.

Imagine that…

And bring on:

The dawning of the Age of Aquarius.

Funny thing – *belief,* it still seems to be the one utterly irrational, yet very ancient mindset, which constantly undermines and completely defeats mankind. Pre-dooming His civilizations and undermining every half-baked revolution in between.

The cerebral womb of that quaint, *yet lurid insanity,* we apes espouse, ostensibly uphold – and act out indignantly … *then* smugly label:

Moral Certitude.

As a relevant aside on defining this particular semantic point – Herewith,

~Memes~

[*In the non-unimmortal words of Sir Terry Pratchett*]:

"*Humanity had arrived as a nasty shock. Humanity practically was things that didn't have a position in time and space, such as imagination, pity, hope, history, and belief. Take those [~Memes~] away and all you had was an ape that fell out of trees a lot.*

Intelligent life was, therefore, an anomaly." – Thief of Time, Terry Pratchett

And so, it is … with *~Memes~*

Thump
Ook?

Today, and more succinctly – right within the indifferent sunny bosom of this highly imaginary Universe – the common, or concrete-garden type *Homo Sapiens'* prevailing *~Memes ~* are not quite so aligned with the good Sir's well detached yet *cut-me-own-throat* razor-sharp perspicuity.

"Great" Naked Apes accidentally managed to lay opposing thumbs on advanced computers, only to instantly realize mass-ventriloquism … through manufacturing baying chorales of smoldering outrage embedded into early 21st-century Big-Tek cyber-entities like Facebook, Twitter, and wam-bam Instagram *et al.*

Modified algorithms more The Shit than Jesus since … erm … well since He ostensibly disappeared [Probably nipped off for a quick joint] in a billowing cloud of smoke along with some alien-looking fellas hovering about on giant wings and subsequently – *Good Lord God That Hurt…*
  … forgot to come back.
  Which, (*in an aside*) gave rise to:

All sorts of wild apocalyptic speculations – indefatigable bloodlust – extortion – cross-dressing – slavery – torturous inquisitions – money-laundering – kicking the everliving heath out of Moorish heathen arse – coupled to the odd bit of horny flagellation – lashings of sadistic frigidity – ruthless Clerical real-estate acquisition – the artistic & intellectual development of something dark, funky and weird called Satanism – along with multilingual blasphemy (mostly aimed at His Mom) – hideously ghastly stake burnings[1] – and coupled to the sweaty-plamed pursuit of deeply pious soft-pederasty – for thousands of awful …
  miserating …
  … godforsaken years.

Until The Beetles playing on sixties' eight-tracks stopped all that hogwash and almost instantly morphed into much bigger superstars than his – *Good God Are You Mad?*
  But seriously, one doesn't see Mr. Joe Facebook poking Miss Jane Twitter on LSD™…

Now, do you?

---

[1] To banish the lying *Demons of Science* and cut out the *Porca Madonna Merde Madre (the Virgin Mary is a Pig Shit Mother)* type insults aimed at His Mum

In fact, it's the other way round, and these transistorized *bash-trash-cash* Graffiti-laden chatterboxes *Are* seriously mega-trending and way bigger than Jesus … Uncle Paul, Ringo, and that other Yoko-detesting lad … George – all put together.

I mean, where the smelly doorknob is Elvis when you need a straight-shooting crooner with killer sideburns, a double-jointed pelvis, and a rhinestone-encrusted mancave on Mars to take the blistering heat off on the Lord's Top 40?

A truly ingenious way to intraconnect opposing thumb-sucked notions [Shocking Fibs] halfway around the world. *And,* without going to all the unnecessary fuss and medical bother of Truth trying to put on the shorts of a savagely enraged leopard that flatly refuses to exchange its spots for stripes.

The real reason why El Lie is a Super Platinum Global Traveler with centuries of frequent flyer miles, all suave, natty, and squiffed up to the nines – yet poor pale Truth … still pimple-arsed starkers and busy rummaging around in the cabinet under the washbasin in the bathroom - for iodine, sutures, forceps, arterial-clamps, aspirin, a defibrillator, and industrial-sized Band-Aids.

Exeunt: *The so last season of The Age of Aquarius … tout suite,* and *voila!*

Be Beholden!

Unto … the newly self-ordained, *digitized,* High-Priests of the Sacred Order of Crypto-Minted-Doctrines … Eternally Holy … unto thee Greater Glories of Cultural Marxism.

Amxn.

Channeled, *sans crystals*, to reboot all of Menkind's nudely naked posteriors … *back* into the almost appeased arms of the nearest socially acceptable Big-Tek cyber-deity.

Most especially when firmly and directly re-applied to:

Ultra-Critical Race Theory.

Which, doesn't have solid gender, but is possessed by an anus and yet another forty-nine sphincters … *theoretically* …

Dearly Beloved.

This *Utopic Nouveau Devotionale,* is applied altruistically in the form of anti-incorrect cyber-groupies … catechizing their cute little *sycophant-news-bot-spawn* – to *preach* the non-dark neo-gospels. Followed … endlessly … by incoherent choirs of distortive droll trolls.

Desperate, and needing some sneaky shadow to lurk … then group-chant, and sup-seek on social media for emotional appeasement and vastly irrelevant – *Relevance*.

Keeping the faith – surfing, trawling – *stalking*.

Saintly keyboard-ninjas, aka S.J.W. Corps. Deep-Recon-Delta S-LURP Counter-Kong Brown-bag Zulu-Whisky COIN Operatives …

… armed to the floating amalgam fillings with a smidge more than a soupçon of confirmation bias. Slinging boldly sloganized *eternal-damnation Proto-cartoons* … as hook and claymore [Bendy Part Faces Enemy. Do Not Eat].

Ever marching onward … fingers *triggered* feverishly …

As *blessed* Mass Missionaries ecstatically Frankenstein-evangelizing. *Ad-hominem* …

… ad, *ad-hominem* …

~Meme~ by vexatious counter *~Meme~*

Endeavoring to thus redeem the surface-Internet's flashing veneer from collapsing under the spam of the ancient village curse – in direct regards to the sniggering truth about poorly fed propaganda mal-awareness avatars, and their skinnied side-kick sock puppets.

Toss in the morale-boosting tail of a leopard's pigheaded mono-fashion dress-sense in co-regard to butt naked Truth … and … *you* … *So be done, Boss.*

A trippy functional extrusion of very well-designed … *clickety-click-bait doorknobbery.*

Sleekly peddled by cyber-fakirs[2] to cut-and-paste … *pre-edited imbeciles.*

For Free!

Click, clicky, click, clack
Thump!
Ookook, Oook, Eeeeek!!
Beep

Here in 20/21, I think most sane folks know this dirty-mind-fuzz … *Cyber Rent-A-Policing* … to be a mangy pavement-mutt's hirsute arse-fixture – wagging the furiously lumpy walnuts offa wildly barking bull-turds.

Burdened with a noticeable whiff of *Scrofula* comorbid with acute *Dropsy* … And … if I'm not mistaken – a serious spot of *Inflamed Rickets* and nasty fang rotting *Scurvy* …

… *somewhere inside, that here … smelly Maw-maw … too.*

---

[2] Until it blows up again. Not so much all Egghead and no face – but ends up in a bunch of burnt mangled bodies in some looted shopping mall, or a mere minor genocide that they allow retarded fanatics to organize with their software, while smoothing over a little treason and systemic pedophilia. Hey! Why are you tossing sheep at me?

Meaningful … *Like the filthy matted semi-bald underbelly … of A Dead Dog in a Thunderstorm …
… meaningful.*

But, *Frankly* – my good man – Today, it's just so much easier for any grubby-minded mass-attention seeker to slash 'n hashtag neo-*adroitly* … all for the thrilling sake of *expediently cozy ether-herd immunity* – yet … blindly ignore more individual glaring ultra-hypocrisies – to blithely *maim, claim, proclaim,* indeed *Exclaim* – on any pale snowflake of virtue in the frantic melting-pot moment.
How sweet and cleva …

Especially when it's a floggable commodity on some terrifying *magic-LCD* Mirror-mirror-on-the-wall … any half-witted moron can lie to at will.
Whilst the same system sneezes hexadecimal GIGO right back – *Atchoo!*
… *Perfectly.*

Utilizing evolving AI algorithms, and Orwellian data-mining – to wrench the rabid rabbit from the virtual-ethix hole in real-time lowest-denominator groupthink.

Sense a fresh bout of utter Moral Certitude prevaricating?

Frankly, Dude – An irking percolator that spews mindless, machine-powered, cancel-culture [Cloying, clingy, sub-intellectual mob-insecurity], thereby effectively shutting down adverse rationale surrounding non-Woke debate [Y'all are wrong because We ALL say you are].

Faithful … unto the smirking righteous glory of - *Militant Political Correction.*

By all verifiable accounts – attempts have been made to go as far as arresting English grammar on recently trumped-up charges relating to the theft of historically treasured obscenities, enabling counter-offensive bigotry, and having the audacious affront to produce grubby-minded right-wingery.

All whilst attracting anti-treasonous swarms of humor-laden moderates buzzing in the peanut butter gallery, generally fizzing with logic and reason … *and* popcorning all over the cheap seats.
And, of course, not being palpably *con*-trolled by the Left Hand.

Most noticeably, *a bad-naughty language detained publicly* - without justifiable Probable Cause or effect.
With the bent-cop view to indict and banish toxic "English" completely for warping already moronic minds.

Without facing trial …

However, the broader English Lexicon of Woke has now been rehabilitated, trimmed, and tentatively paroled under a grim *Caveat*.

From now on all those grinning, smirkish type similes … inappropriate touchings of lewd sarcasm … hairy waggling hyperboles, and, *Vilely Offensive* cobwebbed-fanny metaphors – will get severely moderated by the deployment of mass shaming, coupled with a frog-box of hopping-crazy gender conflict-pronouns and ecstatically forbidden Wrong-Wang slurrings.

Forthwith to be interred under electronic house arrest, along with the constant real-time threat of quality-assured outrage, real-world identity cancellation, and firmly locked into VPN defeating mouse-hand satellite bracelets.

There is a sadly dead language that once started with an "E" and ended with a "lish" but that vile form of communication is no longer tolerated. From now on all public communications are to be addressed and published in Expurgated Xnglish.
No deviations!

Be warned. And be scared.
… Be very Scared …

Smacks of the porn industry demanding a sloppy seconds Nobel Award for bringing about earnest thrusting advances into the rarefied field of – *Instant, High-Margin, Synthesized Alternative-Mores, via Streaming Multimedia HD Proxies …!!*

Just as boring, odious, and dreary.

A sadly predictable farce with what appears to be an abundant waste of good wholesome silicone, too much crank and very few discerning doggie treats for men's best friend.

Can you click [Enter]?
                              WELCOME

To … a vivid, *consensual, high-tech hallucination* we now fondly worship as The Internet.

And wow!
At last!
Anyone can be a [250 characters only] *Politician, Priest, or Analogous Pox-Courtier* of utterly *Anything* for all of fifteen enthralling seconds.
Get face in the game on YouTube and:

Smile Baby!

‡§‡

You are The Internet!

If you are, really, *really good* – you might even break it.
How's that for unreal kool?
Lol Lulz[3].

(Whatever the hell that is supposed to mean)

Good grief, one doesn't even need to be a factual one boot on the ground news reporter to practice non-virtual *"Journalism"* anymore either – as long as you did gotta a spellchecker and the hot lemming sells directly into the latest Main Stream Media [Over-cut-and-paste *faked* fake-news narrative], any copy flake can hack away robotically, in any shade of amoral piss in the snow …
… *Currently Trending.*

It seems as though the relatively stolid Fifth Estate has been rudely leveraged.

Looks to have endured a hostile takeover by a shadowy bunch of mendacity-pedaling slumlords. Folks who simply ignore municipal bylaws and Editor's Guild contamination guidelines when it pertains to the blatant disposal of raw human sewerage, and the 24/7 re-recycling of infectious anaerobic garbage for spiteful fun and advertising dollars.
But crafty folks, who multitask by having a most unhealthy practical interest in arson insurance, and political firesale scams …
[All volatile subscribers are to be issued free matches and lighter-fluid.].

Who cares?
Click [Send] – Pay the bills.

‡§‡

The words: Truth, Facts, Reason, Accountability, Ethics, Objectivity, Professionalism, and Impartiality were supposed to be included in the section above, but they objected most fervidly and requested to be penned down in a completely segregated paragraph.

A new page if possible.

Which may, upon reflection – also contain the phrase: *Permanently reserved for Anti-Bullshit.*
A bit beyond me semantically but I reckon the general idea is:

---

3 👍😊👍

After this fashion, attention may be drawn to these terms' actual core meanings, which must be seen to prevail and then undoubtedly retain informative value as pertains to imparting actual, responsible, and confirmed Factual News *... unto the Dear Reader.*

The former sad state of affairs being exactly *How* this squawking electronic flock of mange-ridden alternative-factoid-bots has come home to ... *Rule the Roost* ... here on ...
... *The Post-Truth* McOrwell Animal Farm.

Eyi-Eyi-Ooo...
THUMP

Be this as this ... chimera ... *this Intranet of Thingies* ... may be   besides digitizing ultra-narcissism – *as an earnest thrusting and online high-margin commodity* – what, *if anything*, has changed over the non-intervening decades for *Raped Women* and their *Unwanted* offspring ... except the movies and the dates?

The theatres of *Her* babies' *abandonment*?

Oh yes, those still bounce the staggering numbers all over the globe – Mogadishu, Mumbai, Kabul, Aleppo, Armagh, Alexandra, Baghdad, Sarajevo, Kigali, Sao Paulo, St. Louis, Sharpeville, Belhar, Tijuana, Beirut, Delhi, Khayelitsha, Mariupol, Baltimore, Bangkok ... on and on ...
... and on and on ...

Pin the burning tail on the Intelligence Mule – Anywhere, anytime: Police, Military, Private Contractors, Terrorists, Organized Crime ... Collateral Damage ... the same.

Orphaned, Unwanted children.
... Fatherless ...

Notwithstanding, these re-spawned *Political Conflicts* are coupled with the horrors of *Climate Change* and all those other species of unnatural and multiplying disasters. And more to come, with other dreadful things like encroaching World Hunger, mass starvation and ... *man-caused Pandemics* ... But still, their miserable *Social Medialess ...*
... *third-hand fates* are only the starving circus lion's portion of these developing ... *Terminal Humanitarian Crises.*

According to current estimates, *there are upward of over One Hundred and Fifty Million displaced and orphaned children in the world.*

Back that right up against 20/21 Covid stats.

Put a pin in it, stand back, and have a good long look …

Yet, the deliberate socio-economic, and Social-Media warfare visited upon the fates of *Unwanted* pregnancies has metastasized and is now deeply *Political* too – among many other things.

Get to those *many* other things later … *suffice to say*:

For now – let's change gears completely … depart this crowded sweaty electronic jungle of hyper-dipshit shakedowns … *then come, walk with me and follow the easy money Baby Momma …*

I Don't Want to Split the Party (BLM - Side)

Wing a wing it's Wokesie!
Message on your iPhonzie!
I Tweeps U…
U Tweeps Dem…

Wii All Melt Down!!

This very second more than 57% of all Blacks-Only babies in the United States are being born to single mothers who will become reliant on State Welfare provided by Democrat initiatives that were introduced by LBJ and are still perpetuated by the current Administration as a voting meal ticket to retain the current tipping point of populist political power.

A mind-boggling percentage that is almost triple that of *Unwanted* fatherless non-Blacks-Only American babies.

Another damned good reason to hate Donald Trump.

He who is/was/shall-always-be Dem's *Agent-Orange* and evidently of the appalling, hurtful opinion – that African-American Men need to get off their criminally lazy backsides, get sober, and be doorknobbing smartly to find work.

Surprisingly, the conscientiously abhorred *Doo-Doo Donny* seemed to be making this happen for these fine fellas (pre-Covid), by significantly dropping the unemployment rate, and yet this, despite deeply devout left-wing hate carpet-bombing, which made *the '72 Yuletide onslaught on downtown Hanoi* look a tiny bit like an overenthusiastic fireworks display.

Truly bizarre, all things considered, because *Donald the Double-Creampie unimPeached Twat* also kept on doing disgusting unanal – like fixing the American economy, bringing American troops back home, keeping Her sworn military enemies in stationary check across the board, and trying to unsuccessfully fence out the Fet slinging drug cartels.

Whilst, also admittedly posting highly bizarre tangerine-infused rude *amuzzings* replete with hilarious contra-contraindications on twippy-tweepy Twitter … *causing hysterical twars, and tweel-feel meltdowns among the flocks of murderously incandescent Tweeps.*

Most certainly gave the entire planet a nasty spot of the old galloping *Blue-Birdy-Shits* with giggles … until … …

Weird that, because none of the other contemporary America Presidents ever pulled those former two-dollar bills out of Uncle Sam's psychedelic bunny-hat.

And, he quite obviously remains a highly despicable man for having done all this on behalf of hostile [Insert bigotry] American minorities. Including the looney-tunes Left who labeled him …

‡§‡

… [Ed: And I humbly quote:] an *Amphetamine-fueled Perpetual Motion Felony Factory and Turbocharged Obstruction of Justice Generator, Who Combs His Hair with A Wonky Wibbled Weed Whacker* … among many, many other Woken-upper endearments bawled liberally from the rooftops anyway.

Certainly … *Someone* giving Ol' Dicked Nixon a good run for dropping his lousy schizophrenic dime.

Take a stroll down memory lane …

Amble past Tricky Dickie's Amnesic Memorial Library, and Y'all be sure to hear the sound of skeletal knuckle-bones crackling and popping in *Rage*.

While the very ground rattles and rumbles … to the muted grumble … of a well-nailed-down casket … spinning around like a Huey-mounted chain-gun … fragging the bejesus out of unsuspecting gooks … *in the third person.*

[RIP Dr. Gonzo]

Spooky.

Quite simply the original sleazy slavers winning over hearts and minds by shifting the goalposts of retain-the-endless-Public-Purse. Synthesizing a newer social opiate to re-enslave their demographically bonded skin-servants psycho-politically – as the easily digested fodder of a New World Order.

For one simple purpose.

Gorge unhindered from Deep State's bottomless fleshpots inside DC's glittering Beltway.

Quo Vadis?
Quid Pro Quo!

Or more succinctly: *Stipendia Peccati est … sal*[4] … while doing a killer Wokey-pokey waltz up and down 1600 Pennsylvania Ave hellbent on crashing The Party.

And, this for the relatively cheap tax-dollar price of a couple of food stamps and almost enough squeak to tweak a Twigger for a week.

Limited to the outer ring of the DC Beltway – from saccharine, clueless, pierrot appeasing Canada … to sad, sneaky, greasy palmed Mexico and every sphincter in-between – where all the ravenous gobbling lobby sharks now swim and grin from gender obsessed West to immutable inscrutable East.

Of course.

Poor delinquent victims.

---

[4] The Wages of Sin is … salt

Can somebody say *Amxn?*

Best to ignore the soft ballooning sound of the National Debt ratcheting up a trillion or fourteen Y'all, which is being drowned out by the angry screams of alla them Baby Momma's Federally approved brats.

Pre-destined to be the biggest choking mouthful of the *USA's 25% share of All Incarcerated Humans on Earth.*

No Foundling Fathers.
No raining Amxns *Hallelujah,*
No Malboro Mxn.

Add to this boiling pot of modern Alabama-toadys – the raging bloody cat-fight between *Pro-Life* and *Pro-Choice* in America over the biological meaning of:

When does Life … begin?

An endless circular-saw debate that does nothing more than occasionally step from the darker Red rhetorical shadows to *harass, spam, gaslight, other, threaten, hack, harm, shame, bomb, assassinate* and detract from the ugly reality of:

Unwanted.

Babies who emerge from the human uterine incubator of ANY skin-colored vulva's recesses and whom one and all – have sweet fanny doorknobs to do with Jesus Christ's *ostensibly Faithful Followers* acutely-schizoid, bronze-age, dollar-fundamentalist, *medical opinionating.*

Yet, the same babies are unwittingly, unceremoniously, and grudgingly welcomed into this world … then swiftly cast-off … onto the Federal pro-*status-quo* conveyor …
… and into the grasping arms of loving check-cashers.
From whence they are no longer God's … *congregational* … problem.

Basic religious sustenance for the bright, *ongoing,* deeply-sanctified *glamour* of this particularly glaring and cheaply bought-off burning *hypocrisy.*

No real Fathers, just deadbeat Our Fathers who Art *nowhere near the illegitimate brat.*
Quite simply:
No responsible Men.

On Cue – Enter the growling sex-freaks …

‡§‡

Or, whatever ongoing alphabet-soup stickers the ever over-Militarized LGBTQIA++ixyzzy mob wish to tack onto their self-loathing in combative denialism of their own living DNA.

Notwithstanding that every one of them still sucking oxygen … yes, one can say this with absolute and utter certainty – were conceived out of a heterosexual act of *coitus un-interruptus* between a vagina and a penis, or quite simply – the comingling of human male sperm and a female egg …

… at a cellular level.

[Ouch, what have you just done! Don't poke!]

Yes, yes, it's okay you poor oppressed darlings, back to your nice safe places … off you go …

sigh

Yes indeed, one hears your gentle … *genital-independent* … stridently *non-binary souls.*
Just like the *angels – pure, gender-fluid,* and keeping tabs with a whistle and nasties clipboard.
Well done! Y'all are perfectly correct, if not so undoubtedly vivid in your angry pre-emptive purposes, so let me clarify:

In very, very rare cases a super special doctor can also do it with a hi-tech syringe completely sterilized of "Toxic Masculinity", but the actual baby-batter still needs ordinary messy-mixing into gooey funk that must go *POP* genetically, and unfortunately, the raw material only cums from inside a working cock and cunt …
… at a Cellular Level.

Sorry kids, that's just basic human reproductive biology for you – stinks dunnit?

That's the nasty thing about science, it pays no attention to truly sincere feels or pretzeled gender identifications. Popper-psychology. Wing-Wang-Wokery. However, it might be clearly said, *moreover, very bluntly put to Y'all* - that what you are truly into is:

Plain ol' attention-seeking, emotionally hysterical, deeply sad and grubby Tableaus of … Lust, Lust, Lust … Lust.
Yes, quite simply, very common … or dog-arse licking …
LUST.

The sweaty makeup animal rutting … of a sexually marginal … meaningless and self-possessed …
… Gimp.

Frankly, mate, who gives a thin bent penny what these hilarious, overzealous, aggressively passive-aggressive, ghastly exhibitionists wish to hump, jump, wump or un-bump?

‡§‡

Thump
Frankly?
Frank!?
Dude!!!
Oooook?
EEEEEEEEEEEEK!!!

This is most certainly not about kinks or cranks or anyone's desperate need for dubious imaginary relevance concerning what they get up to after removing their soiled rubber undergarments. Bugger all to with what *Is* or *Isn't* under them either.

It also has nothing to do with warped confirmation bias. That which colorful folks may secretly fantasize [and/or/pay/pray for] when these self-deluded and bare-assed creatures do get it on.
Including when actual dumb creatures with built-in fur knickers become involved and the serious screaming begins.

The criminal and moral aspect of this gonzing is limited to the real flesh-and-blood product of a non-consensual heterosexual act.

Unwanted Pregnancies as the biological consequence of sexual assaults and sexual predators.

This does include the fantastically fabulous millennial breed of neo-biological female imposters who lay claim to having transcended human sexuality, while oxymoronically still owning a "transgender" cock and balls, which at a base animal [*cellular*] level still function as a male penis and testicles, and will, quite *Frankly*, never *vanish* or joyously transmogrify into a female body with a fun functioning vagina, annoying *menstruating* uterus, and sweet naturally bouncy *lactating* breasts – not even utilizing highly creative castrative butchery, pickled generously with lashings of girl hormones, and stuffed with startling amounts of silicone.

And, *unfortunately*, also firmly withstanding all the Woke and forcibly sexualized sex-garbage trying to sphincter fuck the world.

Ancient biology knows better and is immune to silly naked apes' contrived latter-day sex fantasies or hapless and rather queasy attempts at proscribed cartoon temple prostitution.

The only "transgender" mxn that any Woman is safe from *sexually*, in terms of age-old male predation are those mxn whose cocks have been cut off completely. ·
Balls too for good measure. Ask any self-respecting, expensive harem of exclusive sex-slaves.
But that still doesn't make him/it into a "girl" – merely a self-inflicted eunuch.
Is that wild roaring applause from the rabid and equally Militant Feminists, I'm hearing in the background? Yes?

Seems a bit weird that Y'all are not only on the same previous page as these twisty-minded imposters – you're rubbing shoulders in the same paragraph! Maybe STFU and STFD …
… then possibly listen.

You have no middle ground that you occupy in whatever the hell morality is supposed to imply, none of you, and this is not about You either – *You* also copped out - being a male-hating womxn n'all. There is a vast difference between a loving Father and a lipsticked Gimp with a Viagra dick.
Just like Y'all … pillow talking gyrational rubber sybians and censoring the dreaded …
… *M-word* …

Babies simply don't get born from an act of para-surrogate *non-binary* rape.
Not under anyone's fiercely pierced belly button.
See … That's all very basic weirdo New-Age *Gimp-doorknob-Gimp* in da head - Yo!

Ingenious acrobatic sex acts of apocalypse-inducing, thunderbolt-hurling, pantheonic-blasphemy – directed at any mildly interested local Deity – also don't count.
Except maybe to da Po'lice.

I mean seriously – What character of any *"gender-aware alphabet"* encodes being smeared all over with fishpaste and platinum glitter, then ruthlessly double-teamed in a marathon twinky-twerk gangbang by a giant blown-up mechanized gopher tag-teaming two hairless purple trans-polygender donkeys wearing preemptive bukake clear heels …

Does it matter?

What is the set of aggressively relevant Woke Pronouns that must prevail when addressing the key identifying letter as pertains to the social issue of communicating with this bonking brains out through a leaking earhole persuasion?

Is "G" for "Gimp" taken?

Asking for a non-neutered friend.

The dear, very angry, multi-hued - *Emoji-Vichyssoise* navel-gazers do not have actualized skin in the final biological endgame, as such, at any rate.
Poor sweet darling … *Gimps.*

Gimps are, for all intents and purposes, biologically self-designed one-hit wonders.

Tha's bloody-minded common sense wit'a wee Glasgow-kissy to ye kinky-thinker mon.

Frankly (you hairy Pervert), their noisy, brittle, anti-hetero, pro-hysteria, gender opaque - sweeping-opinionistas … mean absolutely nothing to the future of the human race … so to speak *either.*

A bug-infested swamp of Dead-end gene pools and grossly redundant, *irreversible* genital surgery.

… at a Cellular level … Gimpie luv …

Not forgetting, of course, the sexually inglorious religious maniacs - on the other side of the thundering Gimps broadcasting their advirtuous public Lust … those dearly *saved* saccharine souls … grimly awaiting once again - their exclusive but *highly imminent …*

… Rapture!!

The Slow Death faithsnake rattles on America's Left and Right.

Unwittingly hooked up together, and, with *Frankly the Thin Bent Penny* – banished off to somewhere extremely horrible … *likely each other's incandescent graphic novel Hells at last.*

Concurrently, the most costly tedious species of *Whatever* – floating its squally sinking boat while blowing its funki hairdo back, and in the case of the "Rapture", whether squabbling Christian pro-lifers are theologically aligned to "pre-trib", "mid-trib" or "post-Tribulation" … it still happily translates to:

Good Riddance … or … more succinctly …
… Fuck off Directly to Jesus … Please Do not pass Go – or Collect 10% for Him – or hand out evangelical sales tracts at the Door. Just Fuckoff.

No one of You is a *"Special Victim"* – the LGBTQIA trans-knob mob do utterly hideous things to each other, *yet,* even more truly horrific things happen to *Binary Heteros* too, no matter how religious.
Self-audit *St. Gimp.*
Mxn of any stripe or credence are indeed base animals.

The point being:

No Fathers
That is, in every biological or other reasonably sane psychological sense, which could indeed be mistaken for authentic *Human Wisdom.*

Far too few …
… actualized Men.

Then, of course, on the other side of the *bubbly-bubbly-toil-for-troubley Froggy Pond*:

In alarming competitive tandem, more than 60% of babies born in the Bantu ANC's utterly failed *non-Blacks-Only* U.S.S.R. inspired: *National Democratic Revolution* – way down in sunny South Africa, also have no Father listed on their official birth certificate or in residence either.

A frightening majority of them conceived via *indifferent violent rapes* that the mothers survived.

Well, willya just looky-lookie at that!

Two radically diverse countries as things go.
Continents apart …

One, a functional democratic superpower rapidly being overrun with fake-entitlement berobed as pro-Antifa uber-Wokeism, which is in an apparent ideological war with enraged accelerationists and the Proud Oathkeeping Boogaloo Bois – all in a concerted effort to vainly mask the intertwined symbiotic-stench of their shallow, hemotoxic *Machismo.*

Laydeez and Gennelmen!!!

WELCOME TO LAS VEGAS … MAXIMUUUUS!!!

Tonite! Right here! In the Left corner!
Weighing in the same as a six-hunnerd-pound Gorilla!
With two fists full of dead-niggra martyrs and a zillion crack-smack-whack-babies on his back!
Let's give a warm fighting welcome to *The Master of Disaster*! The one and only! *Blacks-Only Killing Machine!*

BEE ELL EMMMMM!!!

Thankew, thankew Ladeez!!! Thankew!!

And here! In the Right corner!
Wearing a MAGA baseball cap!

Toting a fully loaded NRA Membership and sporting *Orange tighty-whitey DT-Fronts*!
A giant Albino Elephant! Right at home here in *The Ol' Johnny-Reb* Arena!
With four hunnerd years of moonshine, undefeated, domestic ball-busting gut hanging to his knees! Give a massive Home-Crowd welcome to our very own, over-privileged, take-no-shit, *Cracker-assed Cracker*!!!

KEEEWWW ANOOOON!!!

Get your tongue out his mouth boy!!! Let's get ready to RUMMMBBBBBLLLLLEEEEE!!!!

Something that does absolutely nothing to advance the democratic image or more worthwhile agendas of the Globe's self-appointed, and *most hooked* - junkie Policeman.

In close contrast, Uncle Sam's shithole Step-Sister Mzansi: (is) a failing, inept, festering African morass of legislated internecine and backward tribal hatred. Primitive detestation directed at non-Bantu Ethnic-African minorities, Pan-African foreigners, and higher European Ideas & Ideals.

Expressed as:

… constant violence – unspeakable crime – regular mass-lootings – widespread arson – numbing ignorance – rampant runaway corruption – starvation – systemic laziness – iron-age stupidity – animist bush-superstitions – resurging 18th-century sicknesses … and all Dominated by mind-boggling poverty, more poverty, and ever-worsening Poverty.

A cracked, distorted, filthy-dirty, and truly butt-phugly mirror – exactly reflecting the Afro-Commie *Nouveau-Riche* – *decolonized-enslavement* … to *non-Blacks-Only Imperialist's* more sickening sins and sordid baser vices.

Utterly possessed by morbidly obese bellies, politically cannibalistic urges, and owned to death by torrid consumerist cravings for expensive, *shiny-shiny* non-Blacks-Only Imperialist …
… *Trinkets.*

Which, somehow never quite offset the trumpeted narcissism, pornographic moral turpitude, and stunted intellectual-pygmyism. Not to mention the glaring but rather hackneyed hypocrisy expressed as limitless arrogance and a swaggering contempt for the Constitution and Laws of the Land.

Or, is that the US government? *Or pretty much most governments?*

Except for maybe places like Singapore, which *Works.*

Regardless of their failures as human beings, or to put it more mildly – *unmitigated failings as decolonized Bantu Men* – either way, as a result – these children, these *Unwanted*, unloved children – ALL of them … are in essence orphans.

They have no de facto – *Fathers.*

Faces on TV, Photos on billboards, and self-adulating T-shirts portraying the depressing mugshots of Afro-Animal-Farm *Heroes of The Revolution*. Toss in legions of menacing Blacks-Only *"Ancestors"* prevaricating through Bantu witchdoctors, backed up with YouTubes and YouTubes of industrial-strength scarlet lipstick slapped on bumble-mumble, Black-Twittering, *militarized-commiespeak* Politburo-Pigs – until Jesus cums for a second time.

But no real Fathers.
No truly loving Men.

Not in the kids' emotional lives and not in the form of any role model from their venal, rent-seeking – slickly CGI propagandized Leaders.
Bantus who seem to collectively miss the point that the millions of Blacks-Only kids who suffer and die horrendously before they do – as a direct result of their sickening actions – are in effect – the Tribe's *ghostly* …

… Ancestors.

Children are supposed to survive their fathers biologically.
Those whom anyone outlives – are in effect one's Ancestors.
When one's own Ancestors are hordes of Unwanted children,
You have utterly failed as a Tribe …
And too, as a collective branch of the human species.

That is the only way Mother Nature works.
… at a Cellular Level.

Go for it – try out any religious or political-gang scam currently running.
Follow the easy money …
Follow the "White Monopoly Capital"-ization of Johnny Walker Blue to achieve "Rapid Economic Transformation" for senior *More-Equal-than-other-Cadres* and see where it leads down the rabid rabbit hole …
Box of matches, petrol, and a bald-tire anyone?

I sense another affirmative shopping spree coming on.

In South Africa, most of these babies' chances of *Proactive Early Childhood Development* then benefitting from a good *Basic Education* are slim to absolutely none – directly because of this dearth of Bantu Men who cannot perform as functional social leaders at any level *without stealing*.

Unlike New Zealand, which is currently being run by a young mom with a tiny baby. And also WORKS.

What has happened in South Africa is exactly the same as the now completely defunct USSR, which re-invented itself as a mega-gangster, top-down malleable secret Police-State, run by a murderous ex-spymaster and where everything goes to the most actively ruthless oligarchs in his inner brutalsky circle.

The Soviet experiment was always utterly corrupt to the core and bound to collapse.
Then predictably descend into organized violence and criminal chaos.
Both then and now the short-lived interpretation of Marxist-Leninism served as nothing more than an expedient vehicle to be powered by usefully polarized idiots and for the sole purpose of silver-lining the pockets of political sovereigns and their courts of patronized support-cast Stalinist apparatchiks, rubber stooges, and gun-toting lackeys.

In the old Soviet system, the mind-boggling inefficiencies and bilge-like economy were directly brought about through the blind actions of stupid, inept, lazy, and above all – spitefully corrupt and greedy people. Many of whom held high positions of actual Civil Authority, which they should never have been allowed to touch with a rotten bargepole. But they did so then, and in sunny SA – they still do – and just because the Cadre happens to be a friend or family member or some staunch acolyte of some connected Party Official's *faction* representing some backward Bantu-Tribes' cattle-rustling bush-agenda.
As these ugly scum like to brag quite openly …
… *"Now, it is MY turn to EAT"*.

A State Official who is ironically supposed to be a democratically appointed *Civil Servant* instead of entirely failing, blatantly coercing, and then re-suppressing the Bantu voting fodder.
Proles which the Ruling Party rob, manipulate, lie to at will and outside of The Party – not-so-secretly despise to death.
KGB trained, and just as morbidly rabid.

Until the next rigged [KFC Streetwise 4 Two + Glorious Movement T-shirt] *iLekshuns*.
Of course.

The main difference between the barbaric neo-Soviets and the dysfunctional, *regressive*, and highly belligerent Afro-commie Bantu Tribes of Southern Africa – is that although the non-Blacks-Only Communists were/are also murderous to the core, as well as being sickening thieves of The People's lives, privacy, choices, futures, freedom, and means – The *CCCP Marxists* thought for themselves.
And still do.

However mendaciously.

They have brain capacity, homicidal cunning, and willpower – and, could and did build their Idea of *Родина*[5] into the other Global Superpower during the Cold War.

Albeit a bitter, angry, all-consuming Bear who survived for a short while until the Communist Party eventually destroyed all the freethinking talent and personal ambition that the country had to offer. Countless millions of valuable lives were obliterated on the expedient Stalinesque Altar of narrow and unsustainable political ideals swathed in imaginary goosestepping Russian Glory.
Barely concealing crass economic banditry.

This, all in the quest for absolute power to be wielded by a feudal underclass overlording an ever more feared and loathed – unpredictable proletariat, which has fundamentally never changed, and is merely hibernating until the next outburst of Slavic murder, war, terrorism, and genocidal mayhem.

What a naked bunch of cock-ups posing as ape emperors over co-dependent bare-arsed mud serfs.

Yet, take a drive through any city or town controlled by the ANC.
A real big-picture worth more than eleventy-million and 2 hundred words.
Ignore the arrogant blue-light brigades, forget the potholes they drive over blithely …

… Look, *count their starving Unwanted Blacks-Only street children* …

See?

An ordinary Bantu child's chances of becoming an inadvertent sociopath through lack of basic human nurture or possibly drowning in a lethal pit latrine at primary school are exponentially higher than passing a Bachelor's with flying colors at an internationally accepted level.

No Fathers.
No Teachers.
No Role Models.
No Cognition.
No Backbone.
No Originality.
No Empathy.
No Compassion.
No Humanity.

Jesus wept …

---

[5] Rodina (Mother Russia)

No brave MEN.

And unlike the USA – this *Blacks-Only Socialist Utopia* was not wrought by petulant, unrequited minority entitlement born out of a twisted nostalgia for re-writing the bloodstained history of American Slavery either.

Apartheid was real on the east side of the pond and still is.

The African National Congress merely absorbed Apartheid's National Party and switched the hated color barrier to "*Blacks-Only*".

Then penned in a spiteful slew of brand-new Blacks-Only legislations, not so craftily reloaded under the political euphemisms of *Affirmative Action/Broad-Based Black Economic Empowerment* and positioned strategically in an *illegal* Fanonist thrall to "*deploying*" connected Ruling-Party Cadres only. With EWC – *Expropriation Without Compensation* still hovering on the not-so-distant horizon.

[Dear Comrade – How to broken doorknob a perishing economy, sabotage national food security, and starve your "Our People" just to spite your very own political farce 101 – *Luv and sweet little kisses – The Market*]

This, despite international treaties regarding universal human and property rights agreed upon and ratified by the very same Bantus in the UN.

The *Marx-Lenin-Mao-Fanon-Mugabeists* also roundly decided to act out their racial retribution and loathe of applauding personal merit in any form – by installing a semi-illiterate, thieving, rape-accused goat herder as President.

Thereby utterly screwing up an even stupider mutated version of the 1950s *Soviet Communist Revolutionary International Economic Policy Theory*.

All the while going utterly bat-gastro from post-terrorist hubris and falling down drunken revolutionary economic entitlement, thereby, in essence – willfully robbing the basic future of every child in South Africa.

[How to blame industrial-scale looting of State Resources on "Other People" including ex-colonist countries and utterly flabbergasted foreign intelligence services]

Using them as a debased political fulcrum to keep clinging onto crudely levered power at any cost. Buying, drinking, raping, and gang-doorknobbing bling, bling, bling ... *like tomorrow will never come.*

Yet, the grinning, giggling, jiving crook and his equally buffoonish minions were so rabidly dumb that most of the stolen dosh disappeared with three Indian fellows who were tacitly allowed to run off with *Revolutionary* blessings and are currently most happily spending the mammoth share of the pilfered Blacks-Only milk-money in Dubai.

They gleefully tricked the gullible Cdes. out of the seriously big-cheeze and in turn, the wonderfully useful idiots got to pilfer their own bacon cuts of non-Blacks-Only booze, pretty non-Blacks-Only threads, with cool upmarket non-Blacks-Only … *Trinkets … Trinkets …*

… [*shiny-shiny*] *Trinkets …*

… albeit with the constant Stalingrading of *annoying Blacks-Only Corruption Trials.*

While these Bantu *so-called Men of Constitutional Oath,* purported Government Leaders who have been ultimately responsible for bringing de facto Hope to these kids for more than two decades – get further inebriated in self-proclaimed fall-down faux-kudos … ever vainly stumbling around in the sweet stubborn fog of a permanent Dunning-Kruger high … and constantly drooling slimy *Product-Expired* political hubris … exactly like a bunch of obese zombie junkies – the *Unwanted* children of their Tribes' actual predestination will be …

Quite bluntly:
Abject poverty – disease - brutal crime - procreating the next wave of completely Unwanted children.
Politically fated to be the uneducated and functionally sociopathic exactly the same way their absent biological fathers are right now … if they survive the physical and expedient political robbery of their childhoods …

Pillaged by gloriously heroic "*Struggle*" Cdes. right from within their own broken and dysfunctional Bantu communities …
… crammed with *Unwanted* tin shanties full of child-headed households.

Moving on … up, all the way to the Honorable floor [Infantile circus] the lying, narcissistic, Afro-Commie African National Congress/Economic Freedom Fighters – *filth* … strut about on, *soooo ultra-importantly* and infest, like smelly dung beetles [Profuse apologies to actual dung beetles] – labeled Parliament.

Much as, or exactly like mainly Blacks-Only run Democrat cities in America, co-existing either side of the boiling-amphibian puddles really.

Rotting step-apples don't fall far from either side of the socialist Tree.

Here in 20/21 … the International Black Lives Matter movement, apparently vis-à-vis … most violently prevalent in the USA *concurrently* – is urgently financing blame onto a similar *highly select "Race" of people* and rather successfully too.

And, to deflect singular attention away from the glaring inability of predominantly Blacks-Only [*formerly*-Bantu] *"Men"* in America to live up to that most very basic of adult-human sexual responsibility – *Fatherhood.*

‡§‡

No birth-control.
No interest.
No responsibility.
No loving, present, and in-residence Fathers.
No functionally *Adult* Men.

Yo! Homes! Ain't no skin color hatchet job Bro. No bomb. No beef Yo!

Just a giant, smelly, hideous elephant-turd [Profuse apologies to actual elephants] in the room Y'all can color-in any way BLM feels like obfuscating:

Absent Fatherhood.

Your Blacks-Only children … abandoned, unloved … Unwanted …
… By You!

And, these so-called "*Men*" who are way too lazy and hopelessly self-centered to be functional and caring *Fathers*, are of course demanding *Hard Money* from the entire USA's messily fondued melting-pot demographic.
To fantasy-finance their unowned miserable failings as opportunistic deadbeats.

The very same political identity gameplay as the effluent Big-"*Men*" of the ANC, the dirty yellow adolescent brat misogynists of the crimson-handed EFF, and all the other self-serving sleaze-fest-Pastors, meal-in-mouth Priests, craven Economic Parasites, and other useless leeches attached to the Afro-Commie Bantus self-proclaimed *revolutionary* doorknob-over down in South Africa.

This particular hypocrisy is etched so deeply, and so hideously propagandized worldwide - that a certain violent drug addict, better described as a Sociopathic-Narcissist Felon – once broke into a pregnant woman's home with his *Blacks-Only* gang-banger friends, then threatened her with *a loaded firearm pointed at her swollen womb* … so they could rob her of her few belongings *to get high for a couple of hours.*

A real prince of a man. But, nothing new there in *Any* frogless boiling inner-city.

However, this very same *Blacks-Only* Punk later hit the real Posthumus Jackpot and went on to feature as the superstar in an opportunistic amateur snuff-movie – after being unsuccessfully apprehended by mostly *non-Blacks-Only Cops.*

A fateful, [politically edited] *Drama*, which played out over some nine minutes on a Woke spectator's phone because the perp in question, had until then, been throwing a noisy, drawn-out drug-addled tantrum on Police Body-Cam and flatly refused to be taken into custody …

… *Peacefully.*

This, now *Globally Acclaimed*, Scumbag, ceased to be of this or any kinder world from what the final autopsy report [very vaguely] concluded were complications from a COVID-19 infection, along with a mild heart condition – but, *comorbid* with a lethal, illegal, medically-unprescribed, drug-overdose *Cocktail* - metabolizing in his system [surmised and unproven but most likely self-ingested to avoid further criminal charges] at the point of irreversible cardiopulmonary failure.

The Report confirms *Medically*, that the deceased had [non-politically]:

- No facial, oral mucosal, or conjunctival petechiae (*Deceased was not strangled*[6])
- No injuries of anterior [strap] muscles of neck or laryngeal structures [cartilage, glottis] (*Deceased had an uninjured, open, unrestricted air passage and was breathing freely until brain death occurred*)
- No scalp soft tissue, skull, or brain injuries (*Death was not caused by brain injury or trauma. The deceased did not suffer gross physical assault of any nature*)
- No chest wall soft tissue injuries, rib fractures [other than a single rib fracture from EMT CPR], *vertebral column injuries, or visceral injuries* (*Deceased had NO traumatic injury to ANY PART OF THE NECK OR CHEST. The deceased did not, and could not have died due to firm external muscle pressure applied to the back of his neck, shoulders, or back.*)
- Incision and subcutaneous dissection of posterior and lateral neck, shoulders, back, flanks, and buttocks (sic) all negative for occult trauma (*Deceased had no internal or external traumatic injuries. The deceased was not noticeably beaten anywhere about the body physically*).

Ergo, in short, poor ol' George Floyd did not die because of an overt act of violence, committed by either himself or the unsuccessful arresting officers. Medical science cooly asserts and proves this unequivocally, in utter disregard of Woke expediency.

So, broken down further, what exactly did kill the ugly toasted doorknob?

A *broader* study of the Hennepin County Medical Examiner's Office (Autopsy Report), in conjunction with other similar autopsy reports (of suspected Fentanyl OD's), including literature provided by the DEA and further research materials into the prevailing opioid crises in the USA[7]…
… *Reveals*:

---

[6] Hennepin County Medical Examiner's Office Autopsy Report.- Ed: (*Comments*)

[7] Look it up.

Serious, peer-reviewed, and irrefutable data, which in correlation to Floyd's post-mortem, appears to be pretty conclusive, unequivocal even - regarding what factually whacked him – *Scientifically.*

… Again, *Woke Politics* be damned.

- *Concurring*: There were no physical injuries to any part of his body externally or internally that would have led to much more than a cursory visit to an ER or drugstore. Not even the need for sutures. In other words, he had a few nasty scrapes and some mild bruises from struggling violently against being handcuffed and unsuccessfully interred into a Police vehicle.
- That is it.
- His toxicology report, however, weaves a much clearer and truer tale of BLM woe altogether.
- The levels of nicotine and cannabis along with the high uptake of methamphetamine in his system were certainly not within lethal limits.
- Not so the Fentanyl. That particular substance was way off into the lethal overdose range.
- The amount of Fentanyl in his blood post-mortem was 11 ng/mL. According to a CDC document, which monitored fentanyl overdoses in a New Haven hospital for Federal research into the proactive use of Naloxone (Narcan) when administering an EMT response specifically regarding suspected Fentanyl and Heroin ODs … *Exactly* 11 ng/mL of Fentanyl was found postmortem in two separate unresuscitated DOAs that arrived at the hospital during the data gathering period. One a male, the other a younger female in her thirties. Both corpses presented post-mortem without the presence of Norfentanyl in the bloodstream – meaning, they had expired from acute opiate poisoning before the Fentanyl in their respective bloodstreams had the chance to metabolize into the Norfentanyl metabolite that the living body produces when breaking down this particular synthetic opiate into base morphine.
- The amount of Norfentanyl in Floyd's post-mortem bloodstream was 5.6 ng/mL, which suggests that George had a way higher than a clinical dosage of Fentanyl already metabolizing in his system - and then ingested more! Enough to kill him outright almost immediately even if he wasn't on anything else already.
- The presence of 4-ANPP in the bloodstream at 0.65ng/mL is indicative that the Fentanyl in his system was of poor or street manufactured quality - because 4-ANPP is one of the precursor chemical compounds used in the manufacture of Fentanyl, and should not appear in a quality-controlled end-product downstream, meaning there is no accurate way to gauge how much Fentanyl he ingested, or, in what form or ultimately … *What lethal concentration?*
- Furthermore, at the onset of a toxic overdose of Fentanyl, the affected person will suffer something medically termed *"Wooden Chest syndrome"*, which is when the diaphragm strap muscles go into a rigid spasm making it intensely difficult to breathe, even though an open unrestricted airway is present. In this case, as co-indicated by Floyd's very loudly proclaimed *"claustrophobia"*.

- Wooden Chest syndrome also makes CPR very difficult to administer and consequently, his autopsied cadaver presented with a fractured rib post-mortem from the EMTs trying to unsuccessfully resuscitate him.
- Notwithstanding, the science also seems to agree with the visual observation made verbally by the one Police officer on Body-Cam, querying why Floyd was foaming at the sides of his mouth shortly after exiting the *"non-claustrophobic"* SUV, another classic, and highly observable early symptom of a massive Fentanyl overdose.
- Undoubtedly, had George Floyd not lied to the police at that exact point about being under the influence of a highly controlled and very dangerous substance, he would have probably gone into cardiopulmonary failure and died anyway, because, according to CDC research - even if the EMTs or the unwitting Police had administered an emergency dose of Naloxone spray, he would have crashed out within twenty to thirty minutes all the same, unless immediately O2 intubated, given an epinephrine shot to the heart and placed on a wide-open Naloxone drip in an attempt to present an adequate blocker to the opiate receptor in the brain *timeously* and then fight to flush out the toxin. He would have never had made it to the ER, or survived, exactly like all the other ODs on Federal record.
- *What* killed the rotten thug was the Fentanyl. Way too much of it. The very same genocidal poison that robbed the lives of some 100 000 unwitting Americans in that very same 20/21 time frame.
- As to *When* the opiate killed him *exactly* – that was when the high uptake of methamphetamine [keeping him viably conscious and verbal with a functioning sinuous heartbeat] became completely overwhelmed by the complete occlusion of the opiate receptor in the brain – the toxin shut down his entire autonomous cardiopulmonary system instantly before it could even begin metabolizing – killing him deader than a frothing rabid dog.

This factual cause of the fatality simply occurred happenstance to his [?] ingestion, concurrent willfully resisting arrest, and then lying to Police Officers about the illegal drug intake.

Call it seriously bad timing *on the part of both parties* - during a career criminal's commission of yet another felonious crime.

From the moment he was approached, on the driver's side, *of the SUV he was seated in* – this lowlife ex-convict willfully resisted obeying all reasonable instructions from Police officers.

Instead, he protested, denied, wailed away for his mother, gasped tearfully about suffering claustrophobia, and flatly refused to be handcuffed.

A friend warned him from the sidelines that he was going to have a heart attack and advised him repeatedly to surrender to the Police - stating he could not win that fight.

But, instead, the wildly Woke Hoodlum kept on wrestling, fought his way back out of their vehicle …

… all whilst groaning, babbling for Momma, and claiming to choke for breath very loudly on the struggling cop's Body-Cam.

These former Police officers, *who are now in prison*, were attempting to legally detain and question him on the reported suspicion of committing a criminal act involving the uttering of an alleged banknote forgery, which had occurred shortly before his smash-hit snuff arrest …

… but, despite these hard cold irrefutable Facts …

The … poor dumb doorknobs stepped right into the glaring spotlight and onto the snarling worldwide Woke stage, where everything is a Theatre of the Self Damned, Law and Order is the Enemy, and reality and reason … lose all value and meaning.

Now, the baying Voyeurs of this same dead-junkie scumbag are triumphantly trumpeting his gloriously-OD'ed name Globally as an *Immortal Saint* and the *One True Martyr* to the cause of the deeply mythical, yet *so unfairly alt-Right targeted African-American Wakanda Male.*

A highly polemic entity whose demands echo those of the enthralled popcorn-munching snuff-fans and all seems to boil down to being immediately given lots and lots of tax-Free Dollar$$$ - by other hard-working American citizens who must gratefully *Take-The-Knee*[8] at this huge honor to unburden themselves of inherent *inherited* financial and *cultural* racism all non-Blacks-Only Americans suffer from birth.

Ostensibly for *American Slavery Reparations.*

And, only when given Enough Dough … might consider stepping up to join the American Dream as a law-abiding citizen, in the manner of everyone else pursuing and paying for it – including those decent, *Sober*, honest, hard-working, albeit chocolate-all-over African-American fathers so sweetly labeled Sold-Out *Coconuts.*

Thousand shipping containers of *Oreo Cookies* anyone???

Asking for a girl-scout friend *whose Grampops surname was Sowell.*

Regardless of their luridly infantile race antics, the unholy truth is BLM's African-American so-called "*Men*" … *are craven sexual predators utterly incapable of statistically functioning as Normal Decent Fathers.* Hence the need for mass-demonizing some other handy *Male Race* here in the early 21st century as The Great Scapegoat for undeserved gain and shrink-wrapped dressage for showcasing the reloaded period-drama *Victimhood.*

The non-Blacks-Only Devil made me do it Massa … *Wokes me up n'all.*

This so-declared Saint, now an uber-paragon of Blacks-Only Consciousness, the glittering poster boy for BLM and way too much ugly urban graffiti – also fathered *Unwanted* children with various women he felt utterly no compunction to raise or care for like a normal decent dad.

---

[8] Is this a symbolic act by *non-Blacks-Only* in solidarity with that *non-Blacks-Only* cop's knee? Maybe if all of them *non-Blacks-Only* Give-The-Finger at the same time it might deliver the message.

Remember, this is regardless of, and, has absolutely nothing to with the bizarre circumstances surrounding *His Glorious Holy Demise*.

St. Georgie Floyd (*The Ice-T Minnesota Junkie*) *vs.* Lord Jesus H. Christ (*The Serial Tithe Cashier*).

Spot the pious sparring difference, when the only similarity is a *Name* gratuitously abused, over and above *Passive-Aggressive Whining* – to justify violence, power-grabbing, acquiring cheapo pity bling, surpassed by amassing of vast boatloads of empty fantastical virtue signals to drown *Enemies of the Racial Gospel* in.

Relaying *The Lore* vs. *The Man's Concrete-Jungle*.

THUMPPP
Omigod!!!
Somebody Call 911!!
SOMEBODY ... Call a Doctor!!

Can you believe this reeking lizard-piss *pavement-animism* was paid for with my US tax Dollars?

Exactly like the ANC/EFF – A *doorknob-thief, sob-sobfest Saga ... of re-written historical virtue – entirely of the Pulp non-non-fiction genre.*

Mega-producing their very own proxy-murders as full Blacks-Only productions.
Wherein Blacks-Only children get killed in Blacks-Only dog vomit because of the pursuit of Blacks-Only Excellence. *And,* where the non-Blacks-Only Devil, who is the singular cause of Blacks-Only suffering and pain – actually has a non-Blacks-Only name:

Jan van Riebeek made me do it ...
Cecil John Rhodes made me do it ...
P.W. Botha made me do it ...
Johan Rupert made me do it ...
The CIA[9] made me do it ...

Dat dere honkey Debbil is done be mekkin' I do it Massa ...

Donald Trump Did IT ...

The outcome ... ongoing Gender-Based Violence ... *and more and more and more –*
Fatherless Orphans.

---

[9] *Okay maybe they did, never know with those creepy bastards.*

This self-defeating behavior can best be described as Blacks-Only Excellence, AKA – Hanson's Razor with a stropped goat corollary.

The coarser definition being:

A species of excellence specializing in cunning malfeasance, expressed as deeply complex pseudologica, which is solely underwritten by a verified mythomanic tranche of irrefutable fantastica.

A well-developed, yet, most uncomfortable alternative truth - that does indeed provide an irrebuttable presumption on the burning issue of eternal victimhood and the felonious values to be embellished regarding the hopeless tragedy of having suffered historically-arrested moral development and non-genetic irreversible Infantilism Syndrome, in a chronic contemporary faceoff with owning zero responsibility, or human remorse.

Hence:

No Fathers.
No collective Wisdom.
No refined Men.

A former South African High Court Judge expressed her dismay concerning this exact topic to a friend privately.

The *friend* then promptly *Linda-Tripp'ed* her up … and *riposted*:

All Out There

… on that very final frontier of moral virtue-signaling – *Dear Auntie Social Media* …

To writ: *"(You) Want to read my (case) files: rape, rape, rape, rape, rape, rape of minors by black family members. It is never-ending, women tell their children it is their father's birthright to be the first, and that gang rapes of babies, mothers, and daughters were a 'pleasurable pass time' (For men). In their culture, a woman is there to pleasure them. Period,".*

This heartbroken horrified and deeply sickened Senior Judge was promptly hounded out of the SA Legal Profession by a vicious, *snarling*, public *mob* of enraged Bantu jurists.

Ostensibly defending their unquestionable Constitutional right to Blacks-Only *Male Dignity* and decrying her *Criminal Racism* towards Them.

Only THEM.

The entire South African Blacks-Only legal profession could not utter *one word in defense* of a single Bantu baby born out of the crime of *culturally endorsed incest and rape.*

Not one - *Except for Her Honor.*

Not a tiny whisper of objection on their behalf to ratify the world acclaimed Constitution and Bill of Rights they all swore to uphold.

To this day … still nothing.

Except for that thunderous Main Stream Media roar of … BBC's-only … slapping-on-the-table … canceling-non-Blacks-Only … cultural appropriation contest.

Brass Doorknob the Law and the Roman-Dutch gorgon the blindfolded Bitch sailed in on.
It's like the old courtroom chestnut:

If the law is on your side, stick it to the Law.
If the facts are on your side, stick it to the Facts.
If neither is on your side – slap it on the Bar, slap it on the Bar, slap it on the Bar.

Curiously, the good woman moved to the USA.

No Fathers.
No Justice
No moral boundaries.
No conscience.
No Taboos.
No #*MeToo*.
No decent, *just*, or honorable Men.

But all is not lost – we now have new-and-improved: Gender-Based Violence Activism!

Yaaaaaay!!

This doesn't stop the sexual violence, sadistic abuse, or hideously depraved homicides.
It never will.
But at least now the horror show is being admitted to as *Something happening … out there…*
… Somewhere …

Look, there are even Marches, Awareness Campaigns, and even Super Important People who make super even Important Speeches even in decolonized English on TV and even that.
They're mega-serious about even being *Seen* to be even more mega-serious.

Even that *Comrade in the Glorious Freedom Movement* even only accused of raping two eight-year-old girls. Lots of pol-miles and even revolutionary anti-apartheid's quick-money for even #MEtoo …
… if even you get my drift Cdes …

In this new multi-fronted theatre of the newer War of Attrition, marching on grimly toward the nascent miscarriage of mankind's collectively bleaker future, relentlessly frameworking a fast-looming extinction horizon – it seems patently clear that nothing will change for the *Unwanted* peer populations of orphaned kids going forward either.

And why should it?

Cause and terminal *Gini/Geno-effect* with – NOTHING in it for *Anybody*, and no good reason to *Tweep*.
Want to take a trip to the Middle East?
How about an ISIS, Afghan or Syrian refugee camp?

Or skip over to the DRC, where gang rape and the targeted femicide of civilians is a militarized political weapon of terror.
Or, how about the Far or Near East?
India? China? Chechnya, Thailand, Serbia, Eastern Ukraine?

How about inside the mind-bending hell of a suffocating steel container full of teenage sex-slaves shipping out of … well pretty much anywhere?
South America? Balkans? Durban?
South-East Asia?

Anywhere?

And … count the numbers and tote up the Real Global Cost of *Unwanted* rape-babies you find in their wake, *while you are at it …*
The USA and RSA are simply the two biggest political extremes of *an identical, common Hate Crime against Humanity.*
Plenty of sweaty doorknobs hard-epoxied to raving political psychopaths, but …

No Fathers.
No responsible Men.

Far, far more serious, and with much longer-lasting and definitively fatal consequences for all of mankind. From the pedophile billionaire safely bundled away in a luxury private jet surrounded by the usual coterie of slithering lawyers – right the way down to the thundering squall of unrepresented rape-babies being born far below.

I have only one question to ask *Anyone* who might have a problem with *Anything* I have said above:

What do real pigs call a truly filthy and utterly disgusting pig amongst themselves?

Komrade Glorious Lipstick Leader!!

Nah, just kidding … a blood brother assured me that my motives would be questioned and the rigid stance I have taken would attract plenty-plenty *ad hominem* mutterings.

Hell, I may even be dragged for odious monologuing and generating enough friction to meltdown an avalanche of snowflakes.

The best-case scenario is being hashtagged a bad naughty *persona non-grata.*

A man who likes to drag-race sniveling snot-yellow squitty doorknobs of Any Skin Colour. Dicks who haven't got the hirsute man-gooleys to be actual dads to their *Unwanted* children.

Lulz lol[10].

So actually, the real hardnosed question to cancel is:

Have you personally decided to stop being part of the reason why rape-babies get born and then abandoned as human beings?

Consider realistically.

This is not a rhetorical question, and it isn't a - Yes or No Answer.

So, I would gently suggest that you do not attempt to answer to yourself (but absolutely no one else) – just yet …

However, do please keep in mind that evil flourishes when good folks choose to do nothing …

All we need is love … Luv …

… Love is all We need …

---

[10] 👍🏻🖕🏻👍🏻

Ex-Vitro

Self-pity is as valueless as self-loathing,
But self-disclosure has a purpose.
So do giggles.

2008-05-15 / 23:19:37 – Stellenbosch Mediclinic, [OR-B2]

The Ob-Gyn adjusts the reach of the scalpel in the cold glaring theatre lights, and … cuts.
Swiftly, all the way through the Betadine painted dermis …

Exposing the glistening fatty layer below.
Scalpel is re-adjusted.
Rapidly cuts through the same lightly bleeding incision again.
Yellowish tissues part away … Exposing shining, distended red uterus.
No hesitation, one more cut …

A flood of very dusky waters gushes from the gaping wound …
The midwife presses both her flattened palms down, and pushes …
Firmly towards the opening.
His entire head squeezes out … into view.
The surgeon's gloved hand is instantly under him.
Another firm, stroking push …
His shoulders squelch, out of the darkness,
And then all of him tumbles out …
Cord and all,

Into caring gloved hands …

Tiny,
Wrinkled
Wet, slimy, greyish, blotchy, and speckled with blood.
He rests, trembling faintly …
Eyes scrunched tightly closed.

The World holds its Breath …

And, then … *He softly takes his Sacred First.*

My Son.

At that exact instant in time, I completely reverted from being someone's *Unwanted*, and in a very specious moment, I became, someone else's deeply [terrified] loving Father.

I love my Minkeyboy more than I can ever describe, and strive to tell him this … *often*.

Minkeychild's Mother, who was in fact, right there in the very same room at that time – would have collapsed in a dead faint, had she seen any of this gory business.
Thankfully, the poor woman was fortunately flat on her back, drugged out of her mind and behind a considerately shielded surgical green screen.
Firmly and very safely out of eyesight.
Good call for everybody, all things considered.

Wouldn't have done at all, her running around yelling … wigging out … punching nurses … losing the plot, freaking *everyone* out … *then zonking out cold* into stunned blood-nosed silence … *with only the beautiful Jennifer Rush still going off her joyful tits about the "Power of Love"* on a sterilized Hi-fi blasting away happily in the background.

Later … she admitted – he has been the ultimate best day of her life ever since then.

Be this too as it may …

‡S‡

<u>1963-04-03/04:19:37 – Bulawayo General Hospital, [Maternity Ward]</u>

Unwanted Rape-babies, where do they come from?
Not so rhetorically …

As one myself, I have had to consider several different scenarios in which a fourteen-year-old girl like my mother managed to fall pregnant:

1. Incest
2. Rape
3. Statutory Rape.

Those scenarios cover pretty much all the possibilities and varying degrees of the crime.
In her case, I doubt the latter.

The precursors for Statutory Rape are Sexual experimentation and/or promiscuity brought about by an absent and/or abusive father. With an emotionally absent and/or abusive mother. This may be coupled with limited to no supporting extended family and/or positive socio-

‡S‡

economic structure that may be hindered by fundamentalist religious indoctrination concerning sexual education.

In both cases – this causes emotional isolation and conflict in the child.

Resulting in the need for any kind of approval from men outside of the emotional dysfunction, which the child rightly feels trapped in and does not understand.

My mother came from an as-yet-undisclosed yet ostensible prominent and wealthy family, who refused to even acknowledge me – which means that from the grand folks down to the second cousins twice removed, there was too much "Shame for Them" and it was more than likely, quite reasonably decided – it would be in "Everyone's Best Interests" to have me quietly removed from her at birth.

Exactly like I was.

There was also a whispered but repeated mention of three possible men involved in my conception.

The town I was born in was small and a very isolated nook of the British Empire.

Muted echoes of gossip reached everywhere among the limited population of Her Majesty's subjects. Regardless of social class.

Keeping that in mind lends more credence to what I was told as a small child.

Therefore, I can only logically surmise as a father myself – that my mother was either gang-raped at fourteen or was used for pedophilic sex repeatedly, and one of the men who raped her – was obviously my biological father.

Ergo, *the deafening silence on the old class grapevine in every regard as to his identity.*

No Grandfather.
No Father.
No man.

Blunt fact – the male responsible for my mother bringing me into the world on her own, and more than likely all alone and very afraid at the ripe old age of fifteen – was a *pedophile rapist.*

One who probably never paid for his crime.

Me.

He, or *they,* may have even come from her own family, seeing as I was born in a Protestant hospital yet taken directly into the welcome arms of the Roman Catholics. Who, incidentally, had their own hospital in that little town.

And, Whom we all know, are Collectively absolute masters at spin-doctoring sexual depravity towards minors into *holy-smoke and mirrors.*

‡§‡

Take the mass graves of child native-Americans being dug up on Roman Catholic residential-school properties in Canada currently. Then take a hard look at the pious attitude of the gang of holy pedophiles swanning about in fancy dresses with funny hats.

Demanding good repentant sinners confess their evils unto them in secret … then slobber all over a holy ring … *amongst other holy doorknobs*, while the bearer's practice under-rug housekeeping, and re-counting their Mother's global real-estate holdings.

Less historically amortized bloodshed and the untampered rape of minors.
Of Course.

Transmogrifying systemic crimes that should be punishable by death, or life imprisonment at a minimum – into a mere *Forgivable Sin.*

Which, if it cannot be absolved by a few Ave Marias … can usually disappear under the carpet and fade swiftly into rapidly distant memory with the righteous aid of the *All-Seeing-No-Evil* dollar.

Bless me Holy Father for I have sinned – but I truly think He was totally mistaken when He ordered that a millstone should be hung from my neck and I should be hurled from a cliff and drowned in the depths of the sea.
Better to listen to His Mom then, eh?
Hail Mary, for I, doorknobbed righteousness then accidentally raped innocence.
My papally pious pecker was led astray by a seductive child of the Devil. Not my bad.
So, I'm just gonna go ahead and hail you 24 times, then recite six Our Fathers. Are we done?

The traditional way sex scandals are smothered among the rich and their secretive, scarlet-painted … *sickening whore of Babylon.*

Then … to the – why?

Quite honestly, I don't care *why.*
Fact is, if that crime hadn't occurred, regardless of her age …
I would have known my biological father's Name today.

Yes – these things do happen among teenagers and all too often too, but when they do, the family or legal guardians usually step in and take care of things.
Teenage pregnancies are not a new phenomenon.

But, then again – neither is prostitution, pedophilia, or rape.

The small, close-knit community of Rhodesian colonists that I was born into paid lip service to a *higher-moral Imperialist Authority* and would not have gone to such lengths to distance themselves from my birth unless something truly ugly was attached to my conception.

Like I said:

No Elders.
No Grandfathers.
No Father.
No *Man*.

All that matters to me today is – *I won't rape a woman or pay for sex.*

If that man is alive, he has to live with himself and ALL the others like him for being empty filthy cowards with no human value.

Being born out of their collective sex crime may have been a rocky start but at least I turned out better than him and his forefathers, whomever they were or are.

They can all go to that nasty religious place ... where all useless doorknobs get tossed and melted down.

Even if that hade doesn't exist except here on Earth.

Where you can get born into hell.

Just once.

This is not a lone sentiment on my part. As this unravels deeper, it must be understood that *Unwanted* are different to other people – *yet to each other, we are so very the same.*

What is it like being an orphan?

"What happened if an Unwanted child gave birth to an Unwanted child? It was as though she were in a hall of mirrors, except that instead of getting smaller in each one, she got younger and younger." — Heather O'Neill, The Lonely-Hearts Hotel

"Perhaps there are those who are able to go about their lives unfettered by such concerns. But for those like us, our fate is to face the world as orphans, chasing through long years the shadows of vanished parents. There is nothing for it but to try and see through our missions to the end, as best we can, for until we do so, we will be permitted no calm." — Kazuo Ishiguro, When We Were Orphans

"When it comes to forming your own family, relationships, social customs, life questions, you are in an alien world, desperately grasping at alien straws, hoping to learn something about them to build a small, working shelter — while others are helped by their families to build mansions and houses ...

Through all this cruelty of life, you persist by believing, against all odds, that you have a purpose, that there is meaning in your existence, ... – Kenoi Yan (Quora)

"I guess that's the soft spot for orphans, eh? We're so hungry for a father that we go blind." — Emory R. Frie, Giant Country

"For I was indeed a student of human nature, as every orphan and hooker and Unwanted kid must be."
— Carol Edgarian, Vera

We ... share a *Universal Primal Scream.*

However – what matters to me ... *Matters to me more than any other thing, including this in my own life:* I consider all the rape-babies born into this uncaring Hell – to be my de facto *Brothers* and *Sisters,*
   Cousins ...

Don't get me too weird – this is the only reason why I am writing about Us.
   Not you – *Unwanted* ... Us.
   What makes *Us* – brothers, sisters, *Cousins*?
   For each of us: Our father is a faceless, nameless – *Rapist.*

The other reason why I want to collect hands, then go and find them, and bring them *Home.*

So then? How to undoorknob this *untenable* but ongoing and entirely repetitive human condition?
   Solutions?
   ... Are there any?

Remember my not so rhetorical filter question?

Are you going to continue to be part of the problem by doing nothing and saying nothing while this particular evil flourishes, and grows bolder?

Most definitely, Not - a *Yes* or *No Answer.*

And see, you are starting to do something.
   You are still reading this.
   Thinking?
   Maybe it might mobilize you into sharing these thinks through specific and realized actions of your own?
   Only you will know.

Hold that thought ...

At this point, we also have to take note of the fact that this particular problem originates with men and women being proliferating sexual delinquents biologically.

Something which mankind stubbornly refuses to admit openly and simultaneously seems to hopelessly misunderstand or find the means to manage – from birth to Death.

And, all in dismal defense of primitive, self-destructive, Tribal ~Memes~ in one variegated form or another.

Hence …

¿Qué es la vida?

"Without biodiversity, the health of the planet is at stake." – Google.

To fully sustain the basic scale of human needs, any functional micro-society needs to achieve a singular and common biological goal:

- To live in collective harmony with the natural environment, the air, land, and waters of our planet … To husband the flora … fauna – that which gives us life.
For free.
- To realize that this is our common burden of gratitude for the finite experience of *Being* and an immutable rule by which *We* must guide our cyclic, symbiotic existences.
Forever.

Old Skool happy-hippy psychedelic mushroom scat.

Tediously self-explanatory, quaint, tree-humping … *blah* – but still …
Why, is it necessary to state the bleeding obvious?

If we could express the DNA of all organisms as a singular vast array of co-interdependent vectors in a multi-dimensional cartesian plane – then from the mathematical point of view of both physics and microbiology – We, that is all living human creatures, are no less, nor … (this must be stressed) – more important than the existence of say … a common cockroach, lurking around under the sink, in the kitchen …
… behind a lost polystyrene ball.

The fact that one species will probably prevail by surviving an atomic weapon detonation, which the other species invented, and … probably won't survive … along with pretty much ALL other species who have no part in the ape fight – is both utterly immaterial in the grander scheme of universal things … and only worth noting as a fleeting concession to the terrible yet convenient irony of it all.

At least … *from the surviving cockroach's point of view.*

The humble roach while not possessed of a point of view (*at this juncture*) – yet, ostensibly being the only living creature still skurrelling about in the currently foreseeable future of the planet – is rather haplessly the only one who will be capable of forming one.

However, circumstantially limited due to no discernible brain.

But evolution – through the process of Natural Selection [Whilst being utterly indifferent to Homo Sapiens Creation Fantasy ~Memes~] *and*, … given eons of time and wadges of space – could probably provide the capacity for developing an advanced roach opinion from primitive ganglia.

This time, hopefully, not based on finally producing biological oblivion by fiddling with polystyrene and advanced chemistry sets – then going *Wheeeee* … as everything goes BANG.

They will survive Us, but – *will they survive Themselves?*

Is this looking for the proverbial dead foliage in another species' complex eyeballs?
Batting away the equation that bites the trembling ape-arse closer to the sharper end of the proverbial wicket?

Both species are hardwired to protect and actively propagate their unique DNA. From birth to death. Although, they have vast existential differences when pursuing the latter end.
While one species eats its decomposing dead without exception – the other does not, as a general rule – *without cooking it first.*

But generally, Said *other species* – burns or buries most of its expended carcasses rather haphazardly anyhow. Albeit with great rituals and more often than not – deeply somber religious ceremonies.
Or tosses them in water.
Many times, deliberately weighed down and not even dead yet.
To sleep with fishes and *whisper secrets to them* … apparently.

This strange behavior, concerning spent DNA-bearing materiel, whilst on the surface, may seem chaotic and inexplicable – it can probably be linked directly to the sheer bizarreness of Homo's highly brittle sapience.
A relentless awareness that drives the creature mad with worry about not existing.
In the same state biologically.
Especially when it comes right down to haircuts, teeth, and – *what happens to The Money when everything dies?*

It invented something called Hollywood to perpetuate branches of this fantastical idea by using very quickly moving pictures mixed with sound and music to fool its brain via its eyes and ears. Not satisfied, the weird ape pushes it one step further and fools its psychology with something else it invented – called consumerism.
Which is buying stuff [With imaginary stuff it usually doesn't have nearly enough of] that is purposefully designed to break anyway.

When one gets back there … and back again – *just to finally get down to it.*

Then spin around in circles … before falling out of the tree[11].

But the embattled creature needed to distract itself from a glowing-mud third World War and invented colored toilet paper to deflect, *while it reflected*, reverse-genuflecting to Nature.

After that, the rest of the psychotic shopping frenzy was really to be expected.

Worst case scenario … at least in Homo Sapiens' generally accepted and collective opinion – is being food for a short while, then more horribly … remaining fertilizer for a much longer period. Pushing up sunflowers, and never finding out who wins the next Season of … for … Much … *mulch* longer.

Existentially possessed with – no cooking clue as to what will happen in the Finale – when looking at yesterday made one forget tomorrow – today … sort of important *sophical wossname* … unpunctuated by commercial breaks.

Essentially stone:

Dead.

And while Homo Sapiens has largely avoided being the edible option by becoming the rabid Boss apex-predator around – the only other avenue open to the more urban species, when it becomes necessary to dispose of distressing, yet highly edible carcasses – is turning them into *smoke* and a very bad smell for a while.

Then, back to being ye old dreaded *fertilizer* … sans gently-pink … *loo-roll.*

In one form or another.

Ash is also great for pushing up daisies, roses, clivias, daffodils, petunias (you get the pretty picture) …

In fact, longer than both the sapient and lurking non-sapient species have been around.

Shark and crocodile … food-chain-gang – *takeaways* notwithstanding.

One species *lays eggs in cute little suitcases*, does not meddle about with its reproduction systems, and does not kill its own … unless said own are imminently in the final biological processes of becoming highly re-edible protein of course.

Waste not, want not.

Whereas … the other species indiscriminately kills its own – right from after fertilization to … well, imposing non-biological function on survivors of birth – utilizing all methods it can invent with that fabulously oversized brain.

However, with the distinct exception of tried and tested traditional animal methods like *biting*

---

[11] Absolutely Correct! What you heard was indeed the sound-effect of those stubborn Laws of Gravity being ruthlessly applied to a tumbling tailless monkey … *sans Tree*….

… which remains strangely quite rare – except in popular Hollywood sleight-of-brain fantasies of a very peculiar genre called Zombie-flieks.

Jesus … *the reengineered ~Meme~*
Still flesh and blood swilling, but … *lurching, groaning …*
… gory vengeful dead.

The terrible truth is Homo Sapiens dreads non-existence.
Neurotically and manically dreads it.
Cannot easily reconcile to the fact that this brief existential experience of Being is as entirely finite as the next biological heartbeat you are still experiencing.
Yet, Homo Sapiens' only natural predator is quite unhappily – *Homo Sapiens.*
And not for food and certainly not as a vengeful act of Papal Voodoo either.
Although the latter is up for debate.

[Beginning with debating the deeper meanings within the term Papal Voodoo – as pertains to Homo Sapiens' inherent taste for regulated symbolic cannibalism].

Thirty billion chickens and thirteen billion actual beasts of the field can attest to this culinary balk – albeit on their way to the nearest abattoir to offset the underlying appetite.
A case of carpe jugular meets mad-ape disease.
Although, in the case of thoroughly *devolved,* then deep-fried McDinosaurs … it seems a peck unlikely.

Maybe this has to do with the one species being driven by an unconscious hive instinct and the other by a vividly conscious, highly manic, and insanely paranoid self-awareness.

Something that has driven the wretched ape to believe, collectively, that it is, in fact, the only fully self-aware species in existence.
Yet, simultaneously has come to the grim realization that it is also, in fact, the vilest and dangerous. Ergo, it should brush its teeth and strive to kill not only its enemy honorably but everything alive around it in a completely non-animal way – just to make sure.
For *righteousness's* sake.
This behavior is termed biological self-extinction, and it will be caused by *mass self-deceit.* Something the ape seems to vigorously strive for, then decry foul simultaneously.

For the simple reason that Homo Sapiens is *Spiritually inclined.*
Thus, most certainly not a mute beast of the field.
And, *so totally not destined for non-heavenly Mickey-Deez or the greater unglories of the Colonel and his 11 secret herbs & spices.*

And absolutely, shudderingly *Not* – as some of its own lower kind … *thieves, harlots, heretics, and lawyers …*
Cursed!
As are bearers of wood and mere carriers of water.

[Once again, the words *thieves* and *harlots* are up for strenuous debate, mostly in the sense of To Whom these terms apply. This includes the lawyers representing those *propitious apes* coining and uttering the terms in the first place]

Ergo, a unique Ape among apes.

Self-convinced, *unlitigated*, and selectively ordained for much greater things once completely and utterly stone dead, and rotting.
If … of course – said *select grouping of unique Apes' ordained, unmitigated existences were prayerfully occupied with much higher ends than the slaughter of trees and the quenching of baser thirsts* – by any proxy.

Kiss my holy ring.

Thus, the elaborate rituals when disposing of *wasted* but … terrifyingly holy corpses.

For the most part, these greater promised rewards for diligently destroying life and *embracing death* … for the oxymoronic *Life* that will occur once utterly stone dead, and rotting – always seem to involve some form of non-biological intoxication and sex, or unsex.
With truly horrific punishments …

Mostly to do with the practice of unending immolation – invoked by priests barely suppressing masochistic schadenfreude upon those obtuse souls who would rather pass on with the applied mythical fantasy … and *just be dead and done with it* … all one day instead.
For many of these foolish mis-adherents … the horrific threats of punishments come before death to prove the point as sharply as possible … *Anyway.*

If you catch the ball – you are in the game baby.

Hence, the penchant for atomic weapons, homicidal religions, and good orthodontics.
Which, with great exception – will never rip through a beating human jugular … to feed … with great satisfaction and extremely bad manners.
Exhibiting zero social graces.

A Total Karen's nightmare.

One species is profoundly proficient and incredibly organized – the other chaotic, ruthlessly competitive, and completely beyond rational biological understanding.

The human being, as an animal species – *makes no bloody sense.*
As a human, *being human – makes no bloody sense.*

If humans have no biological meaning outside of the collective – *then why strive for non-biological meanings as a collective?*

Why collectively employ the words … ~Memes~ … to invent warring gods and political systems?

~Memes~

… That once spent … disappear … *with the civilizations that were raised and then razed through their nurture.*

In the graveyards of revered gods and sainted tyrants only edged weapons and sickening greed stalk the living world above. Still soaking the earth in wet blood to appease the fading memories of their crumbling … forgotten … wordless, sacred ape-bones.

Why drive a man to directly or indirectly manufacture killing machines?
Why utilize billions of man-hours in exchange for things that he does not need for existence?
Why choose to be so far removed from his real existence that he cannot live biologically without making things to kill other men?

Q – Polystyrene is key to the manufacture of:
A.) Fridges?
B.) Hydrogen (Teller-Ulam – $fi/fu/fi$) type nuclear weapons?
C.) Cardboard-box energy-efficient thermal ovens?
D.) All of the above?

Why do certain men go bald?
Is it genetics or bad hygiene?

Why is it important?

Can a drive in a luxury sports car cure the incurable?
What the slimy doorknob is a golf handicap?
Hark, can any ape outrun his genetic handicaps and mad obsession with polystyrene?

‡§‡

Why hoard and murder for what he cannot eat and will never give him satisfying happiness or comfort?

Why kill other men, he has never met before?

For reasons that only exist in another man's mind – *like an unseen god.*

A man, *a naked ape,* a singularity of competing cowardice – neither set of warring apes will ever meet.

So sick, unhappy, and slowly dying from another ape's disease of the mind – Greed.

An ape cooking its mind with *envy, lies and fear* – for what that ape does not have and that ape does not need.

The Greed of an Ape, that believes it can possess everything … Including a female's body or her mind.

Primates like the squirrel monkey have highly organized, cooperative structures in their natural societies. Baby monkeys are tolerated just one simian mistake and are rewarded with monkey punishment (*biting*) – the second mistake means death (*by biting*).

A second mistake could mean the end of all the other monkeys (*by being bitten*) – so, quid pro quo … *quo Vadis?* … and all that – no second mistake Naughty Minkey Monkey.

The Big Red Button – switches off everything …

Non-human simians do not fret about biting, that is the collective monkey code applied to retain survival as a species. They are very small in size, so in the jungle, they have to practice social cohesion religiously – and do. Try to grab one in the jungle – *should you be a rather dim cat,* then rapidly survive a rapacious tsunami of hundreds of razor-sharp little teeth biting You …

… *Everywhere.*

Suddenly, grabbing a quick easy morsel between the old faithful incisors turns into way too much hassle for *Everything.*

Except, of course, your own front *teefs.*

And squirrel monkeys have happily survived as long as lately very unhappy humans (*1969, 20/21 & COVID-19 Not Withstanding*), yet did so with normal amounts of corrective biting and none of the Multiple Independently-targeted Re-entry Vehicles (MIRVS), slavery, political assassinations, cannibalism, rape, battery, arbitrary child abuse, war propaganda, and mass suicides, … etc …

So, at the end of the day, or … shortly after some Richard Millhouse-Doorknob Nixon presses "ON" The Big Red Button … roaches will be laughing, or rather – twitching antennae hilariously through the glowing radioactive dust ... while valiantly wending their way back to the endless rave in the Giant Nesting Place.

Another day in Roach Paradise.

Unencumbered, at last, by ape-designed, new-improved nerve gas ... with artificial jasmine fragrance, and extra added funky organo-phosphates [Trademarked Di-Psyn™].

You can't *Phake the Phunky Baby Jesus ...*
You can't ... You can't ...
... phake the Phunk!

Homo Sapiens, at last ... at long, long last – will have defeated its own worst enemy and destroyed that foul-foe Man *utterly.*

Including most of the rest of life on Earth.

All that will remain are utterly filthy oceans, concrete ruins, and a massive oxidizing scrapyard.

Finally ... and beyond last ... *truly last* ... in an arbitrary shifting point on the spinning poisoned globe so-called "The West" ... a gently rotting, catalytic suicide note – titled:
"The Holy Bible" ... will flap away in the wind and ... further disintegrate ... into ye old *fertilizer.*
While a roach, lugging a bulging suitcase – scurries past a non-degradable polystyrene packing ball ... without a passing thought in its *non-existent mind* over the entire meaningless-ape matter.

But here is the real kicker ...

Civilizations have not ever risen because of rape – *they all fall, disappear and die because of Rape.*

Rape is born out of animal Lust, Envy, and Greed. The need to own, control and dominate ...
... At Any cost.

The merciless *rape and murder* of women and children.
The gluttonous *gang rape* of the Environment.

The evil systemic rape *of Wisdom, Morality, Justice, Knowledge, and Truth.*

Welcome to Easter Island ...

Clap, clap, clap, clap, clap ...

Ms. Minkey *vs.* The Banana

A ~Meme~ is defined as:

*"An element of a culture or System of Behavior passed from one individual to another by Imitation,
Or other non-Genetic means ..."*

(Thx Uncle Google!)

Sounds pretty straightforward forward huh?

It is a truly fine day ...

Five innocent jungle minkeys are quietly going about, minding their own minkey business and in the process of almost acquiring juicy windfalls ...
Lovely non-suspicious-looking fruit, which seems to have fallen off some tree into a very *convenient* heap.

... all of a sudden, they are slammed together by strangely elastic knotted-lianas!

Something they hadn't, in fact, actually noticed they were walking on just before.
The nightmare instantly binds them together into a painful furry ball, causing the rainforest floor to hurl away – exactly like falling up into the canopy in violent reverse.

Minkeys don't like to fall long distances.
Ever.
Either up ... or *down.*

Falling minkeys are split seconds away from being *Something Else's Grub.*

They scream and yell their displeasure most dreadfully ... *obviously* expecting to become a late lunch horribly too soon.
This does not help matters, and a lot of prophylactic biting will surely be taking place, *to achieve maximum personal menu avoidance, with immediate social far-distancing,* if enough wiggle-room may be rudely elbowed out the way ... to achieve that sort of thing.

Eventually, a bunch of sad-looking smelly homos come along and lower the terrified little buggers back to the ground, there to rapidly toss them into secure bamboo cages and unceremoniously cart the lot off ... from what had always been a luxurious organic abode of the:

Fifteen-Hectare Rumpus-Room plus *Unlimited Open-Plan Walk-In-larders* … with nearby *Very Handy River* …

… Organic Real-estate … category.

At least the homos have no spoons or spicy condiments on open display.

Have you seen the movie Madagascar?

The one with the narcissistic lion, hypochondriac giraffe, and that supercool megalomanic lemur – King Julien?

Well, these miserable melancholic minkeys also embark on a similar sea-voyage … with much seriously nasty squitting, seasickness, *and* terrible misery.

Regardless … all sea voyages come to an end – *either on reasonably dry land or very wet land called seabed* but come to a squitting end they do.

Moments after sailing past …

… an … *enormous metallic-green lady all dressed up in a flowing nightie … with a matching deadly-looking spiked nightcap … and threatening imminent arson at everyone within her cold piercing gaze …*

The five little battered heroes find themselves back on much drier land.

Albeit resting under a huge concrete jungle in this instance.

From the docks, they are swiftly delivered to a *sanctuary.*

' If one might call it that from the minkey's grim perspective. The grim perspective of The homos haven't broken out the BBQ sauce and pepper grinders just yet …

… but *we are not imbeciles, we are waiting …*

Inside the sanctuary, they find themselves released into what the homos have propitiously labeled:

Animal Behavior Research Enclosure

Something that they, the homos at any rate – consider zoologically *spacious and comfortable.*

The minkeys consider it a steel hellbox.

At least there's plenty of water and sufficient, if rather bland – food.

More alarmingly and rather suspiciously – no homo has, *as yet,* displayed any overt early-warning signs of wanting to launch into a savage minkey-feeding frenzy – the thought uppermost in their collective minkey minds. Still, the minkeys are deeply nervous and keep a very close eye on their sinister captors.

Minkeys are by definition eternal optimists.

Most of this optimism is spent on acquiring anything that takes the immediate fancy, then giving it a quick exploratory *sniff-nibble-and-toss*. So, minkeys being minkeys – they set about exploring their surroundings.

One and all quickly come to the firm conclusion that their stinking surroundings are mostly of the seriously aching teeth category, with *bugger all to toss* … and therefore best left alone in the healthier interests of higher minkey learning.

Next on the list after thoroughly exploring the place, is speedily becoming ever more bored.

After a couple of lazy days doing nothing but being jaw-achingly *sure* … sure enough, a group of homos appears outside the Animal Behavior Research Enclosure.

One climbs up on top of the cage and lowers a narrow ladder vertically through the bars into the center of the floor … to fasten it there.

The minkeys all perk up and look on expectantly.

What's this then, eek-eek?

One or two take a brave run up the rungs to the very top, find absolutely nothing of interest except the cold narrow bars, and eventually amble back down to doing minkey business in the best possible manner when strictly confined to the polar opposite of *a luscious Fifteen-Hectare-Rumpus Room!*

Outside the Animal Behavior Research Enclosure, the obviously well-fed and completely unhungry homos are playing with a shockingly long thinsnake armed with a round shiny head.

It seems entirely dead so … *the little hairy bastards pay it no mind …*

At this point, one of the homos cracks open a sack and takes out a bunch of truly lovely, most delicious-looking … *Yellow Bananas.*

Of course, this immediately captures their most *Undivided Attention.*

They watch enthralled as another of the homos takes a single banana, ties a string to it, then rapidly climbs back on top of the cage. There, that homo fastens the fruit to the bars, leaving it to dangle inside the cage at the top of the ladder.

Free, the Banana!

The minkeys snicker.

They know this one. *It's a trap!*

The moment one of them goes after that mouthwatering nana … *it's all over except for the satisfied belching and a predictable argument about who gets to do the dishes …*

The homo climbs down.
The minkeys wait …

Now minkeys all have pretty much one-track minds. These minkeys are no different.
Each minkey present and accounted for, is calculating right down the minuscule second – exactly how long it will take to bound up the ladder … nick the nana … *and make it back down*!
Much alive and completely unmunched itself.

The homos stand outside the cage … *waiting*.
Doing pretty much nothing.
Nothing.
Nothing to protect the poor, lone … sweet … super buttery morsel!
More waiting … then a bit more.
Eventually, a lone minkey takes that final mortal gamble … *up ladder, grab banana, bolt down…*
… precious prize … *intact!*

The homos – then do …
… *the very strangest thing.*

The dead thinsnake comes alive!!
Sprays jets of icy cold water at the four bananaless minkeys. Instantly *soaking them to their very shivering bones*!

This creates a minkey uproar as screams of profane rage and rank astonishment spew back at their oppressors.
The Oppressors calmly ignore this and observe the lone dry minkey guzzle the nice banana.

Soon enough an uneasy quiet returns to the cage.
The minkeys all dry off, tails settle and they resume minkey business as usual.
Boredom sets in … *until* … the homos return for a second round.

Once again, a banana is dangled … *again* – after a brief bout of careful scheming the bravest little doorknobber makes a break and grabs it.
In turn, the other four hapless minkeys receive another thorough icy drenching.

A more focused sputtering fit of outrage ensues as wet minkeys scream the lengthening list of incensed minkey grievances to be had with homos. *All homos!!*
This, of course, is ignored, yet again and the whole terrorism process is repeated.
Again, and again …

The minkeys are certainly not that stupid, and soon enough figure out that the only drawback to their admittedly comfortable digs – is the exact point at which any one of their number takes an unhealthy interest in dangling bananas.

They don't *quite* put their scheming little furry heads together or *Plan* anything as such, but when the cursed homos dangle a banana one final time … *and,* one of their tiny group makes an inkling of a move for it – the others promptly attack that minkey in no uncertain terms.

Back off doorknobber!

Or rather:
Put down that ladder and step away from the nasty banana old sport!
If you know what's good for you and such …

The infliction of physical violence upon each other … *preempts their collective minkey attentions from wandering off to gratuitous Forbidden Fruit,* no one is sleeted and the minkeys happily (*almost all of them*) continue to conduct ordinary simian commerce unhindered or disturbed.
Vertically available bananas instantly cease to be a potential dietary supplement for any upstanding minkey with brains.

However … *the despicable homos are not quite finished with them yet …*

On a morning, they come to the cage and remove one of the newly graduated jungle minkeys, replacing it with a stranger minkey.
Of dubious educational background.
There' the usual sort of – *Who the Hell are You* and *Do You Know Who I Am* – chest-bump type posturing … but soon enough tails settle down, as quite embarrassingly, those missing identities are relocated.
Then, back to looking for tasty bugs in each other's hairdos.

Of course, the utterly vexatious homos come back with *the dreaded banana sack.*

After the usual nana-dangling homo climbs off the cage, the freshman minkey delightedly makes a bolt for the ladder.
That minkey is already tasting the heavenly, twirling yellow vision above – only to find itself on its astounded furry bum and being harangued most viciously by its brand-new roommates!

Again, and again … nana by loathsome nana – until it learns: *The No-go-nana Rule.*

Peace returns to the cage.
Superficial wounds are gently prodded. Injured Pride duly licked.

Minkeys relax into being hard back at work being bored.
Without luck.

The dreaded homos once again remove another of the original jungle group's members and replace it with an even newer minkey. With the same results – re: *The No-go-nana Rule.*

Until the shocked greenhorn minkey in question learns the ultimate lesson the Hard Way, albeit in what the other minkeys consider … *the Easy Way.*

Thus, from that day forth the forbidden banana *remains unmolested by unenlightened proxy.*

Eventually … Another Fine Day breaks forth …

All the original jungle minkeys have been replaced, a banana has been routinely dangled but no new-Skool minkey graduate will dare to go near the cursed yellow thing –
For justified fear of preemptive violent reprisals by the rest of the group - *as an act of mutual self-preservation.*
A gang-banger beat-down … *It Is as it Is.*
Canceling that minkey's extra-cultural urges.
Make sure its furry noggin hangs pitifully in mass-shaming … if it even *thinks* about nanas.

Never shall it be that any righteous minkey shall henceforth … ever eat a captive nana again.

Even though not a single one of the new class of minkeys has ever been sprayed with icy water for any reason – either.

What can be learned from this is:

Homos seem to serially waste good food and practice the equivalent of waterboarding on perfectly innocent minkeys just to prove that a homo named Jesus will send their evil bald arses to a terrible hell if they ever eat bananas.
Oh, and any sane minkey should stay the heck away from homos – they are all wong-in-peanut-butter-jar – doorknobbing nuts.

That is how non-genetic ~*Memes*~ like Religions and Political *movements* come into existence and sustain and re-sustain themselves – generation through generation.

War after war.
Pope by televangelist.
Republican by Democrat.
Right by Left

Supremacist by Marxist
Honor murder by genital mutilation
Stick by moldy carrot.

It is also how they become easily modified.

You only need one ripe banana and four frightened minkeys to rabidly attack anything that comes close to threatening any dangling *~Meme~*

Blindfold yourself. Properly.
When you are sure you cannot see a damned thing, spin yourself around a few times for total disorientation. Great.
Now take six steps forward. Good.
Turn to the side of your writing hand. Excellent.
Now take another seventeen steps, then stop.
The fact that you cheating because you are still reading this – will be completely ignored. *For now.* Okay, take off the blindfold, if it isn't already, and open your eyes … Perfect.
What you see before you … *is a door.*

Opening *that door…* is going to be a total red pill moment for you.
It is going to be like one of those CSI shows where the sexy, intrepid investigator shines a blue light on a suspicious bedsheet and all sorts of invisible shenanigans pop into the audience evidence – revealing:

Who did what to who,
In which positions,
How many times,
For how long,
Right down to –
Who lit the cigarettes … after?

Opening up this dark portal is going to be similar to that.
It will reveal evidence of invisible *~Memes~* within.

So, you wanna do it?
Be Neo? Drop the sanguine disco-biscuit and all that?
Of course, you do!
The door creaks open … to reveal …

Your best friend and your spouse. Very busy having wild strenuous sex.

Press [Pause].
If you hadn't guessed it – this is an exercise of sorts.

What is happening here, is that we are plotting an ARC. And no, this is not about destroying the Matrix but it might get as messy.
An ARC is a construct that a story writer, most especially a screenplay writer, will use to help the target audience understand and connect with a character better. Emotionally.
The acronym stands for Action; Reaction; Consequence.
What is happening to you …
… is the *Action* part.

And it isn't the two kids on the bed doorknobbing away like demented minks either.
The action part is processing the revelation that occurs when you grab that shiny doorknob …
… and the screen transitions from cheaply painted blank wood … to … *98% likes on Xvideos.*
Right before your very own eyes.
Whaddayado?

This exercise is all about your Reaction to this scene.
You know exactly how you are responding already.

What we are going to do with the camera is follow you around and confirm this.
Press [Play]

Okay, so you open the door – There is yelling …

OhMyGod!! OhSweetJesus!! OhDoorKnob!!!
And you …

A.) Run into the room. Beat the miscreants to death with a tiny ceramic doorknob decorated with delicately painted little blue flowers and very firmly attached to the solid timber bedside table.
B.) Recite a dirge about love's doom then shoot yourself right between the crying doorknobs.
C.) Apologize profusely for disturbing them. Go to the bathroom. Doorknob wistfully to hardcore biker-tranny porn …
D.) Call out … *Has this been paid for!? No free backdoorknobbing! No exceptions!!*
E.) Go in meekly. Kneel by the bed. Beg to be plastic doorknobbed with lots of belt spanking.
F.) Shout – *Here comes Cocky's Chrome Doorknob!!* Rip off your clothes. Join in …
G.) Pull out all your money, toss it on the bed … *roar – Praise your Holy Doorknob Jesus!!*
H.) Close the sweaty doorknob and call your lawyer!
I.) Check your messages …
J.) None of the above.

If you answered (J.) then it's time to put the blindfold back on and go sit in the Fibbers Corner. And nobody cares if you cheat this time. Look at where you are sitting doorknob.

See, each of those scenarios is perfectly plausible.

A.) Diminished manslaughter[12].
B.) Romantic suicide.
C.) Closet celibate.
D.) Retail affection.
E.) Soft S&M.
F.) Group entertainment.
G.) Stark raving bonkers.
H.) Legal retribution.
I.) WTF Doorknob?

And what each of those scenarios does – tells us a bit more about you and your character. In the sense that one of the reactions is closest to what you would do in that entirely hypothetical scenario.

I mean, you weren't supposed to blindfold yourself. Or walk into things [Please don't sue the author.]. Or even open the door.

Okay, okay – so we brought the doorknob to the party and let you open the door.

And, just so we are back on the same page – (G.) probably isn't you but it undoubtedly happens a hell of a lot (in one way or another), *and with a lot more profane doorknobbing than most people think.*

What's truly important – *is your reaction to the other reactions.*

How did you feel about the submissive cuckold?
Or the greedy pimp? Or the religious nut?
You can't be all of them.
Especially the suicide. *Then you wouldn't be reading this.*
And you can't be entirely comfortable with all of the reactions.
Seriously – *Murder by frenzied, rage-fueled … over-bludgeoning? That Messy?*
See, those reveal ~Memes~ that are acceptable to others … *but not so acceptable to you.*
Check out the scenario again.

Nobody from our side said you were a male. Are you?
Who else is in that room? Names? What are their sexes?
Who did all the yelling? More importantly, what is the lawyer's number?
Are you comfortable with the author's use of direct engagement and the third person in plural?

---

[12] If you are French, otherwise we're talking first-degree homicide and possibly the needle, if you don't cop to a plea-deal with the D.A. The Jury is going to look Very Hard at you standing outside the door … *listening...* yet still grabbing the doorknob and not doing one of more of: (B) through (J)… Game, set … *Hot Spike! Doorknob...*

~Memes~, ~Memes~, ~Memes~

Our natural defense is to protect *~Memes~* that assure no threat to what we consider our comfort zones. Other *~Memes~* may be perfectly acceptable to other people, who may find your *~Memes~ problematic.*

The point is: absolutely nothing going on in that room is inconceivable – outside of the difference in the reactions.

One man's sweet 'n spicy basting is another man's prussic acid … Shuggawugga …

The only thing that can come out of that scenario, which is truly unacceptable – less acceptable than murder – is an *Unwanted* pregnancy resulting in an *Unwanted* Child being born nine months later and being left alone in this world.

All because of the *misuse and abuse of rotting Dangling Bananas.*

The rest of the whole sorry business is three skeletons in a room doing weird skeletal things that no future paleolithic type anthropologist could ever hope to explain.

We are biological creatures, in a locked, infinitely beautiful biodiverse system, that is extraordinarily simple to understand.

We all just complicate the granny-humping doorknob out of everything.

But hey, *are you having fun yet?*

Sifting Civilization

Long, long ago … in a faraway place … with some very weird ideas about the bedroom, now known as going greek in Ancient Greece – there existed a great but rather reluctant philosopher named Socrates.

A somewhat *angry*, yet vividly strident Don … rather tenuously attached to the first, finest, and only University of its time. Firmly seated in the greatest Divine Metropolis of the *Known World* …

Athens.

A loose-lived, thinking, simple man of *The People* - albeit one loose-lipped, alleged stonemason by trade. Not as much a Greater Thinker, and, thus inherently called to the *Philosophical Arts* by deep inner introspection *or the weird whispering visions of the bountiful gods* - but rather a scheming fellow employing a truly devious offshoot of blind cunning to intelligently offset - then put the same distance between himself, *serial unemployment*, and his even less mollifiable wife.

Thus, and by obtuse design … a stubbornly proud theorist whose core sophic went something like this:

What are you oedipious doorknob strokers bugging me for?
Can't you so-called people ever think for yourselves? Seriously?
Go A.W.A.Y.!
Better yet, bugger off, and don't come back until you hoary goatbangers have had one original thought on your Very Lonesome Ownsome's.
Can you do that?
Cook up just one new Idea among the whole Tragedy, yet not so Comedic … shitstained lot of you?
Just when a person needs a handy stoic with a soothing soporific, along comes some olive-oily arsed flapper with a rusty axiom to bump and grind.
Piss OFF!!

He had no known friends for obvious reasons but he did have a couple of loyally misplaced students who wrote things down for him. Why?
Well, it's a widely held belief that the poor man suffered from dyslexia.

A word he probably invented himself.

Although, precautionary detractors claim that making up a silly word to excuse a constant rotten and moody hangover, accompanied by a mulelike reluctance to doing any paperwork at all *academically* – is pretty much the equivalent of a badly forged sick note from your mum[13].

But Socrates pissed off all the priests and local politicians - *Royally*, which suited the College Administration just fine because this drew the spotlight rather smoothly off the fact that they also lived in raving unexpurgated decadence and did no discernable form of actual work either.

One fine day a fellow master oozed up to him and said: *"Oi, Socrates, do you know what I just heard about one of your 'orrible butty-boy students?"*

Tit-biting Bollocks!
Not that nasty little compulsive note-taking bugger Plato again – grouched the great Scholar grimly to his somewhat crapulous self. However, to the annoying, weaselly academic most unwelcomingly at hand … he uncharacteristically retrained his embattled and concurrent furry tongue … replying rather smoothly in his own opinion:

Hold that thought, my dear Sir.
Before you get into whatever the hells it is this time and incidentally make my ponokéfalo far worse, I require you, Good Sir, to perform a simple little test before you speak a jot further.
It is called the 'Three Sieves Test'.

'Three Sieves Test'?

Yes, sieve. Round thingy. Lots of tiny holes in it. Stop mimicking and interrupting me!
Before you say another word about my alleged shit-for-brains student, take your time to Think carefully about what you are going to say, by pouring what you are going to say - through three special sieves.
And Sir, I must stress that you perform this filtering process before you make another peep in my direction … Yes?

Er…

Excellent.
Now that we have That sorted out, the first sieve, is in fact, the translucent Sieve of Truth.
So-saying, are you sure … absolutely sure, without any shadow of a doubt, that what you are about to discharge concerning the filthy little bastard in question, is the bare-arsed Naked Truth?
Cross your liver? Hope to die?
Pinky swears?

---

[13] Socrates can't come to school tomorrow for the final Gim exam. He forgot where she left his homework what the dog already ate the last time too. Thnak you always as – from Φεναρέτ (His good old mom 😊)

Well, erm, not exactly as such.

Something I overheard in the baths and no, it wasn't another disgusting discourse on Archimedes if that's what you are possibly thinking.

Dig up Archimedes and bugger his corpse with a dripping wet Royal-Purple soap bar until bubbles come leaping out his demented earholes! But, in the meantime, do try to Think for yourself … if you are so dead set on wasting my beleaguered time, won't you?

My dear Fellow, have you failed to discern that my poor pickled brain is 'possibly' imposed? Failing miserably to devise a corrective for giving glory to that evil, conveniently ephemeron, godforsaken sod of a god Dionysus.

Good Gods Sir! Am I to understand there isn't a shred of first-hand Truth in what you wish to say to me in this state?

Silence!!

Don't think about interrupting me again godsdammit!

Thought so.

Moving on rapidly to the second sieve … the Sweet and Tender Sieve of Goodness.

Are you, 'good' Sir, going to tell me something Good about the vulgar little dog doorknobber you have yet to name as a person?

No, er … not exactly.

Marvelous. So, you wish to intrude, impose, and then unleash grossly noxious vapors concerning all manner of unrevealed deviancy, related solely to an anonymous ratfaced little miscreant … smugly onto Me?

Treacherous bile!

That which is really none of my sodding business in the first place and you don't even know if it's the Bloody Truth or Not!?

Er …

Zeus doorknobbing his muther onnastick!

You people reduce me to being viler in this State … than I already Am!

So be it, squawking Fool!

Last chance! Final Sieve …

Demonstrate, IF, you can redeem your shameless excuse of a mucus blathering anus, by clearly disproving that you are most indeed a feces fondling Idiot of the very foremost persuasion.

And thus, for this final burden of proof, we now turn to the Cold Sieve of Usefulness.

Do tell, Good Sir… is what you are bursting out of your slimy toga to freely repose in my tender mind, have any possible grain of usefulness for Man, Woman, or Bitch Humping Dog?

Not so much … erm … that is to say no …

Not True!
No Good for Man or Filthy Beast!
And, utterly bloody Useless to Boot!
Why in the name of all cursed Hells are you wasting my time and Sacred Pain?
Begone … Turdknobber!!!
Before I am forced to ~Meme~ you to death with a blunt doorknobbing corollary!!

What a great man. Wonderful attitude. Very pragmatic.
Down to earth.
Great inspiration to everyone.
Yes, indeed:

Be *Truthful.*
Be of *Good Intent.*
Be *Useful.*

Use your brain and quit feebly pawing at the mind of some other poor bastard with an ungodly hangover.

Rise within the crumbling edifices of old broken ideas young Athenians!
Rationalize against craven syphilitic politics and the inbred ruling families!
Expose the opulent venality inherent in the squabbling religions of the Day!
Scorn democracy-by-bribe and spit on champagne-socialism!
Rejoice, Fellow Citizen, of greedy hate-filled … failing Empires!
You know Nothing and are certain of sweet fanny doorknobs …
Don't come back till you can prove me wrong!
And … you fried chickendoorknobbers can PAY me for my troubles!!
Without letting the door slap you up your greasy-arses …
… on the way OUT!!

As an unwritten philosophy, this truly does need a more thorough interrogation with a reloaded application in our *not-so-complex* Multiplexed Modern Times.

If one is to quantify *civilizational decay* back here in gloomy, paranoid, barking aggressive 20/21 as an increase in overall levels of poverty, crime, and sociological dysfunction – with a marked decrease in cognitive education … *irrevocably co-related to cogent Employment Capabilities,* among other directly impacting negative factors in any country …
Then birth rates will be linked to the economic health and growth of that particular State.

When Economic Growth > Birth rates = economic health + social development
When Economic Growth < Birth rates = economic *decline* + social *regression*

A synthetic tree will only sustain the nutrient needs of a finite number of Naked Apes before those apes run out of sustenance, turn on each other, and eventually kill the entire Tree.

Where this becomes most vividly apparent is in countries with extreme *"Gini"* indexes.
This measures the so-called *"Inequality Gap"* between …
"Privileged" … those who save, invest and retain wealth *and* …
"Disadvantaged" … those who purchase revolving credit, spend disposable cash, and/or live in bitter generational hand-to-mouth poverty.

For example – In so-called *"multi-ethnic"* societies like South Africa (which has the highest Gini coefficient globally) – the various Sub-Saharan Bantu Tribes and their surviving clans who migrated South from the Congo region to settle there several centuries ago, experience very high birth rates, due to *"Colonial"* medicine and consuming the best food security in Africa from industrialized *"Colonial"* farming but for the most part – all subsist in extreme poverty with accompanying levels of horrifying crime.
Both in rural subsistence and rapidly over-expanding urban tin-shanty township populations.
This is in a marked and very stark contrast to their minority non-Bantu compatriots, who concurrently occupy a significant portion of the embattled, *Capitalist Private Sector's established middle and upper classes* and live in reflecting economic neighborhoods.

Wherever there is a birth rate that exceeds the economic growth of a country like South Africa, it will experience increases in the poverty levels amongst the high birth rate groupings, leading to a decline in socio-economic function.

This has occurred in SA.

Ruled by an over-paid and atrociously underperforming, Ruling Party, constantly draining a dwindling tax base – comorbid with established capital and skills flight, but irreversibly chained to an overall chronic inability of hard-liner *Sparkling Wine* Bantu Communists to create better-paying jobs in free-falling National Junk Status, yet still obliviously bleeding the National Fiscus dry for instant-enrichment – with zero regards as to consequence imparted to their own Tribes … other than legal exposure to themselves, their families, cohorts, henchmen, and close cronies.

In short: *Too many uneducated, unemployed and unemployable Bantu mouths to feed, while in the "Revolutionary" care of too many primitive Bantu liars, sickening drunken murderers, and filthy low-life, backward tribal-gang-bang thieves.*

The low birth rate minority groups can afford better levels of education and make better contributions to the National Economy, re-bolstering the established middle classes but constantly shaming the non-performing Marxists, which is then prosecuted as political resistance to *Economic Displacement* by the self-selective Bantu tribes, to whom the entire National Economy, speciously "*Belongs*" … concomitant to the edicts of post-apartheid, over-the-counter … *Bantu Afrocentrism.*

A luta Continua, vitória é certa …

This *manufactured resistance* is widely propagandized as the appropriated "*White Privilege*" of Left-wing America expressed as "*Apartheid Racism*" … *and* loudly declared the sole cause of abject poverty and grimy social dysfunction among the Bantu Tribal groupings.

It is deceptively simple …

Populist Afro-Marxist/Fanonist (*ex-terrorist*) politicians use the abstract concepts of "*Fighting Colonialism*" and the *potty-mouthed* Bell-Pottinger's so-called "*White Monopoly Capital Influencing*" among other high-contrast shades of acquired race-based baiting propaganda – in their short-cut path to power, and once in power will do everything to fan the deflecting flames of cultural hatred by claiming this to be an *Evil Social Norm* deeply prevalent among *all non-Bantu minorities.*

Indians, Europeans, Khoisan, Afrikaners, Arabs, Coloureds, Slavs, Asians, Latinos, Mixed-races …

… in fact, all economically successful South African compatriots along with Pan African foreigners, who are openly critical of the *Glorious Leadership* … are claimed to be *Racist* against the Bantus.

Especially the ethnic South African *Europeans* and *Indians.*

The tiny eight percent, *European*, very low birth rate demographic – *Most Specifically.*

According to modern *Bantu Nationalist Urban-Mythology*, these non-Bantu folk, all want Apartheid back, because they are all "*Racist*".

They ALL hate on Bantus.

A topical, sweeping, *race-based* bait-and-switch, constantly on the lookout for the slightest reaction to the salted accusations, to gleefully explode into an aggrieved public outrage.
Screaming and wailing bitter …

… Racial Persecution!!

Which does have its intended, *transatlantic* Woke effect …

And this collective of smaller South African minorities is constantly interplayed upon in varying degrees as somehow the sole root origin of every social ill among their own *self-impoverished, deliberately miseducated, high birth rate, regressive* Tribes, including, strangely enough, those Westernized and formally educated tribal members, who are speciously labeled "*Sellouts to the Racists*" and vilely persecuted like the sweetly de-Americanized … "*Coconut*".
Counter revolutionaries. TV Uncle Toms … one and all.

Ubaba Zuma's, murderously hated … "*Clever Blacks*".

The reason why the word "*Apartheid*" has transmogrified into a catch-all Afrocentric MSM *euphemism* for blame-shifting the dire socio-economic ills experienced within multi-ethnic societies, burdened with highly disproportionate birth rates among the various ethnic groupings occupying that dysfunctioning State.

Hence … the urgent need for *Transformation* and … *Non-Racist "Equality"*.

Liberal Equality = (Low birth rates + economic health + natural growth) – (High birth rates + economic decline + political decline + welfare + systemic corruption + socialist thievery + n)

Socialists, being pathological thieves and ideologically incorporated liars, are utterly unable to attend to natural value exchanging systems, and thus generate the means for attracting human capital investment – to thereby grow the economy and create a commonwealth base needed to care for the entire Nation's children, and their futures.

Consequently, spiteful attacks are financed through looted tax, then launched willy-nilly on race-based "*Symbols*" of Blacks-Only "*Racist Pain*" speciously linked to the low birth rate groups – *Politically …*

… As in, the tearing down of monuments, burning of open public libraries, torching of hundreds of Bantu schools, public hospitals, trains, and looting of supply chains, along with the wanton destruction of municipal infrastructures.

And … *Concurrent* with periodic brazen running violence, arson, and *in-class* intimidation – visited barbarically upon "*Colonized*" non-Bantu institutions of higher learning.
Public tertiary-education institutions that were all established by hated non-Blacks-Only to teach and develop for all South Africans the mechanics of modern civilization.

The focus of the race-based Tribal hates being directed at those top *former* globally-rated Universities that the entire beleaguered non-Bantu minority use as the only turnkey to greater economic participation.

Including highly grateful foreign students.

Constantly acting out in infantile spite against every form of civilization that is *non-Blacks-Only* … which for Bantus Tribes unfortunately *and very uncomfortably* … pretty much means raging against *Everything* the communists are unable and completely unwilling to create or contribute to.

Not to mention Xenophobia, which was formally referred to as *Affirmative Shopping* but is in reality, cooking up any old excuse to periodically loot and destroy foreign-owned small shops (Spazas) and businesses.

The Bantu version of *"Decolonization"* apparently:

Greater Equality = (Low birth rates + trailing economic recovery + wilting growth) – (High birth rates + economic decline + political decline + educational decline + welfare + systemic corruption + socialist thievery + n*)

*Where "n" is quantified as (n+X), and where X is an acronym for sporadic gratuitous banditry.

Most especially when applied to *Advanced Affirmative-shopping.*

An upmarket and more refined … ultra-hyperbolic version … which is popularly known as State Capture …

Total Transformative Equality = (Low birth rates + economic recession + capital flight + skills flight + declining growth) – (High birth rates + economic decline + political decline + educational decline + welfare + systemic corruption + socialist thievery + Xenophobia + n*)

*Where "n" is quantified as (n x Z**), and where Z is a quantity measured as (n + Zuptaz + Rapid Economic Transformation Banditry + Rising Costs of 0 prosecutions + Industrial Strength State Resource Looting + Gouged running costs of factional ANC internal fighting) x (Expanding costs of extorting Jan van Riebeek's docking at the Western Cape in 1652 x Current Death-Dive Junk Status)

**Covid-19 Rapid Economic Transformative "July '21 Insurrection/Protests" not weighted, or added to this highly inflammable-fluid equation.

This form of decolonization is not to be confused, in any mildly sane or practical economic sense, with the *Singaporean Version.*

Although, that would be utterly impossible to do anyway.

Can you imagine the President of Singapore running off to South Africa for private medical treatment in a State-run Hospital, because he is as morbidly terrified of his physicians as Glorious Bantu "Leaders" are?

They, don't see the … *Why Not?*

The ruling Bantu Elite have ostensibly proven that a legislated 30% Matric pass rate and a stupefying cauldron of *"Traditional Healers"* has miraculously decolonized paltry Western Medicine to produce the foremost Certified Sangomas [witch doctors] in the entire world.

Hell, they can: *"Make BIG enlarge Penis -- Return lost Love -- Confuse Police -- Disappear Crime Dockets – Find New Lover and make you …*
… Number One Money-Lucky Today!" …

On top of sorting out gruesome embarrassing ailments, grisly violent wounds, or incestuous backyard abortions … you certainly don't want to go to your normal doctor or the cops to find out about.
Besides, your average pill-pushing GP probably doesn't accept homemade beer spiked with old batteries or dodgy live chickens as payment.
Very *holistic.*

The poor previously disturbed man would end up *winging* his way back home, in the proven peak of perfect innocent health … pockets bulging with Ca$h, and with a super-pretty dolly-girl valiantly keeping a lap-dance from developing into a pole-dance, on his ginormous, New-and-Improved -- *trurry most-honallable* –- Not-Number-Two WONG!!

This irrational developing erosion of the primary means to successfully increase the national skills and wealth pool will be cyclically justified by those leveraging to stay in power – for no other reason than to feed at the rapidly dwindling corruption trough.

Insidiously and relentlessly propagandized as a *"fight against Colonialism / Slavery / Oppression / WMC / Advancing RET / etc. / ad-Nauseum"* …

… Utterly regardless of the grassroots sociological destruction visited upon their own rapidly regressing Tribes and clans.

This, while the Comrades get puking drunk and gorge themselves senseless on stolen taxes. Entirely comfortable that, *as … Glorious Anti-Apartheid Revolutionaries,* they exist above "The [non-Blacks-Only] Law" or any reasonably sane form of developed human ethics and morality.

While South Africa is just another sad example of an almost completely failed African shit hole, which tiny *Unwanted* kids drown in periodically, this forcefully applied economic partisan parasitism, by the dysfunctional high birth rate groups, remains a prevalent factor in any country or political dispensation.

No matter how well developed or *aggressively self-deteriorating.*

The United States has experienced a continuous decline in birth rates over the last few decades but the prevailing trend is an exact mirror to South Africa in that higher income groups have the lowest birth rates and ergo, *greater access and control over the National Economy.*

The face of the new Democrat dispensation is one promoting a "*Nanny*" type socialist state that is attempting to *force* unwilling low birth rate groups to take economic and social responsibility for the dysfunctional high birth rate groups. Something that has been going on as blueish smoke-and-mirrors and borrowed against by the New Democrats for far too long politically.
But this too, is a natural dynamic progression, albeit for the sake of debilitating left-wing political *expediency.*

The Hawaiians may have the highest birth rate of all the American minority groupings but they also have the lowest percentage of the USA population.
American Caucasians have a much lower birth rate than African-Americans, yet African-Americans have approximately three times the number of fatherless households than non-Hispanic European Americans do.

The highest percentage of fatherless households by any demographic is occupied by Native-Americans and Pacific-Islander-Americans.
Added together, however, they represent *<7% of the total population of Fatherless African-American children, who come in at a shocking third placed percentage.*

That is … 93/100 Unwanted kids in that demographic are African American.

No doubt about it – absent African-American biological Fathers are, by far – *the greatest number of social deadbeats draining and causing strain to the National Economy among all of the United States' citizens doing so.*

And so, according to commercial arithmetic, they are, by rote – *the largest, poorest, and most regressive* of American-American demographics.

Fact.

Ergo, the attacks launched on recently declared over-the-counter African-American Afrocentrism symbols – linked to the lower birth rate majority groupings, in control of the National Economy – as in the tearing down of historical monuments, the burning of "Red" effigies, and multipronged "Woke" attacks within institutions of higher learning.

This too, with a self-declared view to double down on the imposition of Cultural Marxism as a recognized, dogmatic, social imperative, albeit in shrouded favor of the highest birth rate groupings' complete unwillingness to:

Accept American-American Civic Responsibility for bringing Unwanted children into a free-market economy, that you do not care to participate in, Before … having a screaming tantrum over African American or any other form of Civil Rights.

Wannabe Wiggers, Antifa, and every additional mewling Blue-arsed crack-addled transgender obsessed donkey included!

No one has to call you names, butt ugly is as butt ugly Does.

You … DO THIS … to Your Unwanted abandoned Children!

Children who have the right to be wanted American-American Sons and Daughters too – but that's your basic human Male responsibility as Fathers on any side of any skin color spectrum …

Not Mr. Donald Trump's.
Never was, never shall be.

Woke Equality (Blue Trans Donkey Variant) = (Low birth rates + economic health + natural growth) – (High birth rates + non-economic participation + free political mileage + free welfare + free money for felons + free crack-pipes + educational decline + freed up systemic corruption + Deep State socialist thievery + n)

*Where "n" is quantified as (n + §), a 20/21 rising constantly where § is an acronym for (Runaway BLM Riots x 180 Days) – (Jan 6).

When looking at these two vastly different countries, within this 20/21 timeframe, one has to seriously begin wondering …

Who the Hell is copying Whom?

This leads to an annual US GDP that is unable to sustain both the Woke and their non-participatory *Unwanted* Offspring – without re-borrowing heavily against the Federal State.

Fomenting a continuous downward spiraling, *cyclic,* fake economic growth, founded on an exponentially burgeoning National Debt, for no other reason than to procure and retain Political Power through implementing unsustainable populist socialist ideology – regardless.

Something that buys *Easy-Dope Woke-up Votes* and gets very smoothly palmed off in the West as progressive Democratic Liberalism.

Ergo, when the political rhetoric generated by the failed left-wing high birth rate groups reaches a critical mass – veiled threats will be made to exterminate the lower birth rate groups.

These threats will then be acted out through rioting, violence, looting, arson, and attacks on localized law enforcement. Resistance to this will be claimed as "Fascism" and "Right-Wing Aggression", then used to re-double the violence, looting, arson, and attacks on localized law enforcement. Gratuitously enervating even further violent confrontation.

The sharpest MSM focus will deflect smartly onto equally racist, right-wing reactionaries and other outraged sub-marginal extremists – to gratuitously, once again, underscore the purile virtue of asinine moral outrage, crucial to the validity of the synthesized *peri-Afrocentric African-American Wakanda Male Cause* demon possessing the Woke Far Left.

Ironically, the only outcome of this insanity is less economic participation by high birth rate groupings, leading to mind-boggling increases in crime levels and more reliance on The State to provide non-participatory financial incomes and general welfare – for the fast-expanding, yet non-performing demographics – *Unwanted*.
Including basic Healthcare but not inclusive of the gross cost of Custodial Incarcerations, *grand arson, destruction of private property, and spiteful gratuitous violence – coupled with mass banditry, drug-fueled madness, and misogynistic hooliganism.*

When these types of events can no longer sustain leveraged political power for a populist *"Nanny"* type *"Blue"* Administration, the lurking rapid economic decline will set in … as all the National Debt markers get called upon, leading to direct Woke attacks by the "Democratic" mob aimed at undermining The Constitution and Judicial System - upon which The Republic is founded – leading to even greater social dysfunction, more "racial" and other extremism on both far sides, with the vehement scapegoating of resurgent imaginary ills – completely unrelated to *households with too many babies, too many mouths to feed – way too little money and absolutely no decent fathers in sight*.

(See all socio-economic equations above)

And *Then* …
Straight out of the Not-Blue, *just for shits an' giggles* – along comes a bunch of redneck *chaw-chewin'* GOP cowboys, way down yonder in South Texas – who voted in favor of turning fervent prayers unto Almighty Jesus, *Against Sinful Abortions* – into a binding law *Against South Texas Women*. That whole State being so born-agin' n'all … *it done got permanent stretch marks.*

Effectively depriving these American-American ladies of their Constitutional freedom to make their own *Personal*, life, and *Science-Based*, non-Republican, doorknob-the-GOP medical choices … concerning their own [*dare one say it*] …

… "God-given" bodies …

Way to go Y'all …

Now, you good 'ol boys get down on your knees and do something about them tampon thangs. Unnatural it is. Using disgustin' furriner thangs like that. A pussy board was done good enough for my gramma. It damn well done be good enough for alla them uppity gals too. Besides, Lord knows, the Good Lord would approve. Caring about Y'all womenfolks being led inta all kinda furrin thinkin's on the can n'all. Git onnit fellas …

… Who's gonta gimme a, Amen?

Socrates urged his contemporaries to find Supreme Purpose, and ultimately – Think for Yourself.

Think for Yourself.
Determine your Own Morality.
Redefine everything you think you know.

Finally, when the lower birth rate groups are displaced from controlling the economy by the parasitic political power Woke elites *"Representing"* higher birth rate groups *"Democratically"* – actual sporadic genocide-lite will be attempted, resulting in complete localized economic ruin and the collapse of that infrastructure.

Something the USA is almost nudging towards grudgingly, most especially in Democrat inner-cities, and something that is a long way down the road to already happening irreversibly in South Africa.

The Republic of South Africa.
Home to:
The International Federation of Christian Churches, Zionist Church, South African Council of Churches, ANC/DA/EFF, Sainted dead Mandela [cougherrorists], etc, etc, and:

applause

Their unclaimed, *Unwanted – Three and a half million living orphaned children* - coupled with innumerable *Unwanted* Bantu child-headed households.

What would Jesus say to the *anointed* Pastors in the high-end BMWs and Ferraris?

What did Jesus say to the *Mother of that vast Gathering of Unwanted Child Ancestors* after another kid drowned in a vile stinking pit latrine at dysfunctional Bantu crèche, when was that, wasn't it last week?
Silence?

Now, take a very deep breath … settle yourself … then look to Europe and the massive influx of desperate at-risk refugees from utterly failed war-torn Islamic countries, where every single woman is considered … either *a filthy Whore* … or *a paid-for Object* whose innate living duty it is to submit to being nothing more than a religious incubator to proliferate as many *jihadis* as possible.

Quite openly determined to elbow whinging liberal democracy out of the non-binary way in favor of brutally executing full-blown Sharia Law.

Something that is bound to end in far more suicide bombings, armed attacks, crazed stabbings, generalized bloodshed, justified paranoia, and inhuman crimes against Women and Children with way too many tears …
… way … Way Too Late.

Know thy truly hard-core primitive theosophy, before it cuts out your beating heart … *then devours it … with all your precious Children* … Raw and dripping with Blood … *in the stead of a dangling ripe banana* – to appease the Hideously Vengeful Gods.

Think for Yourself.
Determine your own morality.
Redefine everything you Think You Know.

South Texas Republicans should take a good long look at the Taliban, if they believe they have an absolute proxy choice, through bronze-age religion, over any female Homo Sapiens's body or her mind. *Why the sneaky doorknob? Play it through … shoot the whole nine yards, fellas.*

The Pope could also learn a thing or three from Afghans about desensitizing and consolidating *Bacha Bazi* as an acceptable cultural practice.

If you don't know – it means "boy-play", where a select gathering of old religious tribesmen, gets high, then gang-rape a very young child they've groomed and drugged for that very purpose.

Sounds excruciatingly familiar … doesn't IT – Your Holiness?

And, thank fuck You very much … that *Your "Holiness"* – is in no way mine.

Not even the basest of The Lord's Beasts do to each other what you have condoned your Priests doing and Still Doing to innocent children!!
Let me instruct You …

Padre – your "enlightened" Name, your obscene Gilt Slathered Temples, and everything to do with the vile, filthy, obscenities of self-vanquished Rome …
… are eternally Cursed by God!

Take heed, take deep heed "Padre" ... these words will be remembered by my children, at some close point in future history – as nothing more than an ugly viral sickness injected and reinjected into the minds of frightened, greedy men from generation to generation – for millennia ... until a Stop was put to IT.

It would have been far better if You had taken Your barren thirty pieces of Verdigris Silver and basked in the terrified praises and obsequious mewling adulation of Naked Great Apes on street corners. Exactly like the ancient Pharisees of yore.

Desperate for Your blessings and begging to kiss Your fake Holy ring, while you cower away inside your Bulletproof Popemobile.

Content, nauseatingly pampered, and utterly convinced within Your mind that You live so far above mere fallen mortals and too – the filthy depraved vicars You Rule Over ... that nothing can touch You, except ...

God Himself.
Yellow Coward.

But your gluttony and congregant self-adulation made you forget – The Christ has already declared the price of Eternal Damnation:
The Thirst and life of only ONE Unwanted Child.

The innumerable children's lives that you and your heinous, sexually depraved Priests have fed into the maw of Hell, just through their pedophile inflicted self-hating suicidal sacrifice ... offered to utterly unforgivable evil ...

... is Legion.
The name and true nature of your filthy Roman pig-Latin god.
Fit only to possess a herd of drowned unholy ...

... bloated unclean swine ... clutching in rigor onto other people's desperate Offerings you use to buy silence for your filthy crimes.

In Heaven, under His everlasting Throne, His feet are awash in their immortal Innocent Blood!!
You, and all with you, Holy Naked Ape – are, forever ...

... Eternally Cursed by that Almighty God.

How's that for a cold hard harsh reality?
And *Believe It or Not*, it's all written down in The Bible.

Précised ... *into* a suitably: *Doom-Laden Voice* ... but absolutely all scribbled down in there somewhere.

Amid decline – Be Truthful.

This is the most uncomfortable truth of all in a desperate *Post-Truth* world.

‡§‡

Here's another one – There are too many *Unwanted* births. *Everywhere.*

These births are unwittingly facilitated by an indifferently combined Global Society of highly educated people who occupy low birth rate demographic groupings, coupled with very high incomes and economic wealth participation. *And,* who are collectively able to afford to enforce their political and religious *Wills* vicariously upon women and girls who have never had the same science-based medical choices over their bodies. Not in society and not in any of their sub-socio-economic, religious, and para-political enslavements.

Is that … *You?*

The outcome?

More applause

Runaway Gender-Based Violence *Globally* and upward of one hundred and fifty million orphans and displaced kids worldwide*!

*(Insert long-term human Cost-equation** of sustaining ongoing Political and Religious Choices, but only calculate this when TOO LATE. **See above.)*

Corrupted bargain-basement identity politics in bed with distorted money-grubbing religious ~Memes~ are not going to fix this moral and economic shortfall.
That is a rock-solid truth no one can hack through.

Think for Yourself.
Determine your own morality.
Redefine Everything you think you know.

The ancient Great Scholar considered this the only rational pursuit of one's life mission.

Amen?

The leading Athenians of Socrates' time considered any idea that would lure the Youth from their ambit of manipulation and influence – to be a direct attack on their base of power and a viable attempt at eroding their penultimate authority.

Damn right!

So, they promptly charged the contemptuous philosopher with leading the youth into decadence.

He died for his convictions by self-inflicted hemlock poisoning, an *assisted suicide* ... because he flatly refused to abscond from *The Practice* ... or to *Stand Down* ... from guarding these *Principles*.

Since then, a string of theorists from drippy dick Nietzsche to some cunt called Kant has more or less copied the same idea – *sans the bloody-mindedness and contemptuous hemlock chugging.*

Not surprisingly, if one thinks about it – because it is a perfectly natural philosophy that can be found echoed repeatedly in the core of pretty much all *Independent, Highly Successful, and ultimately Progressive human endeavors.*

> *Think for Yourself.*
> *Determine your Own Morality.*
> *Redefine Everything You Think You Know.*

Socrates also held firmly that any pursuit should be approached first and foremost with inherent *good intent.*

Remember ...

Be *Truthful.*
Be of *Good Intent.*
Be *USEFUL.*

The problem with Political and Religious ideals is that they may have found themselves grounded in good intentions but their final applications utterly beggar belief in their cause – quite simply because of the terrible effects that remain being gouged into an ever-passing yet tediously re-cyclic history.

His greatest piece of advice was the quirky admonition to:

> *Think little of Socrates – and a great deal more of the Truth.*

So be it.

Every single God is real.
This includes all the identified dead gods too.

Angels, demons, and invisible beings are all real.
From every religion that has ever existed.

Ghosts, spirits, wraiths, sprites, and phantoms are real.
In every haunted house, holy-roller revival and present at every authentic séance.

Heavens and Hells are both real.

All of them.
Every single one.

The World religions, being: Animisms to Pantheisms unto Monotheisms, from every corner of the globe and to be found in every nook and cranny of human history, all share the same origin in actualized physical reality …
BELIEF.

But, consider … *Belief* is merely a by-product of clinging to the outcome of Human Imagination. And, *Imagination* while being entirely infinite in scope – *IS* exactly as existential in duration as the *finite lifespan of any sentient animal's living Neurobiology.*

They live …
… Gods do.
In Real Places.

Notwithstanding, each of those *real places* – flows forth from a living Homo Sapiens' *Neurochemistry.*
That warm cerebral womb and ultimate spawning ground of all *human …*

~*Memes*~

No baby has ever been born with any type of "*God*" within its natal neuro structures, *however,* by the time that child can walk and talk, and begins to experience and *remembers Being* – it will be keeping at least one alive for The Tribe.
Exactly like a non-biological parasite or virtual tapeworm in the brain.
Even if it is only a fat old jolly bearded man from the North Pole, attired in a cherry-red suit booming …
… Ho-Ho-Ho!

Doesn't get truer than that Cousin.

This proves that comfortable lies sell a hell of a lot better … *and far* … far easier than one lone uncomfortable truth.
Bought and Sold … to any terrified Homo Sapiens, who desperately needs to moot, however mendaciously – *the true, limited, and restricted … existential Nature of Life.*

It is almost impossible – to benignly offer, or even freely give away – certain intensely hard cold facts … *when Not being Nice, because it's a Fact, results in being inked onto …*

‡§‡

The Permanent Naughty List.

The freest and most unsettling Truth of all?
"Civilized Man" has always required religions of some form or another, co-joined to his pyramid politics and subsequent economic production systems to underpin basic acts of cause and purpose. Ever since mankind needed religion to function personally on the psychological level when dealing with, and filtering an ever-growing self-awareness of death – concomitant to a terrifying conscious dread of incipient psychological oblivion, concurrent to a traumatic biological demise.

Try sell that for a dollar …

The second functional, yet highly altruist and overt practical purpose of religion – is to bind a non-coherent grouping of people into a cooperative socio-economic unit with a "universally" (religion-wide) recognized moral and ethical code that ostensibly serves the Group rather than pandering to the individual.

A lot like minkeys.
Nothing wrong with that.
A great place to start actually.
More than just a perfect place to get back to the drawing board to start over.
The ideal.
Just done differently.

Put a neon pin in that …

It is from this highly objective vantage that one can begin reconciling why *utter horror and true selflessness can spring from the same root …*

~Memes~

Then it becomes increasingly apparent that Men and Women … being *Individual, hairless, Naked Great Apes*, are wholly capable of being Evil Monsters or sweet Blessed Saints, entirely in their own right and … *absolutely by their very own volition.*

Rather than in the acquired *Name* of any imaginary god, political cult, or faux religious ideal.

Those either serve as inadvertent vehicles for individuals quietly delivering actualized compassion with an investment in personal mercy or invariably evolve into shadowy havens to manipulate the *Supreme Purile Excuse* – for ongoing sociopathology … the pursuit of employing primal fear to achieve psycho-dominance over others … *and*, quite obviously giving full expression to an unbridled assemblage of sickening narcissism utterly overrun with greed, greed, Greed.

From the pulpit to the political podium and back again, including the cold voracious boardroom.

The truly worst part of any religion is how interpretations, speeches, and sermons can program, through esoteric language, someone who may be a blessed minkey in their own right – into a replicated member of *a group of evil monsters beholden only to someone other Naked Ape's sick or avaricious imagination.*

The power of marketing and promotional copy.

A lone pen directing the bloodied swords …

That is what makes all religions, cults, and sects detrimental, useless, and very dangerous to the long-term future or benefit of mankind. Secular, apostate, heretic, backslidden body politic, or otherwise.

Take the subjective reality of a "*God*" or a "*Jesus*" …
… or the Great "*Whatever*" out of the equation for a second …

Is religious, political, and identity-based "Othering" along with the fervid preaching of "Hell" – its very creation in societies here on Earth?

Is the Apocalypse of St. John a "prophesy" or some twisted suicidal end-goal to subconsciously pursue with the entire planet as the unwilling scapegoat?

What makes holy water "Holy" when it's just recycled piss that has passed through eons of living biological creatures too numerous to count?

How the Scarlet Doorknob is the Pope's piss and stinking gourmet shit holier than the same of a starving, abused, orphaned little girl?

What is going on Moneywise – when a Priest can spend a cool three million dollars on marble steps for a Roman Church but the average payout to make a child-rape accusation go away, super-quietly, is a mere $90k?

How the holy doorknob can the sanctified kiddydoorknobbers – Il "Pappa", noisily jangling the Keys to Heaven …
… on Global Main Stream Media – actually expect to be taken seriously when he tells the entire world that the correct punishment for a convicted pedophile priest on his watch is:
… "A lifetime of Prayer and Penance"…

And, contrives to give a bear-shit about it still happening in a papal forest of whining evil prayers?

Huh? *Seriously?*

Has this artificial tin-Roman monarch *Ever Read* the eighteenth chapter of the Gospel of St. Mathew? Maybe the deranged charlatan should actually be given a real shit-shovel and sent off swiftly to Canada to help dig up the mass graves of indigenous children on Catholic residential properties currently being discovered there … then firmly drag his odious arse back to the ICC and put him and his scarlet Cardinals on trial with the war criminals, African Strong Men and …
… other sickening human despots of every persuasion.

Or, and this is the touchdown kicker – Without Jesus – What is the real reason why every slick-dick Fundamentalist Pastor and oleaginous arse-licking acolyte – claims it needs [oh so wants] 10% of a Believer's cash or other liquid income for Prayerful, Glorious, Wonderous, Miraculous, Worshipful, Joyful, Gifted, Anointed, Prophetic – *"Sweet Almighty Jesus Ministry"*?

What in Heaven could *"God"* or the missing *"Jesus"* [or, his Mom for that matter] want with money that legitimately belongs to a Government Mint and its Central Bank by Human Law?

Who is committing the Biblical *swindle, money laundering, and tax frauds,* God or his *"Holy Spirit-Filled"* Pastors & pederast Roman Priests"?

Asking for Beelzebub's buddy's butler's big BBF.

Don't you just love the smell of laundry detergent and real-lemon fresh, super whitewash bleach in the morning?
Washes away all the entirely unforgivable filthy stains and briskly sanitizes those stinky sins – without all the song and silly dance!

Hallelujah!!

Think for Yourself.
Determine Your Own Morality.
Redefine Everything You Think You Know.

What kind of Parents entrust and drag their children off to freaks like these … repeatedly?

Make their kids go to private "Confession" or," Religious Counselling", so some sweaty-palmed creep may get a psychological fishhook into their vulnerable developing minds … and once successfully under their Spiritual control – then rape their pubescent bodies.

What kind of "Parent" does that?

What kind of parents accept money, instead of laying criminal charges to ensure that it doesn't happen to other people's kids …
… who will also Never See IT Coming?

What kind of parents actually Enable filth with Offerings to pay off their sex crimes like this???

The true nature and non-DNA transmission vector of the mutated 20/21 *Virus*.
Menkind's most subtle, passive-aggressive – yet mass-destructive of all …

~Memes ~

Showing more and more terminal Symptoms, and getting ever regressive by the day …

Looking at the fallen Greco-Macedonian Empire with all those specious, *vanished*, lavishly bestowed sacrifices offered unto the venerated Holy Priests of their deeply dead and highly revered Gods [who Lived on that Sacred Mountain over there] – one can only conclude, that at some level …

Socrates was spot-on concerning *lethally-toxic, politically-sacred Bananas and their waaayyy past sell-by-date.*

Wow, an actual forth-telling "*prophet*" and a profound anti-cultist worth listening to!
Even if it means ignoring the micro-paradox of him telling everyone to go vigorously stinky doorknob … *then come to their Own Conclusions.*

A bit like that dude Hegel, who reckons the only goldarned thang man has learned from history – is he hasn't learned a goldarned thang from history with the only rare exception being that quantum maniac who locked his longsuffering dead-or-alive cat in a sealed box to ostensibly insulate it from human stupidity, or, and get this … being shot by that Hawkins fella with the funny *slowly-being-strangled* robot voice.

So, why bother?

Ups for that one Cousin, but doorknobbit, it's not …

[Game Over]

Quite just yet …
… so why not duck the highly unlikely quadradrillic bullet and give it another go genius?

Here's another intellectual *self-regulating* exercise:

Strip out all the giddy, *Holy-Spooky, Casper-the-Unfriendly, Ghostlier-than-Thou, Whooo-o-woo …*
Supernatural …
… Claptrap … for another second or triple-six …

Broken down to basics, the currently *Warring, Murdering, Hate-filled – prevailing multimedia*
monotheisms, with their vividly Jealous, Greedy, Spiteful, Love-Bombing gods …

Judaism, Christianity, Islam – ironically, all share the same basic core tenet, which when
précised even further addresses only one single moral imperative.

Do not take anything that does not belong to you.

Do Not Steal.

Do not steal a man's "god".
Do not steal his wife
Do not enslave his children.
Do not steal his property.
Do not steal his freedom.
Do not steal his reputation.
Do not steal his peace of mind.
Do not steal his life.

Do Not STEAL.

These warnings, *Ten Commandments*, clearly defined core moral imperatives, *whatever,* are an
all-encompassing dire *caveat* addressed to all men.

As basic rules within any sociological grouping, they make complete sense in terms of
reducing social stressors and encouraging social cohesion.

Although, it does say something about the nature and character of any man [or his supposed
Creator] when the only way that this simple rule can be *enforced* is via the lifelong threat of the
coming vengeful wrath from an imaginary Deity.
Coupled with the practical infliction of actual living punishment for those archetypal men who
essentially steal from other men.
Especially those men who take another man's daughters to beat, rape, enslave and then
abandon Her babies …
… Unwanted.

Think for Yourself.
Determine Your Own Morality.
Redefine Everything You Think You Know.

The Christian addition to Biblical texts tells the story of Christ's disciples coming to him one day with some questions about Heavenly Power Structure and the available long-term career openings in what they considered to be that *Incumbent Hierarchy.*

Most important, in that conversation, was where they would find personal placement as the elites of His *New Spiritual Dispensation.*

Who's to be *Whos-Who in the Heavenly Zoo* …
So to speak …

Rather than pander to their powerplay fantasies – the writer claims Jesus called a small ragged urchin over to them and then did something deeply out of character …
… He issued them all with a Capital Warning …

He told them as a gathered group – that whoever gave the little girl just a simple cup of water, that act would equate *to an act of Worship.*

The little girl is for all intents and purposes - a Living God
… and an … Empress … in waiting.

He also told them as a group, that now that they were fully aware of this forthwith paradigm shift in the Heavenly corporate mission statement …

… Whomsoever among them that caused harm to befall the little girl, and caused the kid to grow up an alienated and broken sociopath – ought to be put to death because that is the ultimate …

… Unforgivable Sin.

To steal the Holy light and Royal innocence from within any Lost Child … is eternally Unforgivable by God.

Pretty straightforward blanket death sentence … Do this *and More*, as an organization – for thirsty, hungry, *Unwanted*, unloved Children, right here next to you, or – your souls are worth utterly nothing to Me.

Your lust for political power wrapped within the outward appearance of imagined trappings of wealth,

... blinded by covetous illusions that crave spiritual grandeur ... yet also given over to seek these follies ... only to Lord Yourself over others - will most certainly completely and utterly destroy you and those with you ...

... You are eternally Cursed.

DO NOT STEAL A CHILDS LIFE

That closed the conversation and it's been closed, glossed over, and mostly avoided ever since. This is the foremost profound truth about Christianity.

So be it.

This author has the good, *Socratic, Useful intention* of reopening this particular conversation as *Truthfully* as possible and without a hint of *fear or favor* – something you undoubtedly understand by now.

Quite simply, *because it needs to be done.*

It Is What It Is – but, patience – there yet remains: *What this Saga must yet Become ...*

Beyond this dark, uncomfortable and inverted Auto-da-fé ... this *Target* ... I'm busy painting and *have placed squarely upon my own hear*t ... is a Journey over a small shadowy mountain, to reach a unique Garden full of children's laughter ... on the *Other Side of the Vale of Tears.*

Ready to come along for the full bumpy ride ... *and join in?*

The List

RIGHT, … NEXT!

ACTUALLY … JUST HOLD IT RIGHT THERE … FOR A QUICK SECOND SIR …
… YOU!!

YES … YOU!

DON'T THINK I CAN'T SEE YOU, MISTER FAT BISHOP, TRYING TO SHOVE IN FRONT OF THAT NERVOUS LOOKING OLD DEAR GENUFLECTING UP AND DOWN LIKE A SEWING MACHINE NEEDLE! GOT MY BEADY EYE ON YOU – I HAVE! AND IF I'VE TOLD YOU LOT ONCE, I TOLD YOU A MILLION TIMES … STOP SHOVING!!
YOU WILL GET HERE SOON ENOUGH [and then You Might not want to be shoving so Bloody Much … mark My words…]
RIGHT, MOVING ON RAPIDLY [and, you are] … SIR?

SIR, MAY I HAVE YOUR UNDIVIDED ATTENTION … THIS WAY … YES, IN MY EXPLICIT DIRECTION … YES SMASHING, THANK YOU … CHARMING, I'M ASSURED … AND YOU ARE …?

Er … I'm here about the job as Oarsman.

WHAT? … WHAT OARSMAN?
WHAT OFF EARTH ARE YOU TALKING ABOUT?
THERE IS NO "OARSMAN" ON MY LIST!
LOOK UP ABOVE MY HEAD, SEE, RIGHT UP THERE BEHIND ME … IS: 'TRADERS AND SERVICE ENTRANCE' POSSIBLY WRITTEN DOWN UP THERE … BY ANY SMALL REMOTE CHANCE?
NOT SURE ARE WE? THEN LET ME ENLIGHTEN YOU SWIFTLY – NO, IT DOES NOT!
CAN YOU READ, SIR?
WHAT PRAY TELL, DOES IT SAY?

Er … "The Pearly Gates".

OUTSTANDING! WELL DONE THAT MAN!
SO … ABSOLUTELY NO INKLING OF A FRIENDLY MENTION OF AN "EMPLOYEES ENTRANCE" OR THE LESS WELCOMING "AUTHORISED PERSONNEL ONLY" … THEN? MAYBE YOU COULD POSSIBLY BE, MISTAKEN …???

Er … no.

SIR, I NEED YOUR NAME … SO, I CAN CHECK IT AGAINST MY LIST. [Somebody's Always Got to be the bloody Joker]
IT'S EASY …SEE … MY NAME IS SAINT PETER … WITH A BIG PEE AND SQUIQQLEY ESSS
… AND YOURS IS …?

Er … I've got a prayer letter …

A PRAYER LETTER?
WHAT LETTER?
WHERE'S THIS LETTER?

Er … right here.

WHOM IS IT ADDRESSED TO?

Er, your … boss?

GIVE ME THAT …
RIGHT, LET'S HAVE A LOOK AT THIS THEN … SHALL WE?
AND, WOULD YOU MIND TERRIBLY IF I READ IT OUT LOUD … SIR?

Er, no.

HI JESUS [good Lord? … Hi?]
SIR, DID YOU … WRITE … THIS 'PRAYER' LETTER?
IS IT A COPY OF AN ACTUAL PRAYER?

Er, yes.

MMMM … FAIR ENOUGH … LET'S TRY THIS AGAIN …

Hi Jesus
Yo! So, here's the thing.
Remember when you told those twelve fellas
YES INDEED …
… following you around, you know the ones who wanted to know who among them would be the bosses sitting next to you in Heaven – Them. Well, remember when you told them to give that street kid a cup of water if they wanted to be a boss like you? Remember that? And then you went on to warn them that Anyone who caused the kid to grow up an alienated sociopath by treating any lost child as *Unwanted* - should be put to death by strangulation and drowning because that would be a total walk in the park compared to the Judgment To Come. Heavy dude!
HRRMMGHGH, MY … APOLOGIES …
… Remember that one too? You said it was the only prophesy worth heeding. Damn right JC! With you on that one all the way! Don't want to know what's worse than strangulation and drowning, but it's obviously going to be really, really sort of like seriously bad and stuff.
YES, OF COURSE …
… But anyway, so here's the actual thing, remember that other time when you told them that if Two or Three are gathered in your name and they agree on anything in your name, then it's on, kind of thing.
Remember that?

Well, see two of your people tried to take me out, using your name on something called Facebook, where I was talking to other folks about taking care of all of society – by telling ignorant folks to get Vaxxed against Covid-19.

But instead of discussing fools preaching trash-for-cash, in your name and subsequently endangering other people's health, they warned me that you are going to get all Karen on my sinful butt

CERTAINLY, INTERESTING TURN OF PHRASE …

… when I get to meet you in heaven and bow my knee to your glory, or some weirdness like that, and then they both agreed about it. Said so, out loud.

That means you and me have some unfinished business to discuss, right now, about the *Unwanted*. Yes, JC my old mate. *My lost brothers and sisters.*

Unwanted. Them.

I've made a bet with these two fellas as a joint stake sort of thing, so that means I've made a bet with YOU! A big bet. The wager is all the money that the Church is going to give you as a tithe for a year.

The bet was made in 20/21. Too sweet for you? Well, it can't be – they laid the bet but *the vig is on you.*

Cool.

It's against a cup of pit latrine shit from a primary school (thought that was more poetic than that cup of water you were talking about lol) and I'll even sweeten the odds for you and all your righteous Christian people.

If just one in ten of them, has given just one cup of water, to only one of the three-point-five-million of the *Unwanted* in South Africa, I'll go on National Television and drink that cup of shit, then smile, praise you and kneel and DO all those sorts of idiotic worshippy type deeds they say you are going to force me to do in Heaven.

But then it's double or nothing and I agree that this bet excludes America.

When we make that rigged wager - I'll break the whole mansion in the sky but I still want to have fun gambling until then.

So, two years of the Sacred Dosh. Sworn blood convents and all that, Yes?

Spit on it. Spiritually wossname. Yeah?

Okay, you are on. But if these "Righteous Christian" people of yours – welsh out on this bet, and more of the blood of the *Unwanted* ends up under your throne, then I get the job of Oarsman rowing their sorry arses into the Lake of Fire, for the Avenging Angels to toss overboard.

Deal?

And I also get a free pass, to go have a party, in Valhalla, often as I like and whenever the fire gets too rough to go out to work. Are we on?

Perfect, great chatting with you again buddy.

Oh, and I'm not going to tell them what I'm gonna do with all that money.

Why?

Well, they would have done it for the *Unwanted* themselves already anyway, and we wouldn't be finishing up this conversation.

Chat again soon … JC 😊

[… Again soon, again Soon ……whatever the Hell Happened to Amen?]
MMMM, WELL, WELL ……WELL.
I SUPPOSE ……YOU BETTER COME ON IN THEN, SIR ……BUT A WORD TO THE WISE, COME CLOSER …
DON'T BE EXPECTING TO GO OFF TO VALHALLA FOR A PISSUP, RINGING BARNEY AND DIVINE ROLL IN THE HAY, TOO EARLY … BOY …
I'VE GOT MORE HEAVY ROWING FOR YOU THAN YOU CAN SWING A NINE-TIMES DEAD CAT-IN-A-HAT AT.

DO MIND YOUR STEP AS YOU GO …… *NEXT*!

Oi, you! Old man!
Do you want a straight *PEE* with a wiggly *ESS*?

Now, that I work Here … *And All That* … maybe you should be aware … I don't take orders
from *The Doorman*.
You might want to jot that down …
… onto your squiqqley List.

‡§‡

歌曲

Traveling.

Onward through an endless desert.
Feet crunching faintly underfoot. Pace by pace.
Moving steadily.
Stepping toward … a distant horizon.
Never ceasing …
Eye is softened by pale cerise twilight …
Bathing, an endless landscape.
Boundless … yet, without shadows.

Ether is cool. Neither hot nor cold.
A faint tendrilled breeze …
… lightly brushes countenance.
Verdigris sand. Fine. Flat.
Ripples … flowing out.
Vast … and limitless.

Point, far-off … Disturbs the pink sky's line.
Draws attention.
Small.
Almost *Imaginary.*
Insistent. Out of place.
Mind, *dream*? Mirage?
Point becomes an *Object.* More definite.
Gradually rising … Footstep, by footstep.
Ever starker above …
Dusky dry ocean.

A shape forms.
An Image … Of a sacred memory.
A word. *Pyramid …*
Nearer, the rough dark triangle is colossal
Size seizes mind … Consumes firmament
Soars upwards … Devours … ceaseless vista.
Closer still … A living edifice emerges.

Terrible to behold.
Etched with writhing scars …
Marks … Cracks, fissures, twisting turning. Healing. Tearing …
… *Alive* …

Some way off from this …

A Blind Scribe.
Cloak of flowing snake silks. Wide-brimmed hat.
Sits on a plain stool. Before a simple wooden table.

Deft fingers clasp an ancient *Angel-feather* quill.
Agéd and shadowy… Etching symbols true on unblemished parchment.
Leering … Between knuckles, atop an ebony marching cane.
Other fingers … grip
A *ruby-eyed … silver Skull …*

Gazes sightlessly at the dreadful pyramid.
Nib scratches faintly … Writes on … undisturbed.

No other sound penetrates the silence.

Drawing nearer … A strange compulsion awakens …
Within.
Piercing heart and quiet.
Remnant … of what was … once … *Voices.*
Voices … *voicesss* …

Go … Go nearer … Look … Go … find the Substance of Time …Tell Usss … What… do you seee …?
What… might you See for us … in this place without Time?

I See …
Hourglasses
Glass life timers
Too many to count
Piled onto each other
Some big … others small
Few ornate. Countless plain
Choicely polished and too dull
Fading old. Many, many brand new

Billions upon billions of timers; Stacked in narrowing, rude layers; Constantly shifting …
… Sliding … Moving … Striving, *competing* ever upward …

Each one uniquely the same – *in function*.
Each one is utterly different – *in the same flow of time*.

They are bound by threads. *Golden threads*. Some thin; Others thick; Plaited; Knotted. Many, many broken. Badly secured together. Gathered in large groups; Some again small; countless fragmented … almost;

alone

Sands run and hiss as they wrestle. Struggling, fighting … ever rising. Some burst. The sand spills … Glass twinkles; Disappears … another slides into place. Over and over. Countless forgotten rivers of time. Flowing …
Down to the flat dark desert … Of no night.

Go even closer … Pick just one … Look … very carefully. Find … the meaning of Time Within. Again, tell Usss … What … do you Seee …?

I see the sand that isn't sand. Grains that are letters. Small, fine, and cramped together.
Drawn into phrases; Sentences bound … pouring downwards; Spoken into history. Telling that life story unheard in words. Ever becoming less … Until the last sentence.
Then the glass breaks.
One sojourn vanishes. A new tale takes place. Some, good stories; Some bad.
All spin a yarn.
Some, so faint;

unknown

They have no meaning at all.
Appearing; Becoming; Disappearing; Yet, increasing … More and more …

Look again. To the very base of this Chosen Order. Seek out … the Value of Time. Find it for Usss. Search for Usss … Finally … What… do you truly … See?

I see tiny hourglasses. Millions upon countless millions of life stories.
Glass is mostly cracked and dirty. Broken; Battered; Tales too short and terrible to read.
Unlike the ones above; No words within for Mother and Father.
Unlike the ones above …
… Bound apart.

Valueless … With pitted, dull wire. Bent, buckled twisted…
Their ties a curse.
Fractured from inception … Foundation of every Woe … Rising above them …
Unseen.
Unknown.

Unloved.

Born to speak of nothing … In the tale flowing through their sands … But misery, loneliness, and sorrow. Never having treasured the Word: *Belonging* – within … The glass shatters:
Meaninglessness.

Well, Traveler … Did you Sssee …?
Take caution, before you speak … In a place where speech is not.

Hear this unspoken word:

A Scribe's simple Record …
… No life story ever asks to be told. Yet, it flows uninterrupted … A mystery which shall unravel; From a beginning … till an end. Only a living Citadel such as this, is within, able to beholden itself.
That is the gift of light;
Of life.
Enlightenment and Blindness … Are both the same Creation.
The Ten Deadly Thefts … All darkness, from Within.
In everything recorded; Every word its own affairs.
Its Total Time … is… A Collective.

Time … Time flows through the hourglass …
… Time is only now.

To use … or squander … Wasted on squabbling gods; Unforgotten, to exist. Or … To pen substance; Observe, learn, teach?
Spendthrift on frivolous charms; Heavenly riches … far beyond sight. Or … To succor eternal Wisdom; Writing a new chapter deep in the blackest night?
Dissipated … gone; To unleash only once! The finite folly of a self-destroyed hell. Or … Traveler; A choice to treasure … Then Nurture every Unwanted Child?

In a place of nothing… Where no words exist … Construct a New Dwelling.
Inscribe it in the sands.
A Braver World … to extoll Within.
The never-ending story; Wherein, these children all Belong.
This Final Choice remains to be Told … Within each … collective life epoch.

A saga is still unformed.
A Beginning.
And … The End.
But, of What?

If this Citadel perishes … Falls away into extinction … Nothingness … Destroyed by its broken foundation. Greed; Indifference … Brutality … Self-lust, Religion, Politics, Murder; Hate, War, harming any Lost Child … Rape … then,

孤兒

Will be the last. Word …
… Written in the glasses of sand …
That Final choice … will splinter … This… Illusion of Time.

All parables great or small, Malevolent … or, Consecrated, are written in the same … endlesss … Meaningless stardust.
And this … Edifice? A precious waste – of Sacred Words …

Go, Traveler … go, Seeker … go, Warrior … and search for the truth … Find Usss …seek the Foundations for …

*A new… Eternal Empire of our **Mother** … wherein …*

We All Belong.

陰

<u>The Four Cornerstones of Truth</u>

屁

Pi is both infinite and the most perfect of all numbers.

It never repeats itself and contains every single unique combination of numbers that has, or can ever possibly exist.

The biggest prime number that has ever been calculated – Pi is able to swallow like the Eye of Jupiter gulping one tiny segment of the nucleus of a hydrogen atom, chopped up just as many times. But that is hardly surprising because Pi could snack on the Universe like it almost wasn't even there. Pi has Everything encoded in it, including the disembodied voice you are hearing in your mind right this very second.

Nothing can be added, and nothing can be subtracted from Pi.

Pi is the only quantity that can be used in an abstracted equation to measure the absolute smallest point that exists. No other number is big enough to calculate it, accurately.

Every single past and future event is encoded somewhere in Pi – *Now*.

All the Truth, Knowledge, Reason, and every eternal Wisdom that could ever be desired, is to be determined in Pi, but not one letter of the Library of Babel can complement this.
We, do not count or define Pi …

For better or worse … Pi counts, encodes, numbers, and *defines that which is US.*

The Short Answer, and the ultimate *One True Resolution*, we as a species - are seeking as a *Purpose* … is:

$$Pi - 3 \neq 3 - \pi$$

The results might look deceptively identical but one is an imaginary infinite positive, and the other an imaginary negative.
For example, in another branch of algebraic geometry … dancing to the never-ending tunes of Pi – contained in a pure sweet spot, somewhere in between – *parabola* and *prolate ellipses*, is the perfect shape – for a space vehicle's nose-cone to pierce *Our* atmosphere.
When *We* pack a nuclear warhead into that cone, *We* create a machine that will cease to function or exist … the very imaginary moment it is fully activated over an imaginary target.

An Imaginary Negative.

It cannot be anything except *imaginary*, because mass human neurobiology cannot survive a nuclear detonation, which has reduced all its DNA back to quantum particles – including the *imagination* that designed that *imaginary machine* in the first place.

Unreal and *meaningless.*

Every calculation, equation, and measured quantity … every manhour, gram of material, and degree of education – pretty much the same as naught, aught, nothing …

A non-existent Ground Zero of meaninglessness.

However, if *We* choose to pack that same cone with a *self-sustaining, space-proof, and human-friendly habitat* …

We may continue on a never-ending journey into seeing how Pi will measure *Our* ways forward, until *We* have paced off enough places, letting Pi explore Us – *to put living human feet on another planet.*
And, then another …

Ergo, what We choose to cherry-pick in the looming Future of Pi, from this entirely quantifiable Answer, is entirely up to *Us* …

This … is –

THE FIRST CORNERSTONE OF TRUTH

dirt flees
ahead
straw broom swishes
softly
clean feet pad away

茶

The Way, up and out of The Valley of the Shadows of Death - is a Road … far less traveled …

吉祥茶
(Auspicious Tea)

… *It* wends lazily through crumbled rocky terrain, past scraggly shrubs and dead thorny bushes, too indifferent to be green … too sad, and morbidly parched to be brown.

Gaunt grey trees cling haphazardly to sharp-toothed rocks scattered up and down a steep hillside adorned hither with ill-looking lichens, creeping raggedly over barren shale.
Silent, lifeless … *uncaring.*

The Way may have once been rutted, worn … but drenching rains, foul frigid winds, and eons of passing ice have scoured all living traces of human passing …

Yet so, crouched on the skeletal bough of a lone tree's corpse, slashed charcoal by ancient lightning …
… a lone, leering, scornful crow *screeches.*
Withering presbyter's *Curse* … then slowly flaps away … cawing at the wraithlike mists in shock and disgust.

Indifferent, a bullock plods forward. Polished traces creak. Stepping away from the soft endless wooden rumble behind its lightly twitching rump. Harnessed to this gentle beast is a diminutive timber wagon constructed of a distinctly rare and sapient type. Casting brilliant jagged shadows onto the newly unwound ruts … scarring the obliterated spectral trail …

Made of magic wood, found only where such enlightened folk of this world are first to see … Our Sun Rising – and thus worship among these living, *Enchanté Arbores,* within vast forests of their spectacular *Glorifying Light.*

A diminutive compact Temple trundling, jousting along, on painfully grumbling iron-bound wheels … blazing a freshly virgin Trail in the fading twilight as …
… Eternal celestial wars wage fiercely on the side panels.

[Dancing silver Demons … Colorful golden Gods … slashing, advancing … falling … warring]

Flowing images, clashing in an exquisite kaleidoscope of wonderous writhing detail.

Sacred, profane ... colored lights ... leaping out at the dreary dour landscape slowly ...
... trundling past.

Ever down the rocky ... deserted
... broken ...
Hostile track.

On a lightly rocking cart bench, high and behind the docile animal's haunch ... rides an extremely old man.

An ancient fellow adorned in a rough peasant cowl. His wrinkled feet are strapped into battered leather sandals peeking meekly over the worn footrest. Well-greased reins hang loosely wrapped around one leathery wrist. A thinly-knotted simple rope is bound about his narrow waist. No emotion passes across the taut ancient features. His skull shines. Completely hairless except for a bound, silver-peppered pigtail issuing from a tight topknot. Disappears down the recesses of his shadowy back.
A wispy goatee hangs serenely, dangling deep between gently bouncing knees.
Watery old eyes ... gaze. Bushy brows following the fleeing, dark flapping insults ... *echoing* ... *gone* ... into the icy mountain air.

Thin, reedy ... *click-sounds* ... issue softly between his few remaining teeth.

Bullock's horns rock placidly. Heeds Master's *Voice* ...
... and *stops.*

Astonishingly agile, the old driver hops down. Nimble, for one of so obvious great years. Affectionately pats the steaming burdened beast ... ever humming rainbows as he releases the shiny worn trace buckles. Gently halters the tired animal ... to lead it slowly up off the narrow track, there to fasten and hitch-tie it to the stricken *crowless* tree.

Returns to a banded brown barrel - strapped onto the rear of the *wildly strobing* cart, where he collects an armful of thick yellow straw. Dumps this before the passive creature, which gratefully lowers an enormous head to feed. Back to the radiant wagon to unhook a flat, covered wooden bucket. Removes the lid and offers the pail to his thirsty bull. Satisfied, the ancient fellow begins darting about ... collecting fallen rocks. Packs these into a tight circle, then, into this chilly stone ring he quickly snaps off then packs fistfuls of sparse broken brush ... gathered brisk thither about. Pleased, he retrieves from the dazzling recesses of the bawdy wagon, an eerie erotic brasier ... trailing *cerise-tinted tendrils of verdigris smoke* ...

... Opens *Her* ... as Fire.

Pours ash and burning red embers from *Her* cool platinum labia … onto his densely packed kindling bed, then kneels reverently … blow-chants a pursed Zen-zithering melody … *relentlessly* at the shy embers … until …

… a fat orange flame erupts.

Hops about quickly gathering sparse twisted dead faggots, breaking and feeding them into the wild fleeing smoke. Eventually, it is piled high … blazing hot.

Retrieves a blackened steel tripod and a small Emperor's Kettle. Settles them above the chit-chatting flames. Then … collects a priceless skin of *Her* Serene Chi and dispenses … carefully… into the dangling Royal Urn. Corks and conceals his precious sacred skin. Repairs with a black-leather stool and small ornate Tea Table. Places them … just so … between the cart and a fine comfortable distance from the raging fire.

Seats himself.

From within the table's beautiful inlaid drawer, he removes a venerable teapot, two translucent cups, and minute pretty tea-chest. Arranges these with infinite care onto the brilliantly lacquered board above. Fishes inside his faded robe and lifts out a long thin jadepipe. An exquisitely carved, ferocious dragon. Hand darts again to retrieve a soft, wrinkled leather pouch.

Packs his *dragonpipe* unhurriedly.

Rises to select a burning stick … lights the cold green pipe … *small brisk puffs.*

Reseats himself.

Tranquil …

Smokes *dragonpipe.*

Inscrutable wise eyes stare down at filthy writhing pyres … *all real religious wars* … greasy foul flames rising … far off … deep in The Valley of the Shadows of Death … *far below.*

Waits.

Faintly … down the rough ragged trail … comes the distant clatter of small rocks bouncing and clattering.

Observes.
Smokes *dragonpipe.*
Impassive.

Soon … a cursing figure emerges from within the faltering twilight shadows and scrawny swirling mists. Alone … and slowly moving ever upwards. Steadily. Muttering, stumbling … sliding … swearing … clawing … climbing.

Ever nearer to the *flashing wagon* and the old fellow's glowing fire.

The stranger staggers up through the remaining prehistoric debris … littering The Way …
… *resigned.*

Icy and silent at last.

Halts before the old man near the warm campfire.
Bows deeply … hushed but warily circumspect.

Eventually, the old man smiles … softly reciprocates the bow.
Takes a huge puff of dragonpipe.

Speaks:

Sojourner San. Good again, it is … to stumble so fortuitously, across thine blessed personage.

Not so good for me you miserable old fart! And why is it exactly, that you and your creepy-lights wagon keep on popping up, out of the blue … all along The Way?

Warrior San, too weary thy seem … indeed maybe too much thirsty too. Convenient it is, that this humble kettle has now started boiling. Auspicious tea, from Our Lady, I will prepare … then your blessed self will surely rest … to share it with me?

Suspicious tea is more like it! Seems too 'auspicious' that every single time my 'blessed self' has to walk soul alone through the godawful VALLEY OF THE SHADOWS OF DEATH, endlessly searching for the KEY to free the Unwanted – that … somehow, you keep on appearing with that Ungodly Mobile-Disco up on the borders of the equally horrible mountainsides.
    And, why is it, your bloody kettle always seems to start boiling, the absolute very second, I arrive?

Purpose fire has, water and tea too. Your purpose, Traveller San, is to quench thy thirst at this moment. That is perfect for this purpose. The true purpose for this Auspicious Hour.

And what is it always with the Yoda yak-yak? If you want to be a guru or whatever … you don't have to speak fashionably weird.
    Quit being all Riddley!

Guest San, the burdens and most grievous wounds of thine world are what thou dost carry … not only the stone tablets of inscribéd grue strapped to thy weary back. Crude Graffiti they are. Of ancient pictographic covenant and scorned deathly hieroglyph. Of Sorrow, Mind Sickness and Woe. All of broken tribal promises and murder. Old blood oaths that were sworn to the small vanishing cloud-gods of power, crucifixion, burnt sacrifice, and war. Only weigh thee further down will these. Parched and thirsty thine soul truly must be.

First rest. Tea, thee must drink … auspiciously with me.

Okay, you win. And there is no need to smirk at me like that! Let me set down these hideous slabs and fetch the kettle …
… You pour you bothersome goofy old goat!

The scarred, battered … deeply wounded young man, slowly … painfully, … unbinds, then with great care, lays down his terrible Burden.
Collects the billowing Emperor urn, and, momentarily subdued, respectfully fills the proffered Teapot.

Employing exact … unhurried movements … the Old Master serves up … steaming … tea.

Perched before him on the two carved sheets of uncouth stone, the younger man eases his agonized body a little …
… rests.

Sips … blows into his curling hot cup.

Ah so? Student San … Learned much have thee, on this thine latest foray?

Nothing more than ongoing horror, and increasing depths of poison constantly brought forth from the curses carved into these two rocks.
Seen again … the millennia of the countless millions of dead and Unwanted they have borne to Our Mother's Daughters.
Murder, rape, battery … mindless abuse. Over and over …
Every day a fresh sun delivers newer volatile dogmas of political and religious hate, arising, flaring up into consumptive flames from the toxic festering midnight ashes of the old.
She is naked, hungry, so sick, pregnant, and abandoned.
Unwanted.
All alone.
And … I cannot rescue any of Her Daughters from this …

Bearer of Unwanted Children, San … blessings are curses spoken as mirrors.
Best it be for thee to let me help utter them.

Oh, cut it out you toothless old mutt!
How are you going to speak the Ten Commandments backward?
Have you seen what has been carved into these slabs? Have you seen, smelt, and touched the horrors bought forth when sold by those who twist these old words to feed greed for sickening political gain? To buy wars?
It's all just rotten banana vomit.

Padawan San, much of bad grammar I am seeing. Hearing also.
Dark Force, it is … as a way to write or ill motivate a human being.
Nothing else.
This Corner of thine quest for Truth … I freely give to thee.

Oh, wonderful, so you saw the frikkin movie.
For your information – 'Thou shall not Kill' isn't bad grammar old man, it is pretty damned straightforward and direct.

Tea Guest, San … a humble test … I propose now … and such … to thee also give …
Thou shalt Not think about a bright pink elephant berobed in a polka dot kimono …
Thy shall Not Meditate on this talking, singing, Flying One at all.

What guiles of the mind are these you sneaky old Trickster? What is this obscene pachyderm you have unleashed into my miserable thoughts?

There lived once a fine rich prince, many long years past … the humble Buddha he became.
Wise this soul, who advised that 'not' is a word the mind ignores.

What are you suggesting then, Oh thou 'not' annoying Guru?

Her Tea, left to boil on a fire, will eventually be reduced to Chi's essence. The core meanings of those dreaded sentences are what thee alone must deduce … Student San.

I have done this, Sensei!
Do not steal a man's god!
Do not steal his wife! Or enslave his children!
Do not Steal his property!
Freedom, Reputation, Peace of mind!
Do not steal his Life!
Do not steal Truth …

… DO NOT STEAL!!

Very near you are, to what you seek … My Child. The opposite of stealing is … TO GIVE.
Deep satisfaction you will enjoy if you should apply that one rule to these.
But first … Father San, the human opposite of a man is what?

… A Woman … … or, a Child?

Thou dost speak well and True … my Son.

Both they are, and only once bound together as Our Mother intended, like a bird and her chicks … safely in a carefully woven Nest, represent the true collective apposite of Her Love's energies.

The time you must take to meditate deeply, and then rewrite these broken Laws of The Death of Men … into One … Eternal Purpose.

Within their ultimate demise is …

THE THIRD CORNERSTONE OF TRUTH

The young man falls silent. Both men sip tea.
The fire burns down.
Eventually, the old man rises, tosses more gnarled tree bones onto glowing embers.
Relights his pipe.

Waits.
Puffs *dragonpipe.*
Impassive.

Waits …
… smokes more *dragonpipe* …
Waits.

The night crawls.

Eventually … as thin polluted rays from a Coming Dawn begin to slowly cast Light onto the burning … curséd lands below …

Sensei San! Master!! I have solved the mystery!
I have figured out how to re-write the death-ordered curses … as a Single Blessing!
A Safe Nest!!

Son, blessed thee will forever be, for walking this Hard Barren Road … alone … only to truly mine what is deeply buried in thine heart.

The Old Grandfather rises.

Repairs to the … *Suddenly Dark …*
… blank wooden wagon.

Returns with a rough burlap sack. Tosses this down with a dull metallic thump before the highly excited youngster.

Carve Her True Edicts in Stone,
My Precious Son …
Make an eternal Record of …

Mother's Will.

From the sack, the young man retrieves an ornate obsidian hammer and sharpened chisel. Flips the grim, graven-stones face down and begins to chip away in the flickering light of twirling warm flames. On the First blank stone … he hammers away …

… *tink, tink, tink* … gradually cuts and carves:

PROVIDE
TO WOMEN AND CHILDREN:
GIVE EDUCATION,
GIVE OWNERSHIP,
GIVE WEALTH,
GIVE SECURITY
GIVE

The old man looks on inscrutably …
… puffs *dragonpipe.*

Into the Second ancient slab … well invigorated, the battered boy beats the steel music mercilessly. Scribes deep … *eternal* into the cold heartless rock:

PROVIDE
TO WOMEN AND CHILDREN:
GIVE A FUTURE,
WITH
PURPOSE FOR LIFE.
GIVE

As the tired young fellow painfully bludgeons in the very last letter … a now grinning … *Ancient Trickster* … pours another piping-hot cup of …

… Auspicious Tea.

勇士

"But whoso shall offend ONE of these little ones which believe in me,
it were better for him that a millstone were hanged about his neck,
and that he were DROWNED in the depth of the sea."
~ Jesus Christ ~

So, there you have it. Did you find what you went looking for?

Down the Rabbithole, across the Valley? Not really, no.

Why not? It seems pretty simple – spread the Word. Give to Women and Children. Provide them with everything they need emotionally, physically, Legally etcetera and blah ...

Of course, it's blindingly *obvious* when you flip the Ten Commandments around!
Take out the *Nots* then flip them into *Dos* ...
But that's the entire point ... A universal Mission Statement applied quite naturally by *Birdies*, Bonobos, and Chimpanzees.
Easy ... *IF* you want to protect and safely propagate your own species.
The answers are not simply about countering or exposing religions and politics for what they truly are. Any semi-educated idiot with a smartphone and a social media app can do that.
Millions get onboard, believing this to be a form of virtual gang warfare, that they, in fact, feel called to, from some deeply primal place invariably driven by rooted uncertainty and deep-seated fear ... which kinda conclusively proves this.
Stupid and profoundly ignorant people *pay* for what they *want to believe* in and then get manipulated into voting for, or *giving* "Heavenly Glory" to ... and then subsequently catfighting over.
They do this, by being coerced into developing an acquired proxy-grudge, then trumpeting a moral virtue and/or proclaiming an Othering Religion and/or Political Party.
And nothing, absolutely nothing that *Anyone* can say will stop this.

Money changed hands ...
... prayers were offered ... Promises made ...
        Fingers Xrossed
... lay your bets ladies ... Bum-Fight is on!

So why go to all the fuss and bother in the first place? Why dissect the problem with a chainsaw, and smash it headfirst into a doorpost repeatedly, if all it reveals is a filthy mess?

And seriously, you may be right about everything you've said so far, but come on, you're not going to make friends by cursing the Pope or being bluntly racist.

Seriously?
Cursed? Mwuuuah?
The *Eternal Hell the Pope has cursed Himself into* – through his vile criminal actions against completely innocent kids …
… *pre-exists only in His mind, and the … Collective Mind … to Whom He sells that Power …*

~Meme~

He has to hard sell it – to ensure His socio-politic *Influence-base* remains intact while allowing the massive network of high-ranking pederast Priests to get away with their ongoing crimes against humanity.

All it costs Him, at the end of lightly critical mass media, is a little Latin mumbo-jumbo mournfully uplifted with a few "*Christlike*" platitudes. Deftly slung "*Consecrated*" words, like "*Penance*", "*Remorse*", "*Sorrow*", "*Salvation*" and "*Repentance*", with many, many other such mangy, dogmatic, slimy-purisms and worn out heady altruisms … spin-doctored about.

The ghastly alternative?
Every single word I have said … is:

True and eternally Holy, by and before Almighty God. Amen and Amen.

And, "His Holiness" and all his depraved papal Vicars *are truly doorknobbed.*

Including if, said *sick scum* … all did the right thing and publicly relinquished their power … then one and all … *fell resoundingly upon their holy gilded swords of Righteousness* to get led away in handcuffs. Perfectly empty scarlet succubae, mouthing empty platitudes and "*Sacred*" words.
But … for random vulnerable children everywhere … a *Deadly Poisoned Chalice.*
Cursed forever, by *God* and … *now* being swept into the dustbin of … *A History of Men.*

That is how I weight the true measure of immeasurable nonsense … committing real crimes against Homo Sapiens as a species.
But this is so not about a corrupt, childless old fart, using sexual aberrations to dig his political-religious claws into the minds of the superstitious, *paying*, ignorant mob.

This is all about *BEING* something completely *DIFFERENT* in this world.

As a deeply damaged, *incomplete* species.

We have to when it comes right down to truly *caring* and being responsible for All our human offspring and their collective futures.

If we don't – *they won't have one and everything I am saying right this second is utter meaningless twaddle.*

The biological markers of all the terrible Symptoms of these co-morbid maladies, such as …
Climate Change, Environmental Destruction, World Hunger, Gender-Based Violence, The Unwanted, Multi-national Wars … etc., are going to get called in … for ALL of us as an entire species … with even more of these unforeseen consequences manifesting exponentially, *whether this ruffles anyone's imaginary tail feathers uncomfortably or not …*

Stripped of all the political noise within the contemporary maelstrom of conflicting propaganda along with nauseating religious deflections – what is *this* truly all about?

Other civilizations practiced pedophilia and rape.

Violent abuse and crime were rampant.

Sexual deviancies against children and brutal slavery were eventually finally accepted norms.

Why is this newer advent of millions of *Unwanted* orphans globally the very final crux that will bring down all of mankind?

If We let it …

Because those civilizations collapsed.

They are *Dead.*

Their moral codes shattered. Gods forgotten. No longer worshipped.

Bones of their slavish priests and filthy expedient politicians dust. Blood-lust circuses of sadistic proxy-demise … entirely *perished.* Memories of their bourgeoning hordes of orphans and grossly maltreated slaves … quantum ash.

Destroyed from Within.

Good for nothing much more than romantic, derivative costume dramas in a saccharine world of Woke CGI.

But the very same, real evil that destroyed them, is alive, well, and kicking on your TV screen, or popping up in your latest browser as a YouTube hate or snuff movie - only this time there is no longer geographic wiggle room to run, hide or cheer slavishly from the pink-mist spattered spectator seats.

There are simply no other choices …

… but to directly Address This …

.

All those failed civilizations perished outright, but not because of military failures, economic hardships, contagious fatal diseases, or other natural disasters deemed acts of the then imaginary angry gods. Not even a combination of these horrors, which these vanquished societies all eventually weathered, staggered away from, and mostly survived.

Yet …

One and all - they eventually fell into total ruin, and thus cultural oblivion when they destroyed basic social cohesion, by choosing to revert to mindless animal bestiality at the root of their hedonistic endeavors, and thus … inadvertently ruined their base economies …

… from Within …

Every successful civilization has to maintain an elementary set of strictly applied rules regarding population expansion and social cohesion to drive its macroeconomy.

This is applicable from Squirrel minkeys on upward to the USA.
And should be achieved through stringently applied laws.

Darwinian type *Rules* that are invariably applied intuitively concerning *marriage* and sexual mores within all social classes, and with an encoded forward-looking view to retaining a solid, stable, predictably recyclic economic structure along with the lowest burden of disease and social dysfunction. Almost consistently, there is also a religious moral imperative, *as an abstract aspect*, overshadowing and underpinning these fundamental laws within such a vitally functioning society, that is always based on exchanging tangible and visible human values founded on a rigorous moral code.

However, it has been said, the power over life and death always lies with the midwives and priests … *respectively …*

… even for despotic Kings with rotten banana vomit policies.

It is also said - a dead fish decays from the head – and nothing could be truer.
And of course, Power almost invariably corrupts, but absolute power corrupts - Absolutely.

When this occurs in any Empire, Government, Corporate Oligarchy - one whose *Kings, Popes, Presidents, Board Members, Tribal Strong Men …* take it unto themselves to flout or subvert these foundational rules of social cohesion for mutually-exclusive political purposes, and/or callous, entitled, venal indifference – a state of affairs arises in where one set of rules exists for the ruling *elites* and another set of rules for the disempowered, *democratic* plebians … that *restless mind-massaged laboring proletariat*, which always leads to lawlessness, unrest, insurrection and/or complete sociological regression.

Until the common, thinking, *shrinking* middle-class populace rebels.

Which, thereafter - can only be mass controlled through fear, lies, State control, martial intervention, passive-aggressive threatening, and covert violence … thus cementing and fomenting bitter partisan divisions in a fight for control of the higher levers of State Power.

Within the inevitable economic collapse, this provokes, by unforeseen consequence – it also inadvertently creates a functioning organized crime machine … an "*underworld*" dark economy in retaliation as a form of crude preemptive survival.

From the gutter to the highest corridors of power.

This, *foremost*, is what eventually destroys any society. One which may have once laid claim to having been free, prosperous, and possibly, in some ways, *civilized*, even in times of war, famine, disease, or disaster. Apparently, there are roughly seven societal markers that indicate a civilization is headed into irreversible regression.

Check and see how many boxes get ticked off in the following …

Civilizational breakdown almost always begins unnoticed, gradual, *sneaky,* and invariably starts with undermining and then invalidating once rigid laws of Marriage and Inheritance keeping the bedrock of that society's social compact … *cohesive, intact, and functioning economically.*

Starting with the concept of no-fault divorces. Who would have thought?

See, hidden in a no-fault divorce is a denial of the product and supreme responsibility of that marriage – the welfare and future inheritance of the children's *offspring*, including third-party political rights and responsibilities. This first-generation short-term self-interest at the expense of a child born into a marriage, in turn, leads to what could be loosely termed a "birth-dearth", which is then expressed as increased hostility shown towards normative heterosexual parenthood and biological mother/father parenting families, leading to successful – *grandparenthood,* with the open counter-promotion of overt, yet sterile homosexuality, as a chosen lifestyle, along with a rapid rise in sickening pedophilia *as being entirely Normal.*

And this breakdown of the biological nuclear propagation unit – mother, father, offspring, *grandchildren* - leads directly to *Unwanted* first-generation children along with inevitably abject child abuse.

Regression Markers - Three and Four:
- Cutting of family ties in favor of the State
- Perversion of sex and morality

Other furrier Great Apes never allow these aberrations into their basic animal societies. The Alpha males would kill or permanently chase off any Beta male who displayed this tendency. This set of deviances only occurs in certain sentient Naked Ape mega-societies where Beta males have come to promote themselves as being Alpha males through imitating, invoking, and promoting sheer fantasy roles, but, in reality, are not able to functionally lead, protect, feed, or guard their societies through the brute animal strength of selfless example.

Instead, these Apes have managed to gang up together and have leveraged political power for power's sake, to gorge their bellies for very little effort, and of course, have freer access to unabridged hedonism for the sake of hedonism without consequence. It may not seem important, but these bald tailless simians are almost always marked by their urge to publicly subvert then denounce those rigid morals and unspoken mores - silently critical of their self-acquired *so-called virtues*. Then loudly rewrite this short-term fakely martyred history in their own self-declared, mellifluous hubris. Since they have no good story to tell – it's almost always about … *Demonizing the Other Guy* …

Regression Markers - One, Two, and Six:
*   Loss of individual identity to identity politics.
*   *Übermensch, Üntermensch* Syndrome – the US/THEM secular/religious split.
*   Rise of Freud's "Narcissism of Minor Differences".

Alpha males, as a firm rule, are always – vigilant against predators, protective overall of all females along with their young, maintain strict discipline among the weaker and young males, and so, remain caring responsible guardians of the Troop … and, are willing to fight to the death within or without to defend this instinctive function at any instant …
… Alpha males are Mother Nature's successful Grandfathers.

Of all the Ape species, humans are the only ones who can't hack it, and allow themselves to be ruled by a small gang of murderous, insatiably gluttonous beta cowards. Liars, murderers, criminals, and perverters of humanity. Wasters and Destroyers … of their own fragile Environment.

The mendacious hypocrisy of the beta *elite* Apes – priests, politicians, and every voracious thing in between, will continue to erode these fundamental biological rules of society's economic survival at all levels, to suit their greed-ridden and highly short-term deviant predilections. This eventually results in the advent of completely meaningless marriages, hollow rites, and beautiful empty ceremonies, which eventually have nothing to do with creating a legal framework for children and their offspring to find a valid, loving, *responsible*, and ultimately *Wise* forward-looking place in this world to grow up in.

Divorce is then no longer a shocking aberration to have occurred to a family, it almost becomes expected, common, perfectly normal, and thus, marriage contracts cease to be an oath that benefits children born into that context – the entire *affair* becomes entirely what the contract is worth in terms of material possessions and future income of the two signatories – and how it will be split once the contract is dissolved.

Children and the ensuing vicious, sadistic, *custody* battles are very *Secondary*.

And so, marriage ceases to be about children's offspring and turns into something quite meaningless, that perchance involved sex and pregnancy.

And that, in a nutshell, is how any society fails its children and their future, then starts to slowly crumble almost unnoticed until it fails economically on the altar of accepted hedonism and parental apathy and spite.

Not so strangely, and coupled with this, with only a few more quick stops and a long way further down the subway line to *Bolgias District of Hell* – awaits a massive side-attack on normative parent's involvement and choices concerning their own children's education.

With a cunning strategy.

Any resistance to visibly failing State-driven ideological curricula, no matter how absurd, indoctrinating, or indeed blatantly politically controlling – will be prosecuted as social treason, and any attempt at resisting, will be shut down, gaslit, and duly canceled by the socialist parasites hellbent on power and rigid groupthink dominance.

The individual parents then become the *baddies*, the fall-guys, labeled, "Enemies of the State", *domestic terrorists*, counter-revolutionaries, bigoted child abusers, and expediently convicted on that loquacious politically twisted altar, then firmly taken out.

Off to the circus lions or the icy salt-mine gulags … *because fiddling about is good and Rome burning is simply a backdrop.*

In the far reaches of downfall, the last attacks on the children of a collapsing civilization will be an outright attempt to edit, exploit, and outrightly abuse, to the very fullest, the natural sexuality kids were born with and without their politically excommunicated parent's consent.

Look only to the final excesses of the fallen Eternal Cities or the ancient South Americans …
… *See?*

But hold that nauseating thought …

Once this original crack in the normative marriage dike, holding back the unwashed barbarian hordes - has been widened to become a completely acceptable social norm, alternative forms of fake marriage will rush in to become the new instantly gratified normal, with widespread propagation of deeper anti-family sentiments, coupled with socially acceptable parental absenteeism, fatherlessness and hideous child abuse of every conceivable form. This goes hand in hand with rising militant *sterile* feminism, profound homosexual political aggression, professionally approved public narcissism, and every species of hedonist excess imaginable.

In this fashion, adultery and blasé fornication by any legal definition become meaningless, and the offspring of these ammoralized, *fatherless, bastardized people* - will go on to live deeply emotionally damaged existences and eventually sub-thrive on rebellion and criminal delinquency, producing a new generation so poisoned … until eventually, *any* and every sexual perversion becomes commonly acceptable at all levels of society, and perversely … *a Crime to decry it.*

From bestiality … to child sexual mutilations … psychopathic sadism … unto murderous blood sacrifice.

A brand new normal of sorts further evolves – one that always descends ever deeper into completer forms of nihilist lawlessness, flaming anarchy, and wanton brutal violence … along with the collapse of that society into splintered forms of blood-soaked "*revolution*" [terrorism, gang warfare and murderous banditry].

As law and order begin to collapse, the judiciary becomes ever more highly politicized in an attempt to protect the terrified beta elites surrounded by Spies, Assassins, and Praetorian bodyguards … which, if successful, swiftly heralds a rapid return to barbarism and short-lived cycles of primitive tribal power warlords wielding the means to instantly enrich themselves through internecine viciousness and terror using their own clumsy formations of Spy, Steal, and Kill Guards - until everything that defined the original moral code of that fallen higher culture is utterly self-conquered and subsequently almost completely erased.

The broader macroeconomy is then non-existent, scattered, or in utter ruins.

Murder, robbery, and rape become rife beyond horror. Starvation, disease, and the hordes of *Unwanted* rampant.

Regression Marker seven:
*   Destruction of the Environment.

Look across the world, and across history - how many of those boxes are ticked? And, this is not Ancient Rome, The Aztecs, or Babylon *et al* we are talking about in our context.

Who and What lives in the corrupted ruins of their plastic polluted, smog smothered, drug-ridden, and evil war-torn ghetto Empires right now? Tick, tick, tick, *tick* … Tik--Tok

Feel me?

This being true, does it matter who screams that a few ol' stick letters and one stone-cold fundamental truth have smacked a few boneheads together?

There is bugger all "racist" in that.

Demographics are demographics. *Counting heads.*

Anthropology is anthropology and psychology is simply what it is.

Looking at the worst of the worst - from the above-mentioned spectrums … *Honestly.*

When over a hundred and fifty million tiny little heads are currently orphaned and *Unwanted* in this world, going to total rotten banana vomit *Sherlock*, then we need to take a very hard long look at the long-term biological health of our species.

From a Mental Health point of view.

The collapse is already descending upon us.

There is simply no more room to blameshift or put a bright partisan pin into a force-fed choice between twisted religion and violent identity politics.

Regardless of how many murderers, thieves, and rapists these cyclic toxic ~Memes~ produce, at any level of society – repeatedly. They are already far beyond redemption and cursed into the dustbin of history and will surely perish within this self-created regression. If …

… there is to be One.

The skin color of any baby is completely meaningless to the baby.

Tell me, seriously, *WHO* is the Most Important Person … *Right Here* … right now?

Now, as in this endlessly existential moment of … *Now?*

What kind of question is that? What do you mean 'Important' … what now? You are?

Don't be ridiculous, really? Come on. Think.

Well, I don't see myself as more important than you or anyone else, so it can't be me.

Exactly … but … there is *Someone* else right here … *walking in this Garden we are going to plant.*
Someone … who isn't here yet.

More than one … *Someone.*

Stop … quieten your mind, and listen … *very carefully …*

Because *right this very second …*

… a Real biological woman is being beaten and raped somewhere by some sick, evil piece of filth, and nine months from Now … that baby Someone is going to enter this world utterly Unwanted and unloved.

Tell me, in terms of *outraged … counter-offended … offensive counterpoint …*

What color is that baby's skin going to be? What Race? What Ethnicity?

What religion's "God" has just decreed that Unwanted child into this greedy, indifferent, hate-filled world?

Why send the mythical 'Stork' to drop the *Unwanted* brat off in the first place?

Should I care about the meltdown point of any Woke, seriously ignorant, brainwashed snowflake, when all I hear is the lonely screams of the real *Unwanted* inside my head? You wanna Race?

Let's talk straight flat figures against a verifiable *Failing First World* backdrop.

African-Americans make up about thirteen percent of the population of the United States of America. Yet, the cold hard numbers reckon that African-American Males are accountable for more than *fifty percent* of All the aggravated assaults, rapes, robberies, and murders … on American-American home soil.

Take the city of New York. In the last decade, nearly seventy-five percent of all criminal incidents involving firearms, that triggered arrest reports by the NYPD - were committed by perpetrators identified and classified as "Black" on the individual's rap sheet.

And those are *only* those perps the Democrat-defunded and serially hated cops caught …

Yet, counting heads, African-American *males* only make up roughly about six percent of the US population.

Cold hard fact.

Do you want to count heads another way?

Nearly two-thirds of the murder victims in the USA, *annually*, are African-Americans.

Two-Thirds!

And, over ninety percent of all those murders are committed by African-American Males.

So basically, you have a demographic representing only six percent of the entire US population but is committing over ninety percent of all the murders, and still counting heads, two-thirds of the dead victims were once African-Americans themselves …

… until their lives were made worthless and taken away by gang-bangers, thieves, junkies, hoppers, psychos, homicidal baby-daddies, and absent rapist fathers from their very own "Race" of people.

Numbers are numbers, and *race* is a convenient excuse.

There is no excuse.

I'll say that twice – There Is NO Excuse!

Race?

Black Lives Matter is the most sickening race-based farce on the entire planet and more than likely in its entire miserable history. For six months this opportunistic left-wing front went on the rampage … the epitome of a *grand mal – fuck-up, fuck-you, fuck-over …*

As … they robbed … trashed … smashed … committed arson … doing whatever else mattered to their barbaric little Blacks-Only hearts in that highly specious moment … yet most of Woke Wigger America stood by, or joined in … grinding their teeth in sympathetic rage … *clasping onto their poor Blacks-Only previously-enslaved hands,* with mascara rivers flowing down pale peeking Antifa cheeks … camouflaged appropriately with appropriated "Blacks-Only Pain", and infested by weeping DC swamp alligators … *to, in repentance - bend The-Knee to their Sacred Racial Idols.*

That's grassroots Far-Left Democrat and twinning Bantu voting fodder for Y'all.

Bawling fake tears, over freshly rotten banana vomit, and for *fake human beings,* all the while yearning to be high-rolling … *Cashable Professional Victim$.*

And yet, *Somehow this was all Donald Trump's fault …?*

You could stuff that nasty Tweeting tassel-footed orange doorknobber like Mao's motheaten mummy, dump him in a quiet spot off the 16th …with his grinning cadaver *propped up with a 7 Iron, and* the ongoing BLM *crime scene* – would still be *his* fault.

That cost-effective runaway public tantrum, which went up in Woke cheers, dumb slogans, rocketing flames, and boiling acrid smoke and mirrors - is being priced somewhere far north of a billion dollars to the people … *the other American-Americans in the US.*

Taxpayers, who also have a right to *the same Civil Rights* as these opportunistically *politicized* deadbeat punks, expending and burning through unearned tax dollars in the United States of America.

Besides, most of these tiny *Unwanted* heads I'm busy counting in Afro-commie South Africa, as well as in the good ol' blue donkeyfucked US of A … *all* seem to share an astoundingly similar type of DNA, which they undoubtedly inherited from their absent fathers *of a certain melanin persuasion.*
Poor little buggers.

Doorknobbed, *before they were even born.*

By loser, cracked, smacked, tweaked … *Baby Junkie Daddies* – with only just enough cunning to guilt out other people into paying for their *Unwanted* and *everything to do with their barbarism and violent crimes* … ANC/EFF/BLM …

The entire frothing bulk of mass hysteria surrounding BLM is yet another contrived *Internet Religion* being used to mass-mask one more hate crime against humanity.

Only this time *cultural self-subjugation* via inverted self-hate … *deflected at a Subjective Object* of spiteful sociological and economic envy.
Crab Buckets in starker terms.

What the doorknob is a Coconut?
 Some guy … just *Some Guy* …

But he *Works*, *Pays* his taxes, and *Loves* his wife and kids. However, *politically,* he's apparently a sellout to the dumb doorknobbing non-Blacks-Only … *"White Man"* …

… because he does what ALL the other successful American-American Guys of Any Skin Color do …

Works, pay exorbitant taxes, barely covers the mortgage, and loves his wives and kids.
Digs professional sport.
Maybe has a hobby or likes bowling or coaching Kids B-ball.
Probably registered Independent or Republican. Maybe not. Might vote.
Willing and able to serve on a Jury. Believes wholeheartedly in Law and Order.
Was one personally, or is related to a Veteran.
Loves being American. Is a legal gun owner.
Probably attends a church every once in a while.
Sometimes bets on the Superbowl or World Series at work.

Follow me with this …

So-called *Evangelical* "Born-Again" Christians claim we *Humans* are *Born* separated from their "*God*" because according to *Them* we are born *Sinners* … [Usually Democrat-brats].

BLM claims non-Blacks-Only are *Born* separated from *Humanity* because according to "*Them*" non-Blacks-Only are born *Privileged* and *Inherently Racist* … [Usually Republican-born-spawn].

Unless all of "US" Sinners/Racists come to Jesus/BLM … Genuflect/Bow-the-Knee … go to meetings/rallies … evangelize/ecstatically Tweep … and most definitely hand over some Money … it's all fried crickety-snickets baby.

Then along comes a bunch of puffy-faced *self-enlightened Vegans* who claim *meat-eaters were originally-born Vegetarians* unto Gaia … *until we all Sinned against Animals.*
[Both Democrat and Republican-born-spawn this time, but lesser holy-dead-donkey Democrat-brats of course]

Each *Sect, Cult, Doctrine, Gospel, snarling Dogma* … attempts to overreach human developmental psychology by laying claim that the *Ad-Virtue … The Original Sin …* in a holy war against their particular …

~Meme~

… was, and Still Is … propagated … Genetically.

Us-*Them … We-They … Mi-Xi … McMickey-Broccoli …*

When the Biological nature of the entire claim can be best described in layman's terms as:

Liquid Male Bovine Excrement.

Even so … the quasi-religious gaslighting, vicious offbeat recriminations, relentless cancel-culture, and … nausea-inducing … *virtue-signal porno loop* … goes on and on … With brand spanking, new mutations hopping out of browsers to make themselves at home - shit Woke diarrhea all over the lounge carpet … while crabbily vying for further *extortive* brat-like attention and phishing for Woke *"Sins"* every day. Did I perhaps mention egregious face spanking?

Us-*Them … I Demon.*

The Happy-Clappy mob would call *That Guy* … and *all the Other Guys Like Him …*
… Unsaved, or *Lost Sinners …*

Instead of an *Oreo-Cookie* or *Uncle Tom's Coconut,* and all his buddies outside of the Gospel According to BLM …
… Racist Pigs.

Vegans would flay that poor unsuspecting doorknobber as being …
… A Face-Eating Animal-Rights Abuser …

Just like you cannot challenge "Born-Again Christians" … never try to out-preach any of these new-fangled religious identity mooks.

To dare to challenge them, in any sane sense – immediately casts you as the DEVIL …

… but remember … one is "Called" to cast out Devils … One does not Reason or Debate with Devils!!!
[… this does mean you … yes, You!]

So doan Y'all gan' be de DEBBIL 'n mekkin' Dey'all be doin'it now, Y'all hear me, Boy …??

BLM is nothing more than a new-age *political-cult* … Cover … for an LMFAO at Y'all dumb doorknobs … *Televised Crime Spree …*

‡8‡

They murder, rob, rape the hell out of their people, and abandon their own children mercilessly, for a quick cheap bop and drug hit - yet have somehow contrived to make sugarcoated donut-*whities* pay the full manufactured moral and contrived biological price, by twanging perfectly fake *Christian Guilt* …

… like a toothless gospel country Song … Sung at you with crystal methodist halitosis.
Enough said, okay?

Dude, sterling advice – sidestep … *race-based, diet-based, sex-based, climate-based, pandemic-based, energy-based, agricultural-based, politically-freebased* … instantly gratified, and brightly virtuous rotten banana vomit dressed up as the latest propagandized invocation of …
… The Seriously Pissed off Fake Jesus.

All of it, and I do mean *All of It* – is a carefully calculated kindergarten rejoinder, loaded by the self-absorbed filth …

… to gaslight, Other, and then Demonize - for the sole purpose of cooking up rent-free space in other people's heads to fill the gaping emotional void all secular religions create when applying this clumsy cultism in the form of carbon copy evangelical templates with brand new contrived dogmas.
And this for fun, easy money, the joy of languishing in a self-defined gloriously righteous goldfish bowl and angrily coerced infantile attention.
As for BLM …?
Entirely, so that they can do whatever the stolen doorknob they want to … *anyway.*

And, get away with it for that matter.

Do you want to know how it works?
Come, let's quickly jack this grim turd-fondling-festivity up to another level and put this poor little *Unwanted* nipper to bed once and for all … *shall we?* Cool.

You …
… Yes, you Cousin …
Have you personally decided to stop beating your dog?

What on earth kind of question is that?

Just answer.

I'm a pussy-person baby, so I don't have a mutt. And, I abstain, because it's a loaded question. Answering either - Yes, or No, just confirms that I get my freak on by thrashing my poor pooch.

Bravo! Bravo …

So, moving on rapidly … *have you decided at last, at long, long Last … that You … being a non-African-American, have realized deep within your cold pale heart … Your Hate-filled Racist of Racist Hearts … that Black Lives really and truly Matter?*

Oh, go screw yourself. Okay, I get it … fair enough.

Sure? Hmmm?

Or, do we need to scram from peering not so fearfully into burning Democrat inner cities and go and re-jack this right down to the bottom of the *Pit of Drowned Toilet Children* and take a hard long look at Sister South Africa?
  I've got plenty of time to waste on poking holes in putrid proclamations uttered by *qazi-religio-politico … Filth.*

Show me BLM and I'll show you financial parasites, *emotional vampires*, cheap grinning grifters who would never spend a cent, even less expend yet another violent public tantrum or weep one cold crocodile tear on the Real-World Slavery and Human Trafficking …
  Going on all over the Globe …
  … right this very second.
  While downstream from their VictimHood Ca$h and Sing Big Bling - Cartel bosses and shady gun dealers rub their hands gleefully … on the way to the nearest laundromat.

Show me a born-again Christian and I'll show you, *someone*, who has never given an orphan a mere sip of water, let alone prepared a meal and shared it. Does not now, and probably never will know the name of a single *Unwanted* child face to face … *by Independent Choice*. Every single *"righteous"* action is measured entirely in their own passive-aggressive *"spiritual"* self-interest and absolutely nothing else. Including, in rare exceptions, when photo-op orphans are pimped as *spiritual currency*. Show me a Christian and I'll show you someone who thinks they can genuinely buy *"Heaven"* for 10% Ca$h, and use anything or anyone to transmit the pathetic virtue signals of their very narrowly defined and entirely metaphoric self-righteousness.

Show me a Vegan and I'll show you, *someone*, who is utterly clueless about biodiversity, has no interest in understanding basic biology, and, in the extreme will do something as absurd, abusive, and mentally ill as transmogrifying animals into their even narrower virtue-signaling anthropomorphic echo bubbles … then attempt to convert a pet cat or dog to *vegetarianism*.
  Show me a militant urban vegan and I'll show you someone who couldn't hack it for three weeks on a real permaculture farm work cycle without at least one self-absorbed tit-fit, and storming off in outraged tears … trailed by fist-shaking recriminations.

Fifty shades of rancid fast-food hypocrisy, no matter how you wanna slice it up, baby.

Out to exploit *emotional something* for nothing. *Money, Sex, Power, Attention.* Pick the order. Pick them all.
Lowest Common Denominator … groupthink - *Narcissist Filth.*

Worth nothing to the transhuman challenges facing off against the far future of *this* planet …
We claim to be …
… Our World.

Point made Dude! Point made … Fair enough, got it … so what would you do with a rapist?

That's not the point.

Yes, it is. You make it very clear that rape and fatherlessness are at the root of all society's ills.

I made a point about parasitic political systems and passive-aggressive predatory religions being a core part of aggravating this oncoming terminal train smash for failing modern civilization, through the active enablement of recycled misogynistic narcissism.
So-called *"Racism"* is simply a race-based enabling device masquerading as a social othering religion. Be it the KKK, ANC, Hamas, Nazis, EFF, Antifa, Daesh, or sainted BLM … *et al.*
Same Day, same old rusted-solid, low-minded, savagely bigoted doorknob.

Identifying a problem is not a solution.
That is merely the first deconstructive step in any analysis.

Okay, so what would you do with a child rapist?

Is it really necessary to go there? This is supposed to be the beginning of moving away from all that. And by that, I mean all the Torquemadaesque infantile revenge fantasies I can see percolating away under your beady bonnet.

Why not?
If you want to leave it behind, get it all out in the open.
You talk about the ultimate solution to dealing with rape babies and orphans, and you mention all these other transhuman "Someones" … listening in to our conversation from the future … Speak away. Deal with the pedophiles, pederast Priests, and rapists first. It follows that their Unwanted offspring get to live in hell. What would you do with someone like your biological father?

‡§‡

There is no point.

On a personal level or otherwise.

I cannot re-engineer society on a whim, especially one hellbent on instant gratification along with wanton self-destruction, and besides, when it does come to me – how the invisible doorknob can you hate someone you have never met?

Really? And why for goodness sake?

Am I willing to lower myself to the point that I am so weak and pitiful, emotionally parasitic … that I choose to define myself as the zero-sum outcome of Other people's irrational fear, indifference, human failures, and stupidity? Drink poison and hope someone else is gonna die … like I said … Seriously?

Besides, what it would take to achieve something like that would be almost impossible to implement, *without further wars*, ergo it cannot happen.

Simply because *Wars* … my dear Watson … facilitate rape, child displacement, and the *Unwanted* in the first place.

And, centuries of previous wars created the slithering religious hierarchies, in which the pederast network of Priests safely prowl, harvest *Unwanted* children, and operate.

Deep in the Holy-Spook, … shadowy, Six-Six … Sick … places.

It is *How* they keep on getting away with pedophilia decade after decade. It is why that horror is happening to a whole bunch of pubescent *Someones* …

… right this very second.

If I were a Roman Catholic, I would get a worldwide "Roman Spring" going and book it on WhatsApp. Then round up and physically defrock the entire sworn-to-celibacy kiddydoorknobbing lot of them.

Imagine … on a certain beautiful new day … chase one and all out of the churches, rectories, seminaries, and everywhere else they lurk, cover up for each other and hide … behind some fake bejeweled cross and a bunch of painted plaster statues.

Then lock, chain, and barricade them all outside, *banished*, without harming a pimple one of their sickening arses.

Not even in the slightest.

Don't touch a hair on their sacred doorknobbing heads, but leave the bastards out on the streets…

… Naked and *Ashamed.*

Exactly like just ONE molested little boy … all *alone* … and *deathly afraid of disappointing God's Holy Anointed Padre, and wickedly rejecting His Glorious Holy Spirit …*

… by spitting it out.

After that, the folks who had the man-sweetmeats to do this … can sit down … wherever they are, and decide for themselves like actual married grownups, with kids – what it means to be a follower and imitator of Christ in a world up to its evil eyeballs in abjectly abused and abandoned children. I can't expect all of them to stop believing in the airy-fairy Jesus and Marychain bull malarkey, along with all their pretty little blessed Saints … but at least *maybe* they will stop using the spooky Roman crap as smoking cloak-and-dagger for feeding greed, relinquishing personal power, and abusing other people's children sexually.

Hahaha … The media would have a fatal gang seizure on the spot. Getting interesting. Coming on with the uber harshness. So, Cousin … fantasize that you have fantastical unlimited power for another day or a year – what would you do to fix the problem of rape?

Do you want to hear this? Because I couldn't care less about curing societies' systemic failures.

Countries have secular laws and judicial systems that are supposed to deal with the crime of rape effectively. It is their given problem. *By the People for the People* and all that.

Exactly, but according to you, they just exacerbate the problem, although funnily enough, the demographics seem to agree with that broad supposition. As I said, speak freely.
As we both agree … many Others are listening in from the transhuman future …
What would you do?

If I answer, the topic is closed.

Please understand, that I'm not here to discuss improbable hypotheticals with you.

And when I answer, we can discuss it point by point, but you may only rebut with questions. Fair enough?

I do not want to waste my precious time on redundant political farces or fallacies.

Fair enough, Shoot.

First, tag the DNA of the entire population, and second, supply compulsory birth control to all high-school and college students, concomitant to mandatory State medical and educational support services.

What!!
You do realize you are still living in 20/21?
Year of the Definitive Conspiracy Theory?
A badly compressed mini-epoch, in which a very dangerous flu is vainly struggling to compete with urban paranoia running wild all over the freaked-out planet!

According to Google, right this very second, Bill Gates is ostensibly in advanced secret negotiations with Tic-Tac Aliens, who gave the virus to the Chinese, so that the New Illuminati,

secretly headed by George Soros, Putin and Donald Trump – could use Covid-19 as the propaganda vehicle to micro-chip the entire planet via hypodermic injection … On an exact date, 5G is going to activate every Vaxxer and they are all going to go Full-Zombie, and then …
… Are you completely squirrelshit crazy?

The entire Globe is ten times more bugshit bonkers than it usually is on any given Monday, and you are suggesting that: One – you would create a Global DNA database that plays right into the Globalist Cartel Conspiracy Theorists, that incidentally, waaayyy too many utter idiots take very seriously and Two, you would basically give teenagers open season to gazump each other senseless?

Absolutely.

Any given country has some form of unique identification, which is required to be presented, on-demand, to the relevant authorities. ID's Passports, Social Security, Driver's License, you get it …

Banks are now switching to fingerprint biometrics as a first-level identification fail-safe to protect account holders from thefts and fraud. Iris scanning will be soon to follow.

It makes absolute sense to take it to the Global DNA level.

In the last couple of years breakthroughs in mapping DNA sequencing through family trees has opened the floodgates to solving cold cases that have stumped law enforcement for decades. This could see arrests for those kinds of murders and sexual assaults within hours.

Oh, and when I said rebut with a question, I did mean as pertains to the point or points at hand, rather than crassly questioning my dubious sanity or to showcase the smoking bugweed-crazy fantastical antics of Messer's Gates et al, al la mode, al la … *~Meme~*

Stick to the pertinent topic *Willya*!

Yeah, yeah, I hear you and concede that a bio-matrix identification system, is a sensible State requirement.

But Cousin, DNA is considered way too invasive, too internal as it were.

People will never go for it.

It's not just harvesting Federally-approved snot, grossly removed from your skull by Law, it's almost like the State giving you a rectal exam on video, with a POV enema for a rising finale, by proxy sort of thang … horribly too invasive and way too disclosing in terms of personal privacy and all that.

The Left would go Scrat-looney chocolate-balls and pick another vicious cat-fight with the Right.

Just on principle.

I mean they are all totally into identity politics, just not with the ability to pinpoint any voter Personally – beyond any shadow of a doubt.

I'm not asking people to go for it, this is just hypothetical.

In fact, I would microchip everyone alive or dead with the key to their electronic medical and DNA bio-matrix profiles.

The biological and medical benefits would be beyond enormous.

Law enforcement would cheer!

Aha, yeesss. Well, I better agree in theory (as I avoid listening to the eerie distant sounds of a mad scientist laughing her crazy-bitch head off), but it would still be insanely hard to sell.

Only a tad less difficult to get out there, past glowering parents, than issuing condoms and birth control straight into the unsupervised, sweaty, trembling paws of horny teenagers.

Name me one PTA that would agree to go for that?

You are looking at this entirely the wrong way and asking an utterly irrelevant question.

In any given high school, right now, teenagers are engaging in unprotected sexual activity, resulting in STDs and *Unwanted* pregnancies.

Gender fluidity, gender neutrality, binary gender, cisgender, transgender … rotten banana vomit …

… is being relentlessly forced down their throats.

Kids with psycho guardians are on puberty blockers without informed long-term choices. Sick doctors cut them up and pump them full of sex hormones.

An entire generation is being orphaned from themselves - *within their own minds and bodies.* This instituted mental disease will probably soon become some sort of insidious law, claiming to protect and "*educate*" them.

But the *Unwanted* pregnancies and assaults *still happen despite this.*

Suppressing, psychologically twisting, and subverting children's physical and burgeoning sexual urges - is so totally not any rational answer, even though it is already being done to them, without realizing that this is being done against the natural development of their sexual psychology and any sane biological parent's will.

Why is this so fucking abusively evil?

Because it *objectifies* them very narrowly and they in turn begin *objectifying each other* and most especially themselves sexually, to protect their real internal issues of developing identity. And, *that* leads to all sorts of serious trouble, as they begin to act out on the dually emerging, knock-on-need for a sense of valid, reciprocated, emotional cogency.

Promiscuity, acquired gender confusion, voyeurist public onoism, and more importantly, *sexual aggression*, passive or overtly victimizing - then becomes some weird type of peer pressure. *This multiplies through Social Media into, and past, newer boundaries of sexual antagonism.*

Pornography of every imaginable tag becomes entirely innurable, boring even, and women are relentlessly demonized and thus labeled terms like "fuck bitches". Overt verbal and sexual abuse towards women is entirely the new norm. Bitch, bitch, bitch…

Most affected by this are young girls, who further become the extended sex-prey of boys engaged in *role-playing* as socially accepted *female queers* by laying claim to being a *"Woman"* through their chosen, *"fluid gender identity"* – and thus, very freely invade all female sexual hygiene spaces with utter disregard to the emotional discomfort or backhand abuse of the real biological girls going through puberty in those spaces. Creating more resentment and anger, with deeply polarized hatred.

Boom! A brand new social internet-driven religion, with disgusted heterosexuals as convenient demons living in the *sin* of sexual bigotry.

But, unchecked, Legal and ALL in the politically holy, and virtuous Woke name of *"safer gender neutrality"* and *"equality for transgenderism"* … and any resistance to this insanity labeled some new-fangled *"--phobia"*, that must be protected against outraged *Parents* at all costs, or *Else You Will Be Cancelled!*
Meaning:

Little girls with fannies just have to accept that they are just gagged institutional fuckmeat …
… for big bad Woke Wolves with lady cocks … dressed up as frilly testicled Grammas.

[So do their legally disconnected, FBI tagged parents …]

A very clear and overt symptom of the fatal venereal mind disease that buried many a dead civilization.
Along with all its [Woke] politicians, cunning failed professors, enlightened chicken-gut oracles, fake soothsayers, and slimy sellout priests.

The full amortization of … *Liberal Socialist Democracy* … on demand and *on its way …*

Let me ask you a question.

Who, as a group of teenagers, growing up together in a knitted social group, that all go to school together, play sports together, live co-ed together, and work together – have the lowest demographic of *Unwanted* teenage pregnancies and overt sexual deviancies anywhere in the modern world?

Er, Amish kids?

I said the modern world, not the simulated seventeenth century!

No, the answer is Israeli Sabras growing up on Kibbutzim. Sabras might not be for everybody. The way they grow up is very open, practical, incredibly tough, and direct. It is also very culturally immersive, which is why all of them identify as Jews but mostly detest religion and politics. They are also very blunt, demanding, and expect the same from all of their men and women.

Equally.

This includes compulsory military service at age eighteen. To outsiders, they may appear arrogant and aloof but they are genuinely dedicated to the safety and survival of each other and their country. And they treat one another with mysterious unreserved respect that they give to no one else. When these folks have babies, it's usually because two highly-committed heterosexual people disarmed themselves, swore an oath to each other before their god, and then relinquished their defensive weapons for a bit.

Haha, yes, I've heard about the Sabras. Not to be messed with figuratively or literally.
So to speak.
Still, you are not going to sell that story to any PTA.
And as sure as syphilitic bears shit runny popes in the burning woods, most certainly not in light of the Palestinian conflict.
Don't go there.
I mean really, are you suggesting that because of the kind of unshakable cultural and moral framework Sabras grow up in on Kibbutzim, they are more natural and responsible about their bodies and sexual identity than other teenagers worldwide?
Including their sworn to bring on total Jewish annihilation, rock with rocket hurling enemies, who occupy the exact opposite of that theological spectrum?

Exactly.

These kids have seen each other naked since they were small, there is no mystery. They live together. Eat, sleep, work, study, and play and they are religiously indoctrinated, giving them a strong moral framework for living. The only one they have ever known.

However ... if you consider their not-so-secret attitude to religious topics and politics, in stark contrast, to their deep, actual commitment to each other as a people and country – a picture begins forming of What May Be ... along this *Journey* we are on.

Are you steering this conversation?
Because it seems like you are steering the conversation.
Please don't do that.

Obviously, I'm steering this conversation!

And, I would like you to take note of the little solutions that we are discovering along the way. Think of them as useful objects because they are going to come in very beneficial indeed.

Weight and sea.

Groovy, so tag everyone kicking and screaming, including everyone not, then turn teenagers into sex-mad, gun-toting Sabras. You made the point, what's next?
Remember to steer this back to dealing with rapists.
What is your next move?

First, literally, *disarm* and gut your conclusions.

You should emphasize to yourself that Sabras rarely have *Unwanted* pregnancies among their youth, or find the need for boys to "*identify*" as girls, and for the most part, are happy and well balanced - rather than focus on their prescribed livelihoods.

Focusing on a vivid emotional trigger, out of context, entirely misses the point – that's a snowflake trick used to deflect, then score cheap brownie points completely off-topic.

I did ask you to stick to the valid points.

To my mind, there are deep values to harvest and lots to be learned here … beyond dealing with enforced evil socialist social engineering and normal teenage hormones running wild.

My apologies, it was a comic book picture that stuck in my mind.
Although, you are right – I can't quite re-imagine a mixed squad of armed, teenage, desert-soldiers with a couple of young mommies juggling bottles, blankies, and grenades … scattered throughout an infantry patrol.
Once again, I hear you. I will agree to put a pin in their "framework" or "useful object" whatever. And I concur, they are truly remarkable people who turned a barren desert into an utterly amazing, first-world … war-torn paradise.
Let's move on – what's next on your list?

Cousin, their framework is not perfect, but it is real and does warrant deeper further scrutiny as an objective social subject, of immense value, but yes – Moving on.

The third thing I would do after DNA tagging and implementing mandatory State-provided birth control is to fully legalize prostitution.

Encourage it socially, and privatize it as an industry with similar compulsory State-mandated medical support for all sex workers both casual and professional.

And indecently, to make this work … only allow American citizens who are registered high-school graduates, and who passed the SAT with a score above 1000, to be issued with a biometric linked voter's card … to be able to vote legally at State and Federal level …

… and then *legalize drugs.*

WOW!! You can say that backward … Wow.
Okaaay?

Explain ...

Yes, you may say it backward but in fact, in Amsterdam, you can see a girl walking alone late at night and no one will bother her. Well, at least the last time I was there.

Why?

Because in that city retail affection is legal and a highly organized business.

Once again, another *working* framework. One worth a deeper inspection.

However, not for practical purposes in our specific and very different journey. We probably won't need that kind of social relief, and no, it is not a perfect system but it does work.

The Dutch introduced things called "*Tippelzones*" a while ago, where it is legal to pick up tarts or johns during certain hours.

Within two years of introducing these zones into certain cities, the incidences of rape fell by up to forty percent in those gerrymandered redlight areas. This, despite the dangers co-existent to the drug trade linked to sex workers and the risks attached to illegal, foreign, and unlicensed street prostitution.

Well worth looking at.

Especially if safe legal drugs and temporary licenses could be bought over the counter in any zone. The license is issued after completing a quick, simple, clean bill-of-health blood test.

A bit like a vaccine passport.

And I would make it cut both ways – Johns need to get a blood test too, before shopping in the zone. And a license must be anonymous, free, and only valid for one day.

As for drugs and the "War on Drugs"- the only people who benefit from illegal narcotics are violent cartel bosses and violent political drug Tzars. A multi-billion dollar industry on both sides of the table. A zero-sum game where dead junkies, prisons full of mules, and butchered, bullet-scarred neighborhoods pay the final price.

And the core reason why high school grads, only those who pass the SAT above average, get to qualify to vote for State and Federal governments ... is that they are far more likely to make better-informed political, and more appropriate *Economic* choices that will directly affect the social health of the entire Republic. Since these kids have already proven that they are willing to work hard enough to improve themselves in life, they will more than likely become higher-end taxpayers and thus capable of holding the incumbent government to scrutiny.

Ergo, they have earned, and deserve, that exclusive educated choice when selecting an *executive* political administration. You can be assured that anyone who does not fall into that category, is either too lazy to have a say, not smart enough to make informed choices, an indifferent criminal, or will seek out anything to fill a declared victimhood belly for free. The reason why the Greeks filtered qualified voters rather than gerrymandered sheer quantities to leverage elections the socialist way.

Now … you may start yelling at me.

I don't have to yell at you, the mere "zero-sum" suggestion will attract screams of Woke outrage, like flies smelling runny dog shit … then zoning in from nowhere. Allow me to shimmy away … a safe distance from you in particular … but do carry on … I'm all ears.

Ha, Ha. Five, legalize the aborting of all *Unwanted* pregnancies but tag the DNA of each fetus.

The mother of such a fetus must then face involuntary sterilization and/or criminal sanction together with the DNA tagged father of the aborted fetus, who must also face similar sterilization and/or criminal sanction. The criminality to be determined at the inquest will be weighted in terms of exactly how the pregnancy was coerced, by whom, and how it occurred medically without the use of *mandated*, freely available birth control.

Sixth, all marriage licenses must be scrapped in favor of Birth Licenses.

Marriage licenses must be replaced by common law business and domicile contracts attached to the Birth License and ultimately the child.

A Birth-License will only be issued in the event of a planned pregnancy between a couple or licensed surrogate and becomes ratified and attached to both upon birth.

Marriage ceremonies are then replaced by confirmed pregnancy rites and birth feasts.

The Birth License contract will exist in the sole social and financial interest of the child. With political riders.

Parties will be held financially and socially accountable for the child but may enter into third-party transfer-of-responsibility agreements with other childless couples for adoption purposes.

Each child will be legally attached to a birth contract until the age of eighteen, whereupon they inherit their own, political, financial, and legal Civic Responsibilities.

Until that coming of age, that child's Civil Rights will be rigorously defended. After that age, each adult male loses all civil rights and falls entirely under the jurisdiction of Mandated Civil Responsibilities, which is each male citizen's law-bound duty to uphold on behalf of all other citizens but most especially for every female-born citizen who enjoys the protection of Civil Rights.

Seventh, all GBV cases, regardless of sex, should be processed through the judicial process entirely by biological women who were born girls.

Female legislators, judges, advocates, and juries, must hear evidence collected and processed by specialized female police task forces, evidence analysts, and medical practitioners.

Convicted perpetrators must receive the maximum allowable penalties under the Law and be segregated to specialized prisons where they will spend their entire sentence working in embedded, viable, outside commercial industries, running within the prison, as fully paid labor. The prison will provide shelter, clothing, and very basic meals along with social and medical attention.

Anything else must come from the convict's pocket through work.

The bulk earnings of each convict will go to paying for the costs of processing the crime and bringing it to trial, as well as paying structured monetary reparations to the victims.

For non-lifers, another portion will go into a legitimate bank account. The rest goes to the prisoner to pay for telephone calls, television, groceries, private clothing, and the like, with a portion going into a prisoner pool to finance general entertainment, recreation, and sporting amenities.

The prisoner will complete paying for the costs of the crime in this manner and will be kept in custody even after sentence expiration - until the entire bill is settled with the State *and with the victims*. A prisoner may also choose to remain in custody after settling the bill to build up a bank balance and must go through an in-depth re-integration program before release.

Recidivists all receive automatic life sentences.

If a child is born out of the crime of rape, the perpetrator will remain in custody for the rest of his life and the maximum portion of his work production will go to supporting the child until that convict dies. The same for child murderers, where the bulk of such a convict's remuneration will go to an orphan program. The same applies to child rapists and pedophiles. Life imprisonment, and working as labor for those children until they die.

Women who falsely accuse men of rape must undergo similar very harsh criminal sanctions and the settling of the judicial bill with reparations to the victims.

Men and women found guilty of child abuse and contractual child neglect must also face involuntary sterilization, the nullification of all Birth Licenses, with similar custodial criminal incarceration, and penalized child support.

However, this remains a humane system, so I would also allow these convicts conjugal visits from sex workers or longer contact and weekends with romantic partners under a portion of that judicial framework. I would also allow convicts working to support orphan programs, under certain very stringent conditions, to correspond with and have remote access to the children's progress and be part of their lives by view-only proxy if they so choose.

I would even go as far as allowing voluntary incarcerations for people who recognize they have a criminal tendency they cannot control, under the same dispensation but with no financial penalties for their labor *if* they have not committed a crime.

Blow me ... and you say those Old Testament fellows were a bit nuts!
Involuntary sterilization! Convicted slave labor ... voluntary imprisonment ...

Are you crazy??

No.

Ask yourself … *Who* … is that form of a judicial system protecting? What is at the heart of such crushing criminal sanctions?

Why draw such rigidly straight legal lines in the sand over the simple human issue of two loving adults having a baby together?

To stop Unwanted kids from being born from indifferent sex and put an end to kids being abused emotionally, physically, sexually, politically, and financially.

Exactly. Well done, so you have been listening.

However, you cannot stop a war by starting another war, that is just common sense. Even if you are already in an unwinnable war and can't evade it.

And, of course, life and the realities of this world are not a silly game of SIMS being played by someone like me.

However, in a practical sense … Disengagement is the way to go.
If you cannot fight it, don't.

Something new … *Completely New* … has to be done about *Unwanted* children, but the solution has to be approached with the realization that no help will come from politicians or religious so-called *leaders*.

That is pretty much the entire fight.

Okay, so where would you start?

PURPOSE.

Purpose?

Yes, ask yourself – what is the purpose of a religion like Christianity?

Lead a good life and go to Heaven when you die, I suppose.

So, the ultimate purpose of life is to die?

No, to get to Heaven.

But there is no Heaven.

How do you know that?

Because quite obviously there would only be *One,* and the future residents would not need to be murdering and bombing each other into pointless oblivion … all in a blood-drenched defense of the imaginary …
One True Lord of Paradise.

That's why …

But a statement like this, while being for all intents and purposes, *intelligent,* does not contain much in the way of collective … *Wisdom.*

At best, it is merely an informed criticism. At worst it creates another moral vacuum hunting for something else to twist and fill.
So then, *quo Vadis* my dear old Hobbit?

What is the key to unlocking the fragile relationship between applied Wisdom, rational Intelligence, and Bloody-Minded Common Sense?

We can inhume like nobody's business …

… But can we … Transhume …???

恩 典

blessed am i
among all living

blessed am i
among any other
DNA
Consumer

blessed be
my tenuous
umbilical
succoring
Her
endlessly expectant
food-chains

blessed be
my each
every
acquired nutrient

blessed be
that which
i am
seeking to consume

ravenously

and that which
is about to
consume me

blessed
are we
who
do

‡§‡

媽媽

Water's eternal … sweet, bright melody tinkles …

Delightfully gurgling, a perfect hollow rumble … trickling ever down … a slanting bamboo tube.

The only Sacred liquid with memory.

Exists everywhere.
A lone catalyst.
Waiting patiently … since before Life began.
Cradling DNA in a deeply precious *translucent* embrace.

Sprawled sleepily as snow on the very peaks of aloof purple massifs.
Boils black … deep inside the far, darkest night of the seas.
That frigid sprawled glacier grinding a mountain to rubble.
Hailed, Queen of Ice!
King of Hail!
And, spawner of Rain … unto every lesser minion, of a thousand given names.
Flying free as clouds, kissing clear blue desert skies … to hurtle breathlessly aloof … with manic roaring godwinds …
… Everywhere.

Runs rivers down the quivering cheeks of the truly relieved mother, clutching her squirming, screaming crying child … *yet, thick as infected snot*, snivels wet … from the merciless nostrils of the despicable … violently shivering …. Guilty … *Evil Fool.*

Lurks invisible, a tortuous dripping tap, yet … thunders down …
… the never-ending cyclic monsoon.

Ever ripping horror and wet death into unsuspecting dwellings and ancient fortitude as it dances wild never-ending barbarian reels to seethe and terrify endless gray oceans full of shipwrecked rocky trenches, and long gone human bones.
Unleasher of Hurricanes, Typhoons … seething mindless water Sprites … armed with powers of gods … lording over the leviathan …
… Lord Tsunami San.

Slumbers deep …
… vanished into an invisible cave …
Has so, for millions of years … ever dreaming of the expired home planet … within the Earth's lightless … adoptive cradling crust.

Always seeking a True Warrior's path of least forceful resistance … launches from the hollow embrace of the neatly cut rattan stalk,
and falls …
… free …

A squat, *balanced*, carved pail below the bamboo tube – momentarily tips over …

Ķtčhőņķ…

… tosses the chill liquid out … to dive down into a clear jade pool, teeming with lazy, regal … red-golden …
… *Koi.*

Mute wandering creatures.
Aimless.
Flashing spotted livery.
Whiskered fat lips …

Carp … carp … muted *opii* … stroking silky fantails … yin … *yan* … yin …
… *yan* … yin … *yan…*

Transluting, splintering water lily lights back at a blazing… *peach-yellow sun.*

Ķtčhőņķ…

A simple wooden rake wanders … rustling through …
… The *Zen.*

Paring faintly hissing bone-white sand …. *Marching…* meandering … inscribing rigidly curved
… non-verbal calligraphy.

Patterning.

The simple wooden teeth moving eons of earth *Chi* …
… calming, perfect …

Serene.

Rake twists.
Wanders on. Measured … purposeful … around a slowly shifting rock … calibrating, erasing, opening, folding … moving … reshaping millennia.
Then stops.

Ḳtčhőŋḳ…

Her smile is the intimate lover of a mysterious sweetness … her exquisite features a royal bequest … that she folds … bows meekly to …

Mother

Delicate feet … pad gracefully away.

The pale old calibration rake, she allows to rest against an ancient malachite obelisk.
Plinthed, between the navigating Babel Fish… and the flat, spheric Earth Dream Device.

Quick pretty toes lead her on to a verdant, somber … *Bonsai En.*
Nearer along … to the flowering entrance of *Her* …

Venerable Sanctuary.

On a narrow pink marble bench, she scoops up very rarely worn garments …
… unhurriedly dresses her tanned naked body.
Readied for her expected Guest.
Sits down …
waits …
…
…

Ḳtčhőŋḳ…

One breath on … past six echoed ticks, of the faithful water gong …

Dmmp! Dmmp! dmmp!!

A muffled hammering sounds abruptly from the shadowy wooden portal to her *Ingress.*

She rises, grinning to herself, most eager to welcome … Her *Man.*

‡§‡

‡§‡

The stout wooden door is bound with a rust patinated steel portcullis, disciplinal, and riveted solidly to very ancient-looking wood.

Timber is dark.
Highly polished.
Its grain and swirling knots seem to … constantly *seethe* and *writhe* restlessly under its gleaming tarnish.
Like moving *magic sludge* trapped in a milky brown puddle.

Like the one he is standing in … as angry grey rain beats down on his matted head … rivulets running down his agonized shoulders … *soaking already damp bones.*
He is dog-tired.
No time for weird.
The slabs on his back have ceased being the overwhelming numbing death burden, *they were,* when carried out of the Valley of the Shadows of Death, *and* into the mountains.
Yet, he has forgotten when every last waking moment is not accompanied by vicious pains, faithfully assassinating his injured back … as he trudged alone … along The Way.
He could use the old man and his Auspicious Tea around about now.

Yesterday.

He is so exhausted he wants to break down and cry.
But he *cannot* give in to a wearisome flirtation with self-pity.
Mendacity only he can borrow, to use as a Lie … *against himself.*
Then he will cease to take another step forward.
Cease to exist.
He has to complete locating *All of …*
… Them.

And this is the Most Important One.

This is where … *the Voices* … have led him …

Faintly … he hears a sound beyond the gateway.

Ķtčhőŋķ…

The strange door swings open soundlessly.
Before him … *framed* in the eccentric ornate arch … is *the most beautiful woman he has ever laid his eyes upon.*

They study each other.

Almost instantly, deadly weariness *flees like a coward* … sneaky, self-pity *dives wailing under a rock*. He is utterly … mesmerized.

How in all of the god's creations, *could someone be so incredibly … radiantly … beautiful?*

He would speak … actually … wants to say something … *anything* … but he cannot.

She is *looking at him!*

Looking at *Him.*

With a beaming, naughty little grin, that legions of men would die for!

Just to get lost in … *forever.*

She reaches, *without hesitation*, takes him by the hand, and pulls him inside.

He is way too bewildered to resist.

And, finds himself on the other side of the arch … as she closes the strange trippy door.

For the second moment, he finds himself completely speechless.

She has so blown all his normal powers of observation … of everything except *Her* … commencing at her shocking … sudden, vivid appearance … that he completely fails to notice what is behind this … this … *celestially attractive girl.*

He is suddenly standing in his road-stained clothes, dripping onto the flint flagstones beneath his boots. Yet, his face is being warmed by delicious, hot yellow sunshine!

She giggles, bursting out like heavenly champagne … and says:

Come, sweetheart … we must get you out of those nasty wet rags. And let us put those precious things on your back … exactly … where they Belong.

She leans in and kisses him gently on his utterly astounded lips.

He is still shivering from biting wet cold and shocked into stasis.

He can't help it!

This woman is insanely gorgeous, beyond any speech or craft of prose … and she just kissed *him?*

… *HIM!?*

Like she's done a million times before?

Who is this ultimate expression of feminine pulchritude?

Why does he instantly just want to sweep her into his arms and bury his nose deep into her skin? Smell her essence? *Smell Her.* Kiss her neck, stroke her wild woven hair, memorize the contours of her heavenly body … with lonesome, *singing* starving fingers.

Make love to her over and over … pour himself … every part of who he is … into her.

Welcome her back. *Again?*

Where is he? What is this?

Still holding onto his cold unresisting hand, she leads him to a second, yet barren plinth on the other side of the Zen patterned … Earth Time.
Gently, she helps him … slowly untying the rough rope and plaited wet rags which bind the cruel stones to his scarred and battered body.
They lower the crudely chiseled slabs gradually to the ground.

Here … help me position them my precious darling. This is where they fit.
Put them back-to-back, so these immortal words that you carved up next to the fire in those freezing mountains … face outwards … with the ten curses trapped unseen … in darkness … never to see the light of day again. Yippee!

He does what she asks him *Dumbfounded with a Capital D*, and between them, they wrestle the two stone-chiseled imperatives, into a snug slot, cut perfectly into the black granite they are standing on.

The Edict he carved looks bright and cheerful.

Nowhere near the intimidating message, *he so grievously fears*, the world will completely ignore…
… Or will it?

She breaks into his gloomy little revery … and pecks him softly on a dirty cheek.

Now … for those icky rags lover … come, let's get you cleaned up. You will feel much better after that. Come, sweetie …

By now, he is just doing anything this miraculous vision of a girl tells him …
But, he is also becoming franticly aware of being terrified that he is going to wake up … and this … all this … is just some fanciful dream that is going to swiftly fade back into a horrifying and depressing reality …
If she would only kiss him again!

And he still hasn't said … A Word!
What is wrong with him?
She's just … a very, very, very … very pretty girl.

She chuckles chocolates and juicy raspberries … squeezes his tightly gripping hand.

‡§‡

Thank you, my baby, you know you are not too bad-looking yourself either.
What? Are you reading my mind?
No … silly … I'm reading you. You.

Stunned into *Silence* again.
She leads them along a twisty path to a deep, lightly steaming pool.

Come, honey, let's undress you and clean you up.
Sure … but first … please … er … Lady, tell me … what is your name?
She releases his fingers … faces him fully … and smiles an emperor's lusted-after fortune … her delicate priceless eyes crinkling up in joyful laughter.

What do you think my name is … my sweet dear man?

Not waiting for a response, she quickly starts undressing him. Now he is shaking his head in perfect, shockingly bemused, Wonderment, *With a capital W …*
Please, please … Don't Wake Up!

She giggles almost uncontrollably, then kneels to untie his worn-out boots. He looks down at the gold-threaded plait running down her perfect back … and just lets her strip him. He could no more resist this woman than he could fight his own shadow. Bite his elbow. Lick his nose. He wants to desperately shake his mind in both trembling hands … clear it mentally. Maybe … *this is a dream!*

But … all of a sudden … *he is Naked.*

And, without further ado … being led into the perfectly hot bath.
He wants to pass out as euphoria rushes throughout his screaming body.
Agony and ice leeching from horrible aching muscles … *unspiking blistered nerves.*
Feels so … sublimely perfect.
An overwhelming release … almost makes him want to cry in relief.
Suddenly … *he is …*

Weeping … into the steaming water, not even knowing why … and not truly even caring anymore.
A burning soul that begins to rack and sob at the horrors … *still raw, profusely bleeding,* and *trapped deep within.* The deadly loneliness that wants to overwhelm, drown … *devour him in its black unfeeling maw.*

He is suddenly aware of her … in the hot healing water with him.

She kisses his eyes, kisses his face … reaches up … looks deep from within the unknown universe into his sorrowful … devastated eyes … for the very longest moment … and then kisses Him.

From that moment everything *collapses … merges…*

He is aware of her hands, his hands, her fingers … his.

She bathes him.

Massages … washes … embraces … touches … soothes.

Then leads him in a swirling daze out of the steaming water.

Their bodies come together … *again* … as if they have always been doing so … thousands of times. He makes slow, slow love to her. She makes joyous love back. Orgasmic. Honest. Naughty. Fun!

She starts to tickle fight him!

They both scream … boiling giggles … roaring in unfettered joyous delight … all over the lush green grass. Chuckling … rolling, fucking wildly … embracing … kissing, yearning into an unrecognizable tangle of limbs and hearts … lost to everything except each other.

Ķtčhőņķ…

The warm sweet dream scurries away back into the lurking mists of sleep … and is gone. His crusted eyes open … groggily.

He breathes deep. His mind is completely clear.

Her smell … everything about *Her* is still here! It is still real. She lies spooned into him perfectly. He clutches at her seamlessly … *very still* … not daring to move.

Not wanting to disturb her … softly inhaling … hair … skin of her incredible neck.

Are you finally back with me lover?
Yes … er, how … did you know?
Oh, I always know when you wake up.

He sits up. Rubs his eyes.

They are on a tatami mat.

She rolls over like a lazy cat … her twitching infectious smile, moist and silvery in the intense shimmering full moon above.

Humbling billions and billions of *suddenly shy stars.*

He looks down into the liquid fathomless mystery of her eyes, leans down, and softly smooches her. Caresses her perfect cheek.

She whispers:

You must be hungry. Let me feed you, my pretty man. Come, you must eat.
Yes … I am hungry … starving actually.
I know. Come.

She's on her feet … grabs him by the hand. Leads him over to the Koi Pond.

Barely hesitating … she reaches into the black night water and plucks out a slapping … struggling wet fish.

Laughs delightfully.

Spins around to kiss him on the nose announcing:

Dinner!

He whups her, on her perfect dimpled rump and she squeals, a tinkling melody … away into the garden full of blossoms.

In the center is a low table. On it is a small amphora, a cutting board, a knife, and two bowls.

Chopsticks rest across them. She slaps the flopping wet fish down and butchers it.

Removes the head … humming rainbows to herself.

Slices into the fins and removes the tail.

Fillets it into perfect *sashimi* … Damascus blade flashing at the peering … *inquisitive moon*.

That gets layered into the Feng bowls with practiced dexterity.

From the shiny Redstone amphora … she deftly pours a dark aromatic sauce over the lightly trembling raw flesh.

Eat … Fill up my lover … then we talk.

He eats ravenously. The soft, tender fish is utterly delicious … tastes like food for gods. She eats with him. They feed each other. She prepares him some more of the delectable fish …

… silently, they complete the meal.

I have never eaten something so amazing. Bravo.
It is all my pleasure. Are you thirsty? You should be.
Yes.

She trots off into the night and returns moments later with a large earthen jug. Stands over him and gently pours ice-cold tasteless water into his open waiting mouth.

He drinks. And drinks.

As he drinks, he realizes just *how truly thirsty he is* … and drinks some more.

She patiently pours … until he is completely sated …

Puts down the jug.

There, that has to be much better. Now … Sweetheart, my beautiful man … time for us to talk.

He gazes at her, *lost into her* … everything about her.

Who are you?

Oh, come on baby … you know exactly who I am.

Yes, you are right … I do.
But that's impossible!

Why?

You are … you are so … excruciatingly familiar … but … you are also … parts … pieces … fragments of every woman I have ever known or truly loved. I know You, I feel everything about you … but you … You seem to be a stranger!
You see sweetie, I knew you would begin to figure this out. That's why I adore you so much.

Are you a stranger?

Maybe, maybe not … right here, right now, I am your first Aspect of me … and, You need to tell me about you … and everything about me … my precious loving man.
I want to hear it all from your mouth.
Look into my eyes, honey. I'm here … you are safe … it is only us … It's Me.
I love you eternally … Tell me everything … tell Me.

Ķtčhőņķ…

He suddenly becomes re-aware of the periodic clonking sound he last heard faintly through the weird magic door.

It's been there like a dull dependent distant metronome. Ticking off the heartbeat to the Milky Way. *A watery bongo rhythm sounding off very slowly in the background.*

It only briefly penetrated his rousing awareness. Moments before he looked into her starlit eyes … awakening from their love …

Her … *bamboo water gong …*

… I love You.
And, I have dearly … Hated You.

I've missed you, and have been empty in heart … and lonely … for You … all of my life.

The agony of longing for you … every time you left me, or have been snatched from me through birth, death, suicide, and murder, is the same unbearable hell, as when you left me repeatedly … because I put you through too much pain.

I have grieved for you, in a devastating loss … and clung to you as my girlfriends, lovers, and wives.

But, from my first waking moment … all I've ever done is search endlessly for You.

Searched and searched for your Love … and yet, never been abler to clasp onto its ever-withering tendrils.

I was born to You … Unwanted.
You probably got raped by someone who was your own family.
I have a rare blood sickness that I could only get from you and someone with that same genetic marker.
I have never known Your Name.
I was taken from you at birth.

Then given unto another you, to be cared for, when You were a given concubine of a vanished god.
In that place for the Unwanted, as a barren temple prostitute worshiping your imaginary virgin mother … you named me after your most revered grandfather of saints.

From there, a poor tradesman … and You, his wife … took me away to make your cold marriage work.
You struck my saintly name and renamed me after the greatest warrior-emperor, who ever lived.
But your marriage was ice and you beat me, and let him burn and torture me over and over.

You both made me bleed and whipped curses into my mind … for as long as I can ever remember.

Ķtčhőņķ…

You took another little girl from yourself, a Ward of the same vestal, frigid courtesans, then You came to live with me. But you beat your little self and continued to thrash me until we learned to hate each other bitterly. We fought over our need for your love, but you were unable to give it, using him … for inflicting more curses … bruising violence.
So, we became like him.
I hit you. You slapped me.
We screamed the same filth, they hurled into our bodies and minds – at each other.

Until … every once in a while … when we stopped fighting … we would play dirty with each other's bodies. I hated myself and you because it made me feel so strange and ugly.
But we could never stop it.
You used to play dirty, to blackmail me into doing it with you, then blamed me at the same time. I grew up with you, hating and wanting you, like that, and not ever even knowing why.
You were with me like that, until I was no longer a child and became a sneak petty thief.
Then I got into trouble and we had to move to a new place.

There, I met You a third time.
That was the very first time I ever tried to love you as a Woman.
But, I forever, first, shed my final shreds of innocence and broke my own heart.

Ķtčhőņķ…

I was so shy and desperate for your love and tried to love you until I found out you were the local gang bang whore. After that, you let me pop my cherry and I stopped playing dirty with the other you.

You hated me for not wanting to lick you and touch you anymore and I hated the other you for fucking five of my friends all at the same time.

Even more, than all three of you … mostly I hated myself for needing you so desperately, even though all you had ever done, was hurt me and hurt me, beat and humiliate me over and over.

Since the day you vanished as my mother, together with the indifferent, vanished god's consort … I had always ever only known You as a cruel manipulative Bitch, without an ounce of love in your selfish rotten heart.

Used, abused, and Unwanted by you and yet, I still wanted you in that ill twisted illusion of love.

So damaged and still so desperately needing … to know the mysteries of awakening your heart's true desires.

Ķtčhőŋķ…

Your beatings and the bleeding darkness in me led me to flee to darker alleyways, where I had to teach myself the pathways of a cruel indifferent world.

But the world's rules found me out and I was sent to be educated and punished in a gladiator school.

I learned the way of a naked warrior and learned to read and write in books.

The school was vicious and violent, so I ran with the thugs and became a mongrel willing to bite anything on a street corner.

And, cultivated a taste for hard drink and opium.

I became a rebellious conscripted soldier, fighting in a war against political parasites. Then deserted my camp to run from opium and drink troubles and became a mercenary, with a foreign army. The soldiers I had left behind, tracked me into a far-off foreign land and there they kidnapped me … to bring me to stand capital trial. But, while in the dungeons, a secret officer came to me and offered me the job of a specialized murderer.

They sent me to a place to get cured of opium's curses and there I thought I had a vision of God. So, I turned away from the path of the assassin and entered the priesthood … of the very same vanished god.

It was in their temple, that I met You for the fourth time.

The terrible festering scars inside me, I tried to keep deeply hidden and thought that I had found your love at last. But we were both the same age and didn't understand sex, and when we tried to … it ended up in guilt and pain and horrifying loneliness again. Neither of us knew, were both looking for a Father, who should have been our actual, loving, living, breathing God.

Ķtčhőŋķ…

The priests of the vanished god uncovered our fleshy transgression.

I was sent out to serve children as a shepherd. In the jungles, tin cities, and bush.

But instead of bringing ourselves … our hands and hearts … the vanished god's priests brought nothing with them except the words of an ancient book.

I saw You on street corners, selling your body.
I saw You as a tiny child with a distended tummy, your hair went red from starvation.
Staring curiously from a mud hut.
I saw You wretched, drunk, emaciated from opium. Filthy, smelling, and weak.
I saw You beaten, bleeding … so battered and worn out that no more light came from your dead eyes.

Then I quarreled with the priests of the vanished god and told them, they cannot feed your belly with empty words. Words cannot stop you from being a toilet, or being trampled under by the disillusions of vicious, small greedy men.
Promises and threats are just words.
They will not reach down to pull your broken soul from the gutter and rake the poisoned shards of deadly heartache from your veins.
I told them to give You a cup of water, a dress, a piece of bread, medicine, some true comfort and create a place to Belong with them – very same words, that the Book so immutably decreed.

They told me they had prayed to the vanished god.
It was revealed to them that I had brought myself under a divine Curse.
I was cursed for being rebellious against the sacred authority given to them alone, by that vanished god's Holy Spirit.
They refused to look at your nakedness.
Refused to hear your screams of desperation and howling wails of pain.
Refused to give your Unwanted babies even a sip of moisture or human sympathy.
They warned me that the words of the vanished god would make streams of living water flow from your spirit because they were called to words of faith and not to worship You as a Sacred Person.

Then they left You to quench your thirst with nothing.
Cast your milkless baby into a garbage pail.
Cast your perished soul into their hellish dungeons.
Eventually, threw me back out onto mean streets.

Chased me from their money-changing temple, where they still stubbornly buy and sell the same greedy words of faith to this day.

I returned to living next to the highways, in drains … once again, insane from loneliness and addicted to drink and opium.

As I left You behind, all alone, poor, sick, naked, hungry, pregnant, bleeding, abused, imprisoned …
Unwanted, human meat to use, spit on and discard – all I could do … was to believe the sacred holy priests,
in the retail sacristies of the vanished god.
They … all had to be right …

The vanished god wanted nothing to do with me. I was Cursed … exactly as their sanctified authority
and Holy Spirit had declared to them … about me.

Nothing and nobody wanted me.
I became wholly Unwanted.
As Unwanted as any human can ever possibly experience.

Knowing, pleading … begging for the maw of this certain hell … to have mercy and end devouring me.

I was searching for a father, but all I found were frightened, greedy Apes … selling a Sacred Gift … for
the same judas silver … ever chasing after the covetous kisses of men and imaginary golden treasures stored
for them … only them … in Paradise.

And, I've never, ever recovered from it.

Ķtčhőņķ…

He stops speaking.
Starts to cry again. His eyes … moonbeam rivers of pain.

Eventually … she reaches across the table … gathers his trembling palms and limp fingers into
her own … to gently kiss them.
Whispers:

Your incredible love for me could never be a curse, my eternal love. The heart of a Curse is possessed by
spite, spiritual greed, and jealousy … hypocrisies.

You are not that man, you are Mine … forever…
Continue … tell me everything.

Ķtčhőņķ…

As you sit here before me … You are three women who found me and tried to love me.
The first time I met you, you had left a boyfriend who then committed suicide by hanging himself in
front of his four-year-old son.

I was working with counting machines and you were a college scholar. You are so stunningly beautiful, so perfect … at first … I believed you only wanted to be with me for some other reason. I didn't understand.

But You did love me, and you were proud to be with me and you were the first girl I ever made love to as a man … and did so with all of my heart.

Everything inside me, was Unwanted, in bleeding scars, that I tried to hide, by acting out the tough guy and trying to out-better all my friends.

The only thing I had to numb the pain, sinkhole of loneliness, and timid desperation to belong … was smoking opium and hard drink.

I swore and screamed at you, hurled things around, trying to force you to do everything … my way. Even though I had lost my job because of opium and you let me live with you, and share your pocket money, just so we could eat.

You are one of the most beautiful girls, who has ever lived in that town and I treated you as if you … were the other heartless Bitch.

Yet, because I had no idea how damaged I was emotionally … I fucked every other you, and other you and other you, whenever any other you would let me. Including most of your best friends.

And, I abandoned You over and over … disappearing into opium dens for days …

Despite this, you still tried to love me.

When we walked, you would cling to my hand and skip along … singing to yourself, those rainbow melodies still in my ears. I made you overflow and bubble.

So happy … just to be with me.

But I continued to betray you and eventually started withholding sex from you, as an emotional weapon … until you turned to my very best friend …

When you left me to live your lives together, I hated you both.

I had never truly understood what depths of blackness the soul can descend into … when choosing to hate. I gathered every dark thing in my spirit and rendered it into utter murderous spite.

I hated you both, so much, that if no one else had been there in the tavern that night – I would have succeeded and beaten him to death.

I despised you so much, for trying to say hello later, that I hurled that rock at you. You were right to have me arrested.

I finally understood, exactly what I had done … to the love you had given to me, when you begged the Peacemaker, so utterly sincerely, not to hurt me. Not to punish me for what I had done to you.

You did truly love me with all of your heart, and I hurt you. Including the day, I found out, you were leaving me for him, then punched you fully in the face. And called you a betraying whoring Bitch.

I saw you, in your wedding carriage, the day you married him. But my hate had evolved, by then, and turned acrid and inward and only towards me. And the hole, the terrible gaping hole that is You, is still as raw as if it were yesterday.

The same, old, terrible grieving nightmare of you, I still wake up to every single day.

K̯tčhőŋk̯…

He looks at her for the longest, longest … moment …
She gently shakes her head. Puts a finger to her lips, and then presses it very gently to his.

Tell me … tell me Everything I need to know about me. Tell me All of it, my love.
You need to … and I need to hear it. Tell me.
Don't hold anything back.

The second time I met You, and you fell in love with me, I was under sanction, for theft, to buy opium again. In the prison, I turned coward, sought loudly … to suddenly re-believe in the words of the vanished god.

The Peacemaker bought my sorry story and ordered me into house arrest for two years. In court, you offered me a place to live out my sentence. In the beginning, you were just my friend and we spent hours and hours together. And, we faithfully went to the temple of the vanished god. Exactly, like I had been ordered to by the Peacemaker.

I never saw you as a woman, you were nineteen and I was thirty.
You were just my very close friend.
After months and months of being in each other's company, every waking moment … you went away with your Father for two weeks.
Then suddenly, I realized, exactly how much I missed You and how much you meant to me …

K̯tčhőŋk̯…

When you got home, you were so sick and, in such pain … from a body infection. Nursing you back to health … made me truly aware … of how much … I … loved You.

And thought it was wrong … because of the vanished god's book of words … those cold words, only useful to threaten any other love beyond the cruel definition of its own. Words of love … that on paper decide, whom it is right to love … and who is cursed … Unwanted and unclean.

But the feelings were real. I could not make them go away. No matter how hard I tried.

That very same day you came back home, a friend of ours came to visit. He asked me if I was fucking you because you were so incredibly sexy. At that exact moment, I suddenly saw you as a flesh and blood woman for the very first time, and, knew he was utterly right.

It changed between us after that. We were aware we had muted mutual feelings … that we believed, we were not supposed to have. Or share.

Always, because of the rejecting words … judging who has the right to true love and who does not deserve bread … empty words written in a book … of a vanished god sold for judas money.

About two days after you got better … that night, you walked past my bedroom, from the bathroom … topless … and, quietly disappeared into yours.

Something truly terrible happened inside me.

Your breasts were so perfect. So beautiful. All I wanted to do was reach out, touch, caress and kiss them. Lick, suck and drink in the honey of your nipples

And hated me for it. It made me feel dirty about you. Like when I was a kid. Only I loved You, truly loved you and had to believe you were not cruel. That manipulative Bitch … all over again.

Ḳtčhőŋḳ…

Her immortal starry eyes draw him in deeper, tenderly squeezing his hands …

Tell me about loving me that much. Go on … tell me … exactly how deeply … don't hold back.

I still don't know if it was deliberate, but at breakfast in the mornings, after that, you would come into the kitchen, and bend down right in front of me. I could see those boobs … so soft, warm, swaying sleepily inside your loose nightie. I could see everything, all the way down to your pretty belly.

I tried not to look, but they were so perfect, and desirable and that's when the lust and self-hatred started driving me mad.

You did more things, like wear cut-offs and very loose shorts. Then lie back on the sofa, bouncing your knees together … while we talked …

But every time you relaxed your perfect dancers' thighs, I drank in all of your narrow vivid panty gussets. Clutching tight to your picture-perfect pudenda, arching up into the shy shadows. Hiding exciting, bunched little pussy hairs, naughty and peeking out … waving at me from the seams.

I wanted it … and I wanted it to stop!!!

It got worse.

I would switch off the light in my room at night. Wait for you to come out of the bathroom … with only a towel wrapped around your waist.

Then I would jerk off slowly, watching you put cream on yourself in the mirror in your bedroom. I craved watching you bend down and spread it all over your open pink sex, then unhurriedly dress in your nightie for bed. It made me feel utterly sick at myself.

That made it ten times worse. I lusted and lusted after you.

All it did was make me feel hideous.

I prayed and begged the vanished god to help me, but still, nothing happened, except you turned into a much deeper object of my animal lust.

One night, the Turnkey permitted me to leave the house and we went to the Theatre. When we returned, you asked me if I wanted something to drink. I said yes, and you left me to fetch it.

I was lying on the carpet in the dark.

That was the night you came back, jumped onto my chest, grabbed my face, and started kissing me like crazy. We pretty much attacked each other after that. And, although I felt up your body and had your pants undone in about three seconds flat. I still never touched you sexually.

I still felt so guilty, because of those words decreeing the vanished god's rules, and what Curses love.

But, in that moment, I also felt immense relief. At last, I could stop feeling sick in my mind about lusting for you like a madman.

We could simply be two people … in Love.

Ķtčhőņķ…

That next day, we locked ourselves in my room, spent time making out and then I seduced you with my hands and my mouth.

It was the very first time you had ever experienced sex and we spent the entire day just giving you orgasm after insane orgasm.

We used to joke about it later … that first day. I would say twenty-six and you would say it was twenty-eight. And then we would try and beat the new record again.

I had no problem with you being my Girlfriend. I was incredibly proud to know you. I loved you, despite the vanished god's condemning words of love's unproven guilt.

But You did have a problem. A very big problem.

You told me how much you loved me, but you wanted to keep us a secret from your father and You as your sister…

Our escapades got more and more wildly intense, until I took your virginity on the floor of your bedroom, by accident one morning.

After that, we had quickies.

Explored the karma sutra.

Held marathon sex events.

And nobody ever found out!

We embraced each other in smoldering, sweaty tantric completeness … every single night … for hours and hours and hours. Month after month. We fucked everywhere … anywhere … all day too.

We set the world record for cunnilingus when I ravished you straight for more than three and half hours..,

But all it did, when you would not acknowledge me as your chosen love, was to drive the black pit of loneliness deeper and deeper inside …

I eventually stopped belonging to myself.
I became completely detached and became a human shadow.
Someone cursed to always be on the outside of watching real love.
Yet, it was happening to you, all the time, with you, for you, and in your family.

I was cursed to be forever unclean. Unwanted.

Real honest love from You will never be mine to know. And I remain aware, that I will never know that same … free … open, honest love … to share with you, from my core … ever.

What led to eventually destroying our love, was the self-declared priest of the vanished god. He lived across the road.
We both left his temple, for good, after falling in love with each other.
So, he sent disciples after me to find out … why?
I told them that the words that the priest was selling to them, had nothing to do with what the same words ordered us to do for free.
Once again, they told me the vanished god, had again, cursed me, and his Holy Spirit was to visit retribution upon me … for speaking out against their anointed prophet.
The priest of the vanished god was far too cunning to confront me publicly … in front of his faithful disciples. So, he summonsed the Turnkey and whispered lies about me being readdicted to opium.
He had cast the high-loaded judas dice, a prize that would see me imprisoned, banished, and silenced from challenging the thievery of their lives.
His wager? Opium would be in my blood and that would prove I was a sinning liar, about him and my humanist lies about words in The Book.

I was taken to prison and kept there, while my blood was inspected.

It came back clean and I was released from the dungeons of those who beat, raped, and murdered You.

When The Turnkey released me from the chains, he asked me … why does that man hate you so?
I answered that I had told his disciples, that he was an emotional parasite who fed off the insecurities of scholars and used them as a cult-driven money trick.
The Turnkey warned me to be very careful of him, the priest of the vanished God wanted to bring me terrible harm.
Then, I told the Turnkey about my love, my incredible love for you, and how it clashed with the jealous words in the book.
He told me to trust my heart.
Just love you and forget about dead words.
Words written down cannot ever teach a living heart.

But, You as your sister had found out about us … and I was tossed out on the street.
Then, you went far away.

But still, no further than you ever were, even in the throes of an explosive orgasm.
And all that time … we fucked like animals for nearly two years, you never once admitted to another human being, that I was your perfect lover.
Or told anyone, how much I loved you back.
And then, you just left me like that.
Never spoke to me ever again in person.
No more either a real friend or an actual man … you claimed in secret, you once loved with everything in your heart … ever again …

It took many years for me to stop hating myself about You. To stop feeling, that I had done something so, terribly, terribly wrong. When all along inside me was an open, honest, earnest love for you … that went putrid, because love cannot be hidden away in secret dirty shadows, hiding from even crueler words that You let someone else choose for you … to dictate the lying, surreptitious shackles of our septic love.

Ķtčhőņķ…

They look at each other quietly in silence.

Do you want to take a rest?

No, I think let us finish this … I have to get it all off my chest.
It still feels so … raw … inside.

Look to me honey, I'm listening … I'm still here … you, will always be my everything.
I am not ashamed of you.
And, I never ever will be …

I will never reject you, baby. If you need to tell anyone … Tell only Me.
Tell it all to me, that's why … the Voices called you here.

I love You.
I truly love you with everything in my heart.
I would want the entire universe to know you are my beautiful, precious man. Tell me in your exact words, the way it felt for You …

Just the way it all happened, that's why I am here …
To listen …

Ķtčhőņķ…

‡§‡

I am going to tell you who You were when you loved me the third time. For the first time perfectly. Completely and utterly perfect.

Until you died.

But not right now.

From the time you left me, to marry my best friend … I tried so hard to find You again …

You became my string of girlfriends, one-night stands, many, many casual fucks. So many of you, and still never found You.

I had learned to play your body like a classical instrument and could make a stone-cold pussy orgasmic.

It became a pattern. You told another you, about me, and then you, told another you, to another you, and you would find me. To chat me up, then I would fuck you senseless.

So many of You.

But not once did You ever get into bed with me, and give me just a tiny bit of what I was willing to give to you. Not once. I awakened your body, connected your sensual mind, and gave you the best sex you have ever had, yet not once did you ever give it back. Doing everything I know to give you every morsel of erotic pleasure, desperately hoping against hope … that sex will somehow make you want me … the same way.

And … awaken in you enough to also love me like a real man.

Before I met you and fell in love with You … for the first time, I got married to You first.

Married You three times.

But I didn't realize until too late that you had such terrible self-esteem issues, which you took out on me.

You wouldn't have sex with me unless you were lying flat on your stomach, and I had to enter your pussy with my cock from the back. It made me feel so horrible about myself … that I somehow wasn't good enough for you sexually … that and my opium addiction … were probably the main reason why we got divorced.

Even though we remained friends.

I know now, how bad those issues were because many years later, you booked into a hotel with me. You had contacted me and openly begged me to fuck you … properly …

That was the time I asked you, why did you force me into sexual starvation … to utterly ruin our marriage? Why wouldn't you just fuck me … while I was still your husband?

Why did you turn sex into a weapon, an issue?

Was it my job as your husband to live alone and choose to let you keep me lonely?

Jerk off in a toilet. Just because you didn't like what you saw in your mirror?

What made you think I wanted to be with that other imaginary woman you were not?

Why reject me because of her?

Was it worth it?

But You didn't know what to say.

It proved to me, once again, that all I was good for … to You … ever been to you … was for sex … Sex … Sex … Sex.

It's how You bought and sold me emotionally, whenever … you wanted. Only, that meant … whenever, and only whenever You chose to feel like it.

In that respect – in bed, You have always been the perfect, selfish Bitch.

Ķtčhőņķ…

In the time before we first met … and you were still seeing your dead boyfriend, I went to a wild party one night and You were there as two others … a forty old cougar and your fourteen-year-old daughter.

The teenager, you came to me in a room, where I was dancing blind drunk and begged me for some pot.

At first, I thought no way, but I knew you smoked regularly, so who am I to play the hypocrite?

As a cougar, you were only at the party to pick up some fresh young cock. You liked to pick up, and fuck all my early twenty-something friends, working your way through them one by one.

I was so drunk, I could barely stand, but I let teenage you walk me outside, into a field and I lay there flat on my back. Lit a joint I had in my pocket.

We drank whiskey. You smoked, then I did. I dragged deep, you leaned down right over me and started inhaling my smoke. Next thing, you had your face on me and we were kissing, kissing. Smoking.
Part of me was annoyed at you, for using me for whiskey, pot … and to make out.

But I thought it was probably better, it was me because I wouldn't dream of hurting you or compelling you to do anything you didn't want to. That's why you were at that party. I said straight it would be better for you to wait for a proper boyfriend … than make out like you were doing with me. I warned you that hooking up with any random guy might end up badly.

So, we smoked, I kissed you some more, then told you that I refused to have penetrative sex with you with either my cock or my hands. I told you to give yourself time and wait for that lucky guy, but I also told you I would make you feel very good, in another way, and would lick your pussy. So, I did. Then, I helped you put your panties back on and went and passed out somewhere.
I was awoken by You, as one of my brief ex-girlfriends. Because after we got you back into your pants, you returned to the party and started puking your guts … from greenies chugging all my whiskey.

As my ex, you came to your rescue and asked what had happened.
You told yourself.

‡8‡

You as Ex and the pissed-off cougar, both furiously accused me of raping you. And told anyone who would listen. I freaked out and told you to go to the authorities.

Ķtčhőņķ…

He wants to hang his head; mute his silently weeping soul … turn away … but she won't let him break her even steady gaze.

Hey lover … my baby, tell me everything.
No matter how bad it is. I'm not here to judge you.
And, I'm here forever. We are not going anywhere.
Be here, be with me. I am with you.
Just tell me. Only Me …

A week later … as the cougar, you came to my local watering hole, looking for me.

You bought me bottle after bottle of wine and wanted me to describe everything that went on that night. In delicious detail.
I knew you liked to mix the vanished god's guilt-trips and sex, by fucking any man half your age … then dragging him into the praying thing with you. Then, while you were interrogating me - I realized … you were getting turned on. You were asking me to describe things that never happened!
I didn't know what the hell to think.

Ķtčhőņķ…

You offered me a lift back home and came up to my room. We sat in the pitch dark and you lit my opium pipe. Then you started making out with me and the next thing I had your pants off and started fucking you. You were really into it, until you realized after about five minutes, that I wasn't playing the vanished god's guilt-trip games. I told you I wanted to fuck you like a normal guy, not talk about the vanished god or get guilted out.
But that was your kink, with all your toy men. You needed a hard horny cock, but you also needed the guilt trip to get your pussy buttons to go off.

So, when I didn't respond by saying the things you wanted me to, you told me to stop and pull my cock out. But I didn't, I fucked you until I was done.

That was when you told everyone that I conned you into a lift home.
Pulled you out of your car.
Dragged you up to my room … whilst you were begging me not to, and, struggling vainly against your will.
You then claimed, once inside my bedroom … that I had attacked you, ripped off your clothing … then raped you for hours.

You told everyone that I had sexually assaulted both you and your daughter.

I told you to go to the authorities and lay charges.

It went on for years, until one day, you as you the older daughter, completely lost your temper at you the cougar. At the time, you the cougar were married to another extremely young man.

The older you exploded in rage, and told you in no uncertain terms … it was never a rape!

And to stop fucking up your life by spreading lies to everyone and embarrassing you about something private that had nothing to do with you!

You, and that young man, whom you got rid of for a new one … both sat down with me, eventually one day. I told you I did feel shit. I should have stopped; it was my fault.

I fucked up because I always make it all about the woman and what she wants, not me.

And, that was the only time I had ever fucked up sex completely like that.

Then you finally admitted, after all those years … that you took me up to my room, got me drugged, and when we were halfway fucking, you got turned off, because you got mad at me for not playing the guilt game … then used it as a way to get me back.

You asked me to pray about it, with you, for forgiveness from the vanished god, right after you admitted this. The same fucking game!

But I just got out of there and left.

Ķtčhőņķ…

Once again, it was something about you, I spent too many long years hating myself for.

One of those stupid, careless things I did with you, to You … all fucked up on whiskey, opium, ravenous desperate loneliness, and lust.

I saw you later, when you were about twenty-three, working in a market. It was hot, so I bought you a six-pack of cold beer. We smoked a joint and I tried to apologize. But you laughed it off, told me to get a life and forget about religious cougar crap.

And You, were also so many other different women, who did drugs with me and fucked me and we fucked up and fucked over each other for money, booze, and hits. We were both fucked up in so many different ways … that is the way it was between us back then.

Ķtčhőņķ…

May I ask you something?

Something terrible, because I cannot bear this other burden alone anymore. I can't …

You can ask me anything my precious heart … anything at all.

In a few moments, after this …

She rises to fetch the earthen jug. Leans down, and kisses him sweetly on the top of his forehead.

Hold out your hands … there … wash your face, my baby. Wash.
You will feel a bit more refreshed. Promise.
See … there you go.

Reseats herself.
The devastation lurks, shallower within … fragments of free-floating sorrow just below the surface … running freely from his eyes.
She looms back calmly in the pale silver light and takes up his hands.

What do you want to know?

Ķtčhőņķ…

… Was it hard … dying?

Every time you have died … you died so horrifyingly … alone.
So violently.

Were your last moments terrifying?
Did you know it was the end?

That man who murdered you, said in court, that you kept on praying and crying to the vanished god to please let him spare your life.
That's why he smashed your face and teeth in, then stabbed you while he raped you and tortured you.

Did you know the vanished god was not going to let you live?

He told the court that you were a white woman that he had to force to submit to him, so he beat you unmercifully, bound you with barbed wire, and then raped you.
He claimed he was curious to know what sex was like with a white woman. Did he tell you he was going to kill you before he shot you in your beautiful face?
Did he laugh and taunt you for beseeching the vanished god with your terrified desperate prayers?

When he pointed the gun and you knew it was coming, did you realize as you experienced that last consciousness flash – your whole life was betrayed by men?

Did you realize in those last moments that there is no vanished god?
That no one was there with you, except that evil man, his gun and filthy beastlike sadism.

Ķtčhőņķ…

‡§‡

When that gang of men was beating you into pulp …
… When they raped and raped you, then strangled you and threw away your precious beautiful body,
like used up garbage.

Did you know long beforehand that they were never going to let you live?
Did you hope the end would come quickly and make all the horror and bleeding agony just stop?

Begged for the blackness to take you from the sounds of your agonizing screams and their sickening
depraved cowardice?

Ḳtčhőṇḳ…

What led you to be so utterly on your own, and so desperately alone, and crushed, and lashed so
unmercifully by the loneliness that you would steal your father's gun to put a bullet into your head?
Was it to stop the unbearable primal screams?

Ḳtčhőṇḳ…

Did you think of me?
Call out to me … in those final moments … lying bleeding, crushed, and dying next to the uncaring
highway?
I should have been with you and protected you like I always did. Treasured you. I would it was rather
me.

I see your faces in front of mine.
The grief of your passing will never loosen its claws.
All I can do is be humbled to have known so perfect and precious love. To have known you …
To have had the incredible privilege of having known, and seen into a mirror of unending love.

Ḳtčhőṇḳ…

She rises, still gripping him by the hands. Pulls him away into the star-washed garden.

Enough for now my baby. Hey, I'm not in a grave … I'm not dead or hurt. Look at me, I'm here. Right
here.
With you …

She leans in and kisses him, softly.
Kisses his face. Kisses … delicately licks away the tears that refuse to stop flowing silently
down his cheeks.
Kisses him passionately on the lips.
Wraps her body tightly against his.

‡S‡

Whispers:

Tell me about the most perfect moment you ever spent with me. That most sublime moment of love we ever knew and shared …

Ķtčhő̃ŋķ…

… They stop kissing.

We were at my place.
It was a Sunday afternoon. We had just eaten lunch and were lying on the bed together.
I was reading a book.

You were lying curled up into my side, with your head lying on my chest.
Listening to my heartbeat and staring off into space in your own world.
I was holding you, mostly to keep that wild bush of hair of yours out of the way of my reading angle.
We had our favorite global music on quietly but I could still feel you humming rainbows to yourself through my skin.
You had come back at long last and loved me like that again. Just being so utterly happy and completely at peace doing nothing.
You suddenly stopped humming, got up on your knees, and all very seriously said you wanted to tell me something.
I grumbled that I was reading, so you promptly grabbed my book and tossed it across the room.
I went all mock horror on you and was about to do something drastic like a tickle or pillow fight when you put up your Totally Stop Right Now Finger and made an I Don't Want To Hear a Sound zippit-zippit … across your mouth.

I wondered what your mission was and just exactly where you were going with this.

But you like surprising me.
Mostly with drop-dead stunning lingerie that I would savor … removing the garments slowly from your perfect body with my teeth. Growling like a very bad, naughty, naughty monster … making you giggle half to death and not so secretly dripping-horny as hell.
You sat there on your knees that Sunday afternoon and then you grinned that same little wicked grin you had when I arrived here.
So, I put my hands behind my head, lay back, and played along.

You never took your eyes off me. Then you started swaying slowly, just like when we danced alone in a crowd. Coming closer never stopped looking into my eyes.
Swaying like a cobra …
Then as a lazy feline, you crawled up on top of me, completely on top of me, bowed down, framing my face with your hands.

Kept swaying and staring into my eyes and searching my face. Never saying a word.
It looked like you were hunting for something, deep inside me … inside my soul. I watched you.
Your eyes seemed to grow enormous, exactly like yours do … and I could see something in them.
It was a depth of Love, I just wanted to get completely lost in. Just like you.
Then you stopped swaying and just gazed with that ocean … of unfathomable deepness in your eyes.

You finally leaned down and told me;
I love you with every ounce of my being. You are absolutely everything that love means to me as a woman. I love you. I love you. I love you. I will love You forever.
Then you bent down and whispered into my ear so that only the two of us could hear it: Please make love to me baby.

And I grabbed you in my arms, crushed you to me, mostly so you couldn't see the tears starting up in my eyes, and told you – you have a deal, but you have to do a striptease for me.

So, you did. I kissed every inch of you then I lay you down and we had hot raw sex and made the most beautiful, passionate honest love I have ever made with a woman.

That afternoon was the first time I ever had a girl make love back to me. Kiss by kiss.
Caress by careful caress … teasing … titillating.
Thrust, by utterly overjoyed thrust … matching me completely in our need to express that incredible closeness … I treasured about you in every way inside me.
That loving honor we needed to give and express to each other with our bodies and minds.

Well, baby, it sounds like we had fun … Wanna go for another round lover…?
You do realize, though, that I am going to have to put some clothes on first?

Ķtčhőņķ…

Ķtčhőņķ…

Conscious awareness claws back up from some faraway lightless place. He tries to open his eyes but he is too groggy. His body feels like an obstinate lump. He cannot move. Well, he can, but he doesn't want to.

It feels like he has taken a rusty instrument and lanced a deep festering wound somewhere and now needs to just lie down and not be … for a whole long while.
A very long while …

So drained … but at least the numbing grey agony has dispersed from his mind and heart.
At the same moment, he realizes with horror that she isn't with him …

‡§‡

And then he *hears* … clearly hears … *The Voices* …

Not straining to be heard … *like listening to tumbling words spoken through a running waterfall.*

He can *Hear* them!
Undoubtedly …

Think he's awake yet?
He should be. Let's find out.

That's when he opens his eyes.
He is alone on the tatami mat. She isn't with him!
He sits. Panic rising, which promptly evaporates, as into vision pops two identical, lithe, pretty young women in their very early twenties, with long dark hair.

Daddy! You're awake!
See, I told you he was going to wake up around now.

Now he is awake! Wide awake.
The girls scamper over and he is enveloped by soft warm arms, maddening tickling hair, and wet plastered kisses, leaving him slightly more stunned than he was yesterday.
He fends them off gently.

Good morning, ladies … Whoa.
Brakes on. Just calm down a tiny bit.

Goodness. And who exactly are you two lovelies?

He allows them to sit back, each excitedly clasping one of his hands.

See, I told you he wouldn't click immediately.
He will, Daddy look at me … Look at me.
Not just her Daddy, look at me too … Look at both of us.

And then it does *click*. Their *eyes* … they have *his eyes*.
Why do they have *His Eyes*?
And does some quick calculations in his head. Suddenly the lightbulb explodes.

But they were never born!

She killed them.

She didn't even know there were *two* of them.

Not even the idiotic bitch who surgically removed his first daughter knew they were twins. She was too lazy or too stupid to take an ultrasound scan.

Removed one of them in the clinic, that *she lied about*, claiming she had gone to visit an aunt in a distant city. Then on the long bus ride home back to him … *her husband* … she lost the other one too.

In a horrifying mess of blood and gore.

His other daughter, also *dead*.

Tiny corpse too developed to flush down a public transport chemical toilet.

She had claimed to have had a miscarriage, but deep down in his heart of hearts … he knew she was lying. That's why he threw her out and divorced her when he found out the truth.

The devastation, the disappointment at losing them, the grief … losing his one perfect shot at being able to find *Her Perfect Love … expressed in his Daughters*, snatched away by the same first, coldhearted, selfish Bitch he had to endure as a child.

How … *why*?

Why … are they here with him?

Girls look, … actually scratch that … wait. I need to know something … erm, where is she? The other One, the one who was with me yesterday?

Daddy, it's Us! Don't you recognize us? See, he doesn't recognize us.

Of course, he does. Daddy, you do recognize us, don't you?

We are your Second Aspect. Can't you see?

All very convenient as there are quite obviously Two of us. Don't you think?

And we called you. We are the ones who have been calling you from far away Daddy.

You know who we are silly Daddy … that's the only reason why you came. Isn't it?

After yesterday, the shock of uncanny recognition, the insane rollercoaster of ecstasy, horror, confusion, and intimacy. The *ripping open of the festering scars …* that allowed this deep nourishing current of … *Belonging to her, truly belonging to Her …* to rise so completely within … he, didn't think he could be almost speechless … *again* …

What is he in for next?

Okay, let's roll this one small notchback. I think I'm starting to get a handle on this Ladies.

Yesterday, I was with you as my eternal Lover and to lay rest the memory of you … and banish the vanished spiteful Bitch. To reveal to you all the pain of longing for you, the remorse from wilfully hurting you, and the agony of bearing mutilations inflicted by you … that which compelled me to journey here.

Are you two beautiful Ladies … the other twin aspects of my pain, grief, and dismal human failures?

No, Daddy … Sweet Daddy!
Do you feel that same agonizing hurt about us inside? You can tell us, Daddy …

Honestly, all I can feel is a terrible sadness … for both you girls and You, the one who killed you both. What I feel about you is … without you, my life will never be complete. I'll go to my grave a Fool. Utterly lost. It's a longing, an unending yearning … for the tiniest little chance to love You … just One Chance. Far more than it is the grief of having ever lost you as I did.
Does that make sense?

See, Daddy … we aren't the love you lost, nor the love that wasn't loved, or the little bit of real endless love that you did find.
We are the love … your love of Us … you still long for, with all of your heart.
We are all of your love. That love you desperately want to leave behind in a very special place in the world. Your journey was not only to reach a safe place and there to bleed out all your grief, mistakes, misery, and pain. If that was your only purpose Daddy … you would not have reached us …
… You wouldn't even be here.

Because … your love, that unrequited Love … is what drives you and brought you right here into our perfect garden.
This isn't a garden of dreams Daddy, that's why it's so real. Why you need to be awake to Be Here …
… It's a place the Love inside you created from nothing.

This is who you are meant to be Daddy. Why you are here with us. Isn't it fun!

Our love is like the water gong. It is the same love … you know not where it comes from, nor where it is going.
It will cradle Life, and be the author of merciless disaster … but like our love for you, and your undying love for us, we bring it into this place to keep it safe. Protect it. Here in this sanctuary.

Make it useful Daddy.

Love is like water. It keeps time for us, reminds us … gives us sustenance. Feeds that which feeds us. Gives beauty and sacred meaning where none exists.

Like our fragrant garden Daddy …
… And then it passes on, into its own … on a never-ending journey … soaking into hearts and minds wherever it can.

We take that liquid love and plant a Garden to grow food and medicine. Raise up gifts of flowers and pretty trees we use for furniture to sit, share and eat.

Then sing and dance and dance and dance … Daddy.
Water is life … and Life is our Love Daddy …
Without it … we are … imaginary dust.

But now, you have found your true purpose Daddy.
You will always be here inside our hearts … ever with us. I love you, Daddy.
Me too Daddy. We both do. We love you.
You are our perfect Sweet Daddy,

We are your purpose Daddy … you brought us here. You built this sanctuary for us, and you built it entirely out of Love.

The highest conscious realm in your imagination and the most valuable gift of all is to search like you have done to find a truly healthy Life Purpose founded solely on Love.
Then, Daddy, it becomes like our water gong in the streams of time …

From this Life Purpose, will flow your passions and your One True Mission in this world.

And see, Daddy, look at where we are sitting because your passions have unveiled for you, what - you are truly good at. And your mission is what has led you here … into exactly what - your world needs.
What you are good at has become - your profession, and what your world needs, shall become - your True Calling.

Now Daddy, at last, at the end of this terrible journey … you have found a true exchange of Human Value … and so rightfully claim the happiness and joy … you deserve.
Do you understand now?

And Sweet beautiful Daddy, there is nothing you cannot reach for, or achieve anymore. You have found your unending True Purpose.

This one purpose … is comparable to ours …
… Your yearning, unfathomable Love for Us … is

THE SECOND CORNERSTONE OF TRUTH

It is Our treasure.

Now, Daddy … we must go … Plant us a pretty flower garden, a big veggie patch, and sweet fruit trees.
Full of lots of singing birds Daddy. Surround it with beautiful animals, and ponds full of fish.
Make a special place there, like this one … and we will meet you … again Daddy …
… as your baby children.

Mother is coming …

… *She wishes to commune and speak with you.*

See you soon Daddy!!

With that, they fling their arms around him, more tickling hair and kisses … jump up …
… and are gone.

Ķtčhőņķ…

陰陽

Part One – The Tao of the Confucian Student

Homo Sapiens …

The *Latinized "Wise Man"* … or so the enthralled Ape likes to muse when contemplating a carefully coiffured countenance in a complimentary mirror … **Grin**

Problem is … the self-aware, bipedal, mostly hairless primate - remains a biologically hardwired … *aggressive, omnivorous, opportunistic* … scavenging mammal.
Albeit one who evolved into a hunter-gatherer that eventually figured out domesticated animal husbandry and subsistence agriculture about a hundred and fifty thousand sun-revs back.

Oh, and sailing … all the way from straddling a floating log in a river whilst dodging crocodiles and piranhas …
… to the Titanic.

Ergo, as an animal, it will always be caught between fight or flight with very little respite in between – depending on the unfolding existential choices the creature makes in order to survive its *ad hoc* local environment … *second by precious second.*

That sadly highly-decried … yet staidly *observant* Ape … Uncle Chuckie Darwin, was entirely correct when mapping out the profoundly uncomfortable idea that "*Survival of the Fittest*" relates to any organism that successfully passes on its DNA to another generation before perishing.
And in the process, creates a slightly different generation of offspring that "evolves" through each new iteration of successfully recombined DNA.
From a T-Rex to a chicken, as it were …
Broken down functionally, within the warm-blooded Animal Kingdom – the most deadly hunter on the planet is probably the breathtaking Orca. Killer Whale. World's prime apex mammalian predator and armed with the largest brain. The most prolifically *reproductive* lactose tolerant? Likely a toss-up between sewer rats and a fluffle of nymphomanic bunny rabbits. One that can live anywhere? Try bats. The fastest? A big ol' kitty cat. Largest on land? A magnificent Elephant.

And so the list goes on until …
… *Us* …

Who, rather perversely, can only lay claim to being able to kill these creatures and each other quite randomly with second-hand impunity.

And this about sums us up as … *"God's Creatures"*.

It is also said that it takes an entire Tribe to raise a child. True.

However, I would take that rather accurate truism a step or two further, and state …

… a Seed of the entire Tribe is planted in a child to successfully reproduce The Tribe one child at a time.

Ergo, for us … our future existence depends entirely on cultivating … *The Survival of The Tribe.*

As animals, we are not able to subsist very easily as individuals, *more like not at all* - and our only way to ensure that we do produce new functional generations of The Tribe …
… is via cooperative social cohesion based on collectivized institutional Wisdom.

A world-famous anthropologist was once asked - what is the quintessential prehistorical factor that indicated Early Man was not merely a self-aware animal but destined to take a long sentient journey into developing complex societies and civilizations?

One might think the answer lies with something technocratic … most certainly *mission-critical* - like controlling fire to vastly extend the nutritional scope of an edible, and digestible diet. Or the knapping of primitive tools from flintlike rock to hunt, strip bark and dig for bulbs and tubers. Or using cured animal skins for warmth and protective covering against thorns, other animals, and the harsh elements. *But no …* the learned academic replied that the core evidence was to be found in the discovery of a healed human femur-fracture … *of very, very ancient origin.*

That set bone fracture indicated *Someone's* ability, *at that time,* to project empathy, with effective sympathetic actions, into a critical, all-encompassing intervention that saved our long-gone common ancestor's life from a guaranteed fatal injury, which no animal would have been able to survive … *in the unforgiving Wild …* without help, and direct *outside medical attention.*
Something … ostensibly not even a glimmer of a psychological or religious concept … yet.

A little intangible, unchanged, prehistoric thingy - A Choice … called Love and Caring.

This is the ephemeral mortar that creates a Family, binds a Tribe, and builds a Civilization brick by brick.

The inverse … institutionalized *Hatred, and Spite …* those ~Memes~ which came with mankind's kings, priests, and gods - is what will always eventually destroy one …
… Exponentially faster …

This uncomfortable but *infinitely positive* fact, quite simply, *is …*

THE FOURTH CORNERSTONE OF TRUTH

I chose not to pursue this final discourse.
Until now.

Felt that it was utterly necessary to seek out the bedrock foundation, building blocks, and fluid living cement. That which *Binds* and *Constructs* effectively … *First.*

It may also prove prudent that I did not cast all my precious pearls of love away … before using my writing hand to cast bright daylight onto a certain evil legion of obese drowning hawgs.

Most succinctly … to avoid yet another cheaply-slung … lukewarm *virtue-signaling* cliché when I define an extrapolative structure to express and actualize something as deeply profound, primeval, proud, and highly imaginary … such as *is* … *Doable Love.*

To arrive *here* … both you, I … and the good Reader, have been … *straggling after Voices …*
… trailing misty sirens …

Deep from within Pi's unraveling depths … *and while not prevailing against … at least emerging through the Dark Valley of the bitter Shadows of Death … mostly unscathed.* Yet so, ever grasping onto very ancient, yet tangible Socratic principles … that so easily unmask Deadly …

~Memes~

Those replicated very bad nasty ideas that bring about the direct cause – to being … *Unwanted.*

Imaginary, *insatiable*, devouring dogmas … lurking within hegemonies co-existent only within mortally greedy, subversive, and terrified Ape's … living minds.

And now … *here we are …*

Be *Truthful …*Be of *Good Intent* … Be *Useful* …

But *First …*

… let me jot the other foundational Cornerstones of Truth onto this handy whiteboard doodad labeled *Posterity*, and thus reiterate … *Yes?*

‡§‡

Amid Civilizational Decline:

Think for Yourself.
Determine Your own morality.
Redefine everything You think you know.

Then …

The First Cornerstone of Truth

Choose an *Imaginary Infinitely-Positive Idea* of the Future.

The Second Cornerstone of Truth

Seek a truly Healthy Life Purpose Founded Solely on Love.

And …

From this Life Purpose will flow – *Your Passion with A Mission.*
Your Passion will unveil for you what – *You are Truly Good At.*
What you are Truly Good At will become – *Your Profession.*
Your Profession will lead you into – *What Your World Needs.*
And what your World Needs, shall become – *Your Life Calling.*
Then you will then have created – *A true Exchange of Human Value …*
Thus, to claim – *The Happiness and material Rewards … You deserve.*

These primary foundational Truths, *when taken to heart … and then unequivocally accepted and expressed as a chosen reality …* need to be critically applied to:

The Third Cornerstone of Truth

PROVIDE	PROVIDE
TO WOMEN AND CHILDREN: GIVE EDUCATION, GIVE OWNERSHIP, GIVE WEALTH, GIVE SECURITY	TO WOMEN AND CHILDREN: GIVE A POSITIVE FUTURE, WITH A TRUE PURPOSE FOR LIFE.

Build a new *proto-Society* out of the world's *Unwanted* on that.

‡§‡

Part Two – The Extreme but *Cautious* Philosopher

And now, my dear old Hobbit, we move on into the mechanics and end application of these *Foundational Truths…*

Plato's definition of social justice grounds itself in an appeal to *human psychology*, rather than to address *perceived* behavior.

One can only imagine that having Socrates as an *Alma Mater* begat the poor Fellow being highly cautious in terms of rocking ocean-going Hellenic Slave-Galleys, all lost at holy political sea, and loaded to the slopping salty gunwales with bales and bales of unquaffed hemlock … *ergo:*

Reason rather than *Dictate.*
Suggest … rather than … Hold Forth…

Cooperation has a far more desirable all-around common outcome - compared to any self-serving internal competition striving away bitterly within The Tribe.
However, fierce competition unswervingly serves The Tribe, as an Entity, when directed outwardly in Cooperation - to achieve common … Living Goals.

The one is positively forward-looking.
The other is negatively inward-looking and invariably obsessed with the unchangeable past, which does cause an improbable and highly uncertain future.

One builds …
… the other foments strife.

And we respond much quicker to genuine human kindness …
… than we ever do to overt threats or fading empty promises.

Competition must be attended by mutual cooperation and genuine respect, with common tangible goals to succeed as The Tribe. And achieved goals must be trailed by living … Concrete Rewards.
Most crucial to The Tribe … is the question – What is the highest, and ultimately … Our most important Goal?

All things considered, *this – is exactly such a Platonic appeal for Cooperation … with a defined Goal.* No more, no less …

‡§‡

… only an Appeal …

Much less a self-righteous, sanctimonious, and smarmy sermon … *that is probably best to ignore* … than a blueprint to a *Life-Path* that contains a true *living* Purpose. One that will work for any individual willing to cooperate for that greater good.

Albeit, consciously understanding that there remains the lurking, essential dichotomy to this, *Our existential experience of Life.*

On the one hand … life is entirely finite. For you, me, *the Voices,* and the Reader.

Meaning. Being alive has a fixed biological time limit and certain death awaits us all – with nothing … absolutely nothing else to expect any further from the exact moment death occurs.
For the deceased, every waking understanding, memory function, and conscious awareness of ever having known sapience … *ceases.* Like it never existed. Meaninglessness.

What was once a *living brain* … becomes *lifeless, irrelevant, biological waste.*

In the face of this disquieting fact - these four Cornerstones of Truth – can gird our existential living minds with *an Infinity Positive Attitude,* that will live on, and on, and on – into an infinitely positive, *Planned Future* … never seen … never to be experienced … but one, that we will have assurances …
… will surely take place.

How?

By simply deconstructing our prevalent socio-economic dysfunction, extracting the core immutable human values that will always remain, and then using these standards to redesign a *functional* non-DNA-transmitted *Aim Orientated ~Meme~* with the sole primary purpose of realizing all Four Truths.

The Four Cornerstones of Truth … *these delimited building blocks* – are simply re-realizing, re-aligning, and retooling most highly efficient … *very Ancient Ideas.* And then *creating* a definitive common long-term Goal.

Fact:

Historically, *H. Sapiens* has always seemed to *Need* religious constructs to function psychologically when self-contemplating the ontology and epistemology of mortality.
Those gordian knots in spatial thinking that theorists, philosophers, and priests alike …

… have All tried to unravel:

Who Am I?
Where do I come from?
And, Where am I going?

As already said - These core queries, and more importantly – *"The Answers"* they engender … lead directly to the secondary functional purpose of a shared belief system. And that is to cogently bind a non-coherent grouping of people, into a cooperative and functional socio-economic unit.

This, with a belief-wide, recognized *moral,* and widely *understood* underlying *ethical* Code that all members understand *instinctively.*

Invariably, it ought to serve the calling creed's higher assembly of faithful, rather than the common wants of a grubby individual. And so it does.

Ironically, to achieve this end, all religions must essentially rely upon an ongoing process whereby penetrating the fabric of subjective reality, by necessity needs to occur for the adherent as an *Individual.* This, in turn, stimulates cognitive dissonance psychologically. To overcome the various facets of knock-on rational doubt and disbelief, a new devotee must undergo recyclic mental persuasion to stay within the bounds of the religious social grouping … by attending regularly convened congregations of similar-minded acolytes … and *listening,* usually with no logical rebut, to teachings of advanced proponents of that belief system. *True Believers,* who are themselves exact mental carbon copies of a self-same re-perpetuating process.

The individual disciple must also intellectually consume all of the rules, diligently apply the doctrines, and be aware of the dogmas that guard that specific temple of ideas. This is achieved through selective religious text immersion along with regular supporting rituals and esoteric observations *enacted* from the acquired text to underscore this public declaration of *"Personal Faith".*

During the process of this cyclic psychological reinforcement, by degree, participants progressively allow themselves to become socially exclusive of all non-adherents of that religious subset's theological framework within any population grouping.

The *Us* and *Them…mentalities, mind viruses, thought pathologies, Syndromes* … that plague the world so vexatiously today.

By falsely advocating that the world is only divided into an *Oppressed* and *The Oppressor, Sinners,* or *Saints – Blessed* or *Cursed* - one merely advocates to create the infinitely negative emotional space for actual oppression and real social decay to reoccur … along with systemic injustice and abject abuse invariably meted out to innocent and *Unwanted* children as a direct consequence … *in an infinitely indifferent trickle-down equation.*

Faith is the comprehensive application of any religious theory that *promises spiritual benefit* solely to the *"Believer" … as an Individual.*

As an animal, and one which *must practice social cooperation to survive,* "Faith" is the only esoteric *relationship* that man can psychologically sustain entirely within his own privately defined and on personally pliant executed terms … *emotionally.*

Sweet salvation and a glorious eternal *Paradise* for the blessed … *lone* … "faithful" *Pilgrim.*

Supreme egotism … *at the expense of all else.* In fact, a deep inward-looking Lie claiming to be something virtuous.

The end product of this illogical, *highly contrary,* socio-biological premise - is the notion that mimicking religious words through religious actions, *in public,* will, in turn, bring *promised personal Eschatological rewards* … beyond the crude and natural mortality of the *Believer.*

Everyone else gets to hot rock it up at Dante's multistory BBQ party.

No grouping of people who have ever gathered around this common *"Purpose"* of the *Individual's entirely intangible Reward after Death* – will be able to serve any *good* or live a primary human Function that can serve humanity selflessly … *secondary entirely* … to the pursuit and defense of that specious *Reward* at any or all costs … *while still alive.*

This defense includes othering, disavowing, and the psychological cancellation of any member or apostate of that grouping. In fact, *any* person who might bring a perceived threat to the *empty theological promises.* Reactions range from passive-aggressive ostracism with group bullying, all the way to screaming firey hell threats …

… *even unto murder my Lord.*

The exact opposite of acquiescing to an agreement, within an open didactic debate, or seeking to compromise and cooperate to achieve a common positive goal. And … while the priests get fatter, richer, and more powerful on religious offerings - not a single *Unwanted* child, *Inherits for Life* … as little as a stale cup of holy water.

By prehistoric *Choice.*

Therefore, religions of any shape or description are in reality … all just *Cults of Personality with a malleable toolbox of proto-morals, used highly selectively, for instant entirely self-gratifying convenience.*

They all eventually end up *Buying* and *Cash-selling* an *Idea* that unvaryingly serves no practical hands-on sociological purpose other than manipulating and maintaining the *spiritual vanity* of each *Individual* within that group surrounding the exclusive religious text.

"Spiritual" Greed has nothing to *Give* to anyone but *quid quo pro* will gladly pay a fortune for *Spiritually Promised* … self-appeasement.
Mirror, mirror on the Wall …
… Who's the prettiest …

Plato's cunning philosophical strategy, as expounded at vigilant arm's length in *The Republic's* discourses - first explicates the primary concept of socio-economic, political, and thus an archetype of *perceived* higher moral justice, and through that specious vehicle derives the analogous concept of responsive … *Individual Justice,* within the natural democracy of The Tribe.

What we are, in fact – busy reconstructing here *theoretically.*

Who are WE?
What did We evolve from?
And, What do We Need to evolve … Into …

He also believed that the citizens of his allegorical Republic, ought to *Specialize* in what they are inherently *Good at Naturally.*

Instead of chasing after *The Role …*
… they Wish to Fulfill in Given Society.

Mirror, mirror on the Wall …
… Who's the prettiest, richest, best dressed … gloriously sanctified in His Sacrificial Blood … and,
The Most Supremely Powerful …
… Of Them ALL …?

This dovetails neatly into everything we've come through in all those dark places perpetuated by politics and religions. If those dark places and their regressive Role-Playing ~*Memes*~ did not exist …
… You would not be reading this.

In my opinion, Plato is crudely and rather prudently defining the failing World … both *His then* and *now Ours,* as:

A Dysfunctional, fractured, dystopian society, wherein most active participants are psychologically self-coerced into playing at least one entirely Partisan Role in this Shakesperian Theatre of Life, and as a result…

… are merely ham actors on a crowded rickety stage, haplessly snarking Punch 'n Judy skits at each other, in a slapstick One Act, cacophonic soap-opera … entitled:

"Doomed to be Ruled by Fools"

Embracing the farce, toeing the line, beating the drum … humping … *humping*. Being ambitious, pleasing the Boss, pulling up socks, climbing the Ladder, racing the rats … *Doing The Job … Kissing The Arse …* rather than seeking to give full expression to what we as random, disconnected individuals are *Truly Good At …* through a simple process of proactive cooperation aimed at a Common Goal.

What are You truly Good At … Citizen?

Why did you quit a stressful high-paying Job … cash in your savings, and leave your loved ones … to be a lowly contestant on …
… Masterchef?

Why Masterchef[14] Citizen?

Go ahead … take a Big Bite of the ripe yellow banana.
Enjoy!
Really enjoy …

This isn't a Cage … welcome back to the luscious green Rumpus Room!

Run … play … laugh, Be Yourself …
… Be free again!

We don't need to reinvent ourselves using tech and squalling new internet-driven political religions – we need to stop being self-manipulated into biting each other and learn to stand together to confront the imaginary bars inside the polluted steel cage … *we are all trapped in.*

We will accomplish far more if we can still cry onto *Unwanted* seeds indifferently ground into the dirt under our feet … than drowning them in endless starving bloodlet greed and stupidity.
Only the smell of our real tears will cause them to germinate.

---

[14] MC Australia, that is. Reality TV Yankees are way too wired on being aggro for aggro's sake to dig really loving to Do something for others for it's own sake. In [Good] Korea, MC Korea is apparently the most watched show in the country … *Mmmm …*

I am telling you this, setting this rock-solid foundation down as firmly as I know how because what comes next is where the meaningless and truly heated pushback is going to start. And it will start with You …

The *Dear Reader.*

This is where *we* …
… if there is a We … (no pressure … always your choice)

Get hardcore and … *Think for Ourselves. Define foundational morality. Redefine everything we take for granted.*

If slimy politicians, even slimier religious professionals, and their shadowy bagmen are at the heart of the current chaos and snowballing world crises, then beyond the small words of this book … resolutions for the realistic future of mankind …

… are incumbent upon You … and Me.

The, until now … Silent Majority.
Or at least a minority of two, one current Reader, and a multitude of future Voices … Lol …

Confucius promised his disciples that he would provide one *Corner of Truth* as the first step in a given method to resolving any problem. But it is entirely up to us … *Auspicious Students* … to seek out, and then determine for ourselves … the other three.

I have searched to hell and back, to return … knowing, and happily treasuring these key human psychological value-systems … *within.*
They are ancient and free.
They are yours to possess. Apply them to your life. Absorb them. Live them and I am convinced you will know actual happiness and the subsequent equivalent of *"Spiritual Reward".*
Your life will make sense and you will come to know true peace and genuine inner joy … albeit faced with disquieting mortality.

However, it is entirely up to You, the *Reader,* to realize, *actualize …*
… BE …

The Fourth Cornerstone of Truth.

For us, that little thingy, that choice, we call *Love and Caring* - is at the very heart of everything infinitely positive and imaginary that … *We DO.*

In my not so humble opinion - The highest and final true Purpose of mankind, if applied with careful *Wise* focus, and carefully constructed planning, using an open framework of these Four Truths – may be able to reverse our currently downward fatal social trends … as humanity resets focus and sights differently in placing transhuman feet endlessly onto other planets. Opening ever newer vistas for mankind … anywhere and across any frontier … *We choose to explore …*

A Common Goal.

However, *at present* - we live in a truly amazing world where millions of people can communicate instantly, and yet this incredible modern miracle is being used for …

… Spewing dirty biased journalism – spawning instantly obsolete consumerism - conducting political gang warfare - reproducing religious parasitism - blasting soulless pornography - running financial scams, trading in casual murder - and, expending endless imaginary energy on the unending ejaculate of professional Social Media … emo-vampires.

Exactly like an image in a magic mirror, entirely inverted, *Negative, and Imaginary.*

The internet can certainly be used to take this tiny tome, *This Idea,* by employing prehistoric *Love and Caring,* along with applied *Wisdom* … as a viable catalyst to neutralize these ~*Memes*~ via complete ideological *disengagement.*
Then shift positive viral focus onto the suggested outline below - to Make a Plan.
There is no excuse in the world not to.

When faced with a daunting task or a massive project, like flying to Venus … *for a game of golf,* any one of us can sit scratching our bald Ape arses, then find umpteen, fantastically brilliant, and utterly reasonable reasons *not to get there,* starting with:

How the doorknob will one mow the fairways if they keep burning up instantly, including the frikking mowers and crew? And don't even get me started on trying to cultivate sports turf with superheated steam!

When all it takes is the simple stubborn determination to grab a couple of solid titanium clubs, slip a few asbestos balls into a pocket, strap thick fireproof boots onto one's feet, bite down hard on a shielded spaceproof respirator, damn the handicaps … *and* MAKE A PLAN …

… to tee off on that hot rocky sphere of utterly inexplicable, emotionally obtuse lady lumps … randomly going … Bang!

Consider realistically, this is only a suggested *proto-Plan.* Put a pin in that word – *Suggested …*

I am going to extricate from *"The Republic"* - Plato's concept of an *Archetypal Function*, which every intentional serving citizen of this coming *planned* Empire needs to fulfill as a *Purpose* – not a *Role*.

Stripped of Plato's weird-assed labeling of course.

Put a pin in that too.

We have a Purpose to Fulfill …
… not a Role to Play-act out.

These *"Functions"* of foundational Purpose … I loosely define practically as being:

- Scribes
- Caretakers
- Artisans
- Farmers
- Carers
- Teachers
- *Soldiers?* Maybe not. *Maybe necessary.* Mmmm?

The idea is *You* decide what you are and what set of functions define your unique purpose. It is in that loose collection of basic functions somewhere.

Then, it is up to you to go, communicate … BE what you are truly good at in your co-related functions … and DO that – with all your significant intelligence and passion.

However, for me, this is about the *Unwanted.*

This is entirely their story, *the one They are listening in on.* Each of us has a life duty to give a kid who has nothing and no one, a cup of water – *at the bare minimum …*
… Do unto others as you would have them do unto you.
Validate our Common Humanity.

But that will only quench a thirst – not provide Life.

To achieve that is going to take more …
… Much More.

And here … Laydeez and Hobbits … is a *rough* Master Plan …

Apply and filter the mindset of the foundational Cornerstones of Truth to:

- Mass adopt *Unwanted* babies globally into a common extended *"family"*.
- Raise them scientifically as politically neutral, socio-independent, *proto-Tribal* networks.
- Seclude them safely in profitable high-tech very large-scale commercialized permaculture settlements they live upon.
- Create a recyclic financial engine of which they are the sole joint controlling beneficiaries.
- Create a legal framework in which they collectively own all corporate assets in perpetuity.
- Institutionalize their inherited joint Adult responsibility for continuing to drive the Initiative, and managing the Trust which rescued them, then brought them Home … *by going back to Step One.*

Stop … go back …

Read that again.

And once again, if you need to … and let it sink in. Deep in.
Meditate on it.

That is the entire aim.
The GOAL.

Nothing more, nothing less.
Can it be done?

This is the final fork in the road.
A one-time-only raincheck meeting with the Devil at the Crossroads at midnight.

An attempt at engineering a self-replicating social construct that will take their lives forward, into an infinitely positive future that preserves them bonded together by good purpose and with Love and Care, into what we might loosely define, for now – A proto-Empire.

Either this is just another book you have read, or it becomes …

… Something Else entirely …

‡§‡

‡§‡

Part Three – The Band needs Brand New Music

Realistically, the mere notion of creating a global movement to give orphans autonomous economic and *secular*, non-partisan, neutral political power is going to raise noisy resistance … better rephrased as - *Invoke Unholy Hell* … but that hardly bothers me.

It is all the truly *unbiased*, Smart People and their *empathic* inquiries that ought to follow this *Idea*, and which we must first put to crude tests … *so that the truly clever kids get on board* and Make a Plan.

For the sake of scratch terminology, we will label assembling the Four Cornerstones of Truth: an *Initiative* … and the *Unwanted* … *Beneficiaries.*

You and me…? Well … [*without jumping over guns just yet*] let's think about this … [*without getting too cheezy either …*]

Each of us represents the functioning Fourth Truth, *that tough Choice to Love* … because the other Three Truths are what drive our higher Purpose. Ergo, we ought to call ourselves … *stones.*
But in this world, as *"stones"* we have had to personally overcome individual horrors and relentless grim life itself, just to reach this *mutually understood* point … that *Love is a long-term commitment and Choice …*

… To Want "This Idea" enough. …

That kind of journey has the potential of relentlessly grinding and polishing unchiseled rock into a *gem.*
Consider then, if a gem, *what kind of gem?*

The most precious and *living* organic gem of all – is the Pearl.

Unlike a diamond trapped in kimberlite rock, a pearl becomes ever more valuable the longer it remains nestled inside a living host. We are organic, we have living value, and the insides of our hearts are precious – how about we think of ourselves being incalculably valuable *Living Pearls*?

This one is not carved in rock, but I'll use it, *for now*, to hang around my pretty daughters' necks. And you have heard my daughters speak out Mother's immortal wishes … if I adorn their eternal celestial beauty with anything other than exactly how truly precious they are, it should be with something as priceless and alluring as … *Pearls of Wisdom.*

Living Pearls strung together by free, natural, organic insight - binding and building together these immutable Four Truths to achieve simple human belonging for those who will never experience *Love and Care* … Unless …

… *WE Choose to be the timeous vehicle of the expression of that Love … unconditionally.*

That sounds about right … [*even if it does come off a bit Gorgonzola Melt and runny …*].

Pearls of Wisdom it is then.

First off, let's look at the archetypal platonic *Functions* because it is in this rough order that key major *Purposes* ought to be tackled, then defined.
I do not carve these applied working disciplines in jade either. This is simply a working start.
Brainfarting …

Scribes: Legal Framework, Diplomacy, Law & Order, Administration.
Caretakers: Financial Engine, Energy, Security, Pl.anning.
Farmers: Water, Food, Medicine, and Natural Materials.
Carers: Medical, Caregivers, and living Pearls of Wisdom.
Teachers: Primary, Secondary, Tertiary, Corporate.
Artisans: Engineers, Mining, Manufacturing, Services.
Soldiers? Defense? Startroopers …? Mmm?

Out of these Functions, an organizational map ought to be outlined, and then transparently plotted.
But wait!
I'm getting *Waaay* ahead of myself … and *you* … [jumping guns is bound to get one's foot shot off] … so, let's retrack this …

In the section titled "*Our Story*" published on the Bill and Melinda Gates Foundation's website, the following is stated:

"Unfortunately, factors outside of anyone's control make it hard for some people to reach their potential: things like when they were born, who their parents are, where they grew up, whether they are a boy or a girl …"

This is regrettably true.

It sadly holds true for most poor children born in and out of wedlock, anywhere in the world, and who are probably the type of target beneficiary the Gates Foundation wants to help – but most of all – that statement penultimately holds fast for the horror of *Unwanted* babies born out the crime of Rape and indifferent sexual predation. Problem is, very few NPO/NGOs, including the Gates Foundation, know how to support these children holistically, no matter how well-intended or altruist.

Why?

Because the *Unwanted* never set those organizations up. And it does not address the core fundamental problem – *Fatherlessness.*

And please, this is not an attempt to knock these good-hearted folk, or their projects - certainly not the Gates Foundation or anyone else involved in similar charitable initiatives.
They all do highly sterling work.
But what everyone has to keep clearly in mind, is that the children born to raped women and abused girls, the offspring of sexual predators ... *abandoned children* ... who subsequently notice and become aware of *Being Unwanted* – almost always have to bear this horrifying burden and a lifelong social stigma – commensurate with a debilitating sense of desertion and primal rejection – and, in reality, become outcasts before they are even born. For those kids who survive birth and childhood, in this fashion – the psychological weight of who *they are not* – among their peers and within their respective societies – *will never leave them*, and very few will ever reach their full human potential.

Absolutely terrible, but horrifyingly true.

Most of them will crash and burn out completely eventually. Then ALL of society gets to pay the inflated and terrifying price, *anyway.*

One damaged child can do more harm and cost a community far more social destruction than the loss of mere money – when it would have been far cheaper to find a solution to take care of the child adequately, at only a fraction of the grievous heartache and involuntary loss of life.
You can throw as much good-meaning, sympathy money at this reality, yet it still going to have the same psychological and zero-sum sociological outcome.
It's undoubtedly a true Socratic gesture, but that is all it is ... so, any contemporary institutionalized attempt to resolve this common problem, *the current way* – won't work.

It has the wrong *Goal.*

As seen, so violently intense and so very apparent on our streets, in youth shelters, morgues, and within our common overflowing prisons.

Here in 20/21, Gender-Based Violence and Sexual Predation have finally found a Voice and come to a place where this scourge is now being addressed *Globally* as an actual issue in many countries and societies. This through very factual, no-nonsense, private/public awareness programs, Social Media campaigns, and movements like #MeToo. But the outcome of sexual predation, sexual assault, and sex trafficking – right down at the grassroots level – are millions of babies, that mostly – belong to no one, and – *whom no one wants.*

And the movement, while brave and necessary - will more than likely eventually get hijacked from within by people with politically narrower and far more narcissistic personal wants, needs, and ultimately self-serving end goals. Another faux sex religion in the making.

The only focal point should remain firmly fixed on the *Unwanted* … what every single word of this conversation has been, and … *Will Continue* … *to be all about.*

Until, by choice, they become … *Our chosen Living Gods.*

It is one thing to decry the appalling lot of GBV victims, focus firmly on the axis of the crime, and apply maximum legal and other consequences to the perpetrators – as a *post-incident means to attempt to arrest this evil scourge within our societies.* It is entirely another to take responsibility for all the unforeseen biological consequences.

In other old news, Childless couples do adopt *Unwanted* babies, for sure.

However, also consider, adoption is a highly profitable global industry for certain organizations and a moral mandate for most reluctant governments and some religions.

People need and desperately want that cursory second-hand *assurance* that Someone Else …

… is *"Taking Care of The Problem"* …

The entire financial model of churches and governments is …

… *"The President"* -- or *"God"* -- or *"THEY"* … are being *paid* and are surely …

"Going to Take Care of Everything" …

Hence, polls, prayers, religious tithes, and misspent taxes, which have indeed led to the historic advent of cruel orphanages, abusive foster homes, lethal places of *"safety"* and greedy contemporary adoption agencies.

But these same elitist folks who bought into this - are also responsible for buying war, sponging up political self-preservation, trumpeting mendacity, and enforcing social apathy.

And while each of these charity streams has varied and somewhat dubious outcomes, most especially when fostering or adopting at-risk children for a *Government Cheque* – the human success story of these faux-familial relationships, is directly reliant on the adoptive/foster parents' - *lifelong commitment* to that child as their own *de facto* offspring.

This invariably exposes their underlying motivations, which more often than not – primarily serve the proto-parent's *fleeting emotions* or highly expedient financial needs – rather than the children's extended psychological future.

Long after the ink has dried on the social compact.

Hence, all the horrifying child abuse that occurs.

However, no matter how loving, caring, and truly committed emotionally – no adoptive parent can deal with, or entirely overcome on behalf of an adopted Son or Daughter – the deep psychological scaring every orphaned child needs to weather in order to lead a healthy and productive life. More so those kids born to raped women and girls. To be reasonable and fair, there are many success stories out there, beautiful inspiring stories, take the Hobbit right here with us for instance, but they are usually far scarcer than the other brutal realities that prevail.

So, unfortunately, the Gates Foundation is 100% right.

Add to this … that these kids are hard currency to certain people. So-called *Poverty Pimps.*

Do you know why it is almost impossible to adopt the *Unwanted* out of natural disaster areas, active war zones, and refugee camps? Because of human traffickers that flock to these tragedies like flies …
… *to harvest human slaves.*

So, this entire problem demands a novel approach. Or an unabridged Encyclopedic Battle Plan, but most definitely one that starts *here*.
If anyone wants a few cheap, *all-encompassing*, *Conflict-inducing* political slogans … it ought to be:

"Rape Matters"
because
"Being Unwanted Matters"

… and once we have dealt with those pressing core issues … we then take it upon ourselves to address all the other *secondary* civilizational pathologies.

There would not be an abortion-on-demand burning *Political Issue* if the DNA-tagged man responsible for the unwanted pregnancy - faced long-term legal sanctions and mandated sterilization after the offense. The same applies to any woman with an unwanted pregnancy who wants a non-medically mandated abortion on demand. The first one is an almost free pass. It comes with tied-off tubes that only a court order can overturn. Birth control and condoms are issued for free. No excuse. This is the dark, evil, and real hidden frontline of this war of attrition being waged upon the *Unwanted* that no one wishes to address. Men and horny boys casually fucking women they have zero commitment to, much less the babies they produce in the process. A woman can only get pregnant once, but an opportunistic penis can bounce from uterus to uterus to uterus without a care in the world for any of the lifelong consequences it will never pay for. While the raging *Political Solution* is to ignore the penis [it has unalienable Civil Rights] and put the uterus on trial to either kill the fetus or toss the *Unwanted* baby out into an indifferent, spiteful world. Same difference … *for the penis.*

SCOTUS: *Wade in Mud vs. Rotten Fish Eggs.*

I suggest that Pearls of Wisdom start at the very bottom of the social dungheap and work their way upward from there.

The greatest problem in both America and South Africa is that people in positions of public trust - *Roleplay* ideological games, rather than *Solve* immediate pressing problems.

Partisan MSM is probably the biggest culprit to apportion direct criminal culpability for this.

However, strangely enough - the chief drivers of ideological rather than pragmatic planning in the US … *are the so-called Conservatives.*

Composed of people obsessed with fundamentalist religious zeal … or a similar type *gainer* of self-declared, extreme *egotism* … they proudly expound as … *Individualism.*

For one, these ideologists undermine the natural ideal of a cohesive, cooperative, coexistent community with a common *cyclic* economic end goal.

They underfund public education because of perverse taxation ideology instead of supporting better compensation. Underfunded public education directly breeds a hotbed of socialist and left-wing subversion … opens the door to cheap lazy "labor" unions that cause increased levels of illiteracy due to curricula displacement in favor of enforcing Woke indoctrination, which immediately lowers gainful employment prospects, and oxymoronically hampers future economic participation. With education successfully gutted by these unforeseen consequences, they then run to resist increases to the basic minimum wage, which is of itself a knee-jerk left-wing palliative against the voracious profit gouging of gluttonous indifferent Capitalists. Karl Marx may have been the poster boy for social envy and spite, but he was right about a few things.

The outcome: Americans who work harder and longer, for less disposable income, while raising badly educated and politically indoctrinated brats who hate their own country – the flip side of which … is religiously brainwashing the very same, for the same living outcome, and deepening the US/Them split … as each hurls political blame, ~ *Memes* ~ and vitriol at the *Other*. This leads to escapism, which turns into various toxic obsessions, along with morbid addictions, and those lead directly to further mental dysfunction, social breakdown, and runaway crime.

Result – *Unwanted*.

Conservatives steadfastly oppose many common-sense policies merely because of this *Ideological Purity*.

Oppose public education because it's not religious.

Oppose higher minimum wages because that would cut into the greed-driven profits of enterprise stakeholders and shareholders.

Oppose universal health insurance because that might affect individual medical choices. Yet, they oxymoronically oppose individual medical choices by women, when the ladies would prefer to end *Unwanted* pregnancies …

Result – *Unwanted*.

Ironically, they also oppose spending public money on infrastructure improvements, because of the tax code deal. This creates a cauldron of apathy and anger, which is then gleefully gold mined by the hovering left-wing Socialists for cheap political mileage *with enormous unearned benefits,* and which does serve to underwrite their deflecting flavor of deep-fake, parasitic, virtuous *Ideological Purity* … and so the show goes on and on and on … descending deeper and deeper into an ever-rabid partisan polarization that resembles nothing more than an ineffective, bitter imaginary war … rather than building onto, what should be a striving, *Healthy*, and functioning Republic driven by a broad democracy to defend its Declaration of Independence and Constitution through the founded rule of Law and Order.

The unforeseen outcome of this mutt-brained ideological stubbornness is a natural sociological vacuum that quickly attracts a swarming amoral left-wing cesspool of howling *"interest groups"*, deep corruption, socio-economic regression, and blockbusting crime – right across the board.

Yet, on both sides – each looks into a talking head magic mirror on the wall and considers themselves …

… The Good Guy …

We need cyclic economies, cyclic energy systems, cyclic permaculture agronomies, cyclic carbon reduction systems, and cyclic self-funded socio-economic programs aimed at one very long term Global Outcome – not stupid recyclic and highly regressive political ideologies, coke-fueled whorish capitalism, slavering gospels of hate – all clawing for power, splitting countries, firing up weapons, clogging the airwaves, wreaking havoc on the environment, fomenting mass mental disease, destroying children's futures while fouling up the Internet.

Result – *Unwanted.*

Understand, extremists cut from opposite sides of the same cloth will be swift to attack this *Idea*. One lot will call it *Criminal Racism*, the other a *Blasphemous Atheist Cult* - in any attempt to cancel the *Core Transhuman Idea* they all stupidly withhold from.

At worst … *The Mind of a Fool* … or … *Hatespeech from an Antichrist* … Lol.

Of course, nothing could be further from that gospel truth, and the more the *Idea* exposes their inherent hypocrisy and human uselessness – the more vicious the pushback … *will become.*

American politics has descended almost way too far into an applied GOP/DEM … *cringing* … whack-a-mole contest … driven by actual raging hate and fundamentalist religious hysteria.
And neither side's plebes are willing to hold their Own Side *accountable*, and very, very few realize they mean nothing. Absolutely nothing. No matter which bunch of wrinkled alligators is running the show.

Puppets on a Chain.
Fools in a Cage of rotting bananas.

So, we query ourselves, are these the people asking the burning question:

Will there be the United States of America a hundred or a thousand years from now, and if there is … *what will that country look like?*

This Initiative should obviously refuse to descend into this bratlike contemporary *Othering* that is so stylishly fashionable … or engage in an infantile level of non-forward-thinking discourse, and similarly, should flatly refuse to be *condescended* to by anyone of that political, religious, or any other backward and regressive persuasion.

No matter how threatened or *threatening* they become.
Expose it all for what it is.
Telling *The Truth* has nothing to with speaking *Hate*.
And then … *disengage.*

So, by answering all the troublesome questions that will most certainly arise, searching for answers that lead to a more definitive *proto-Plan*, and mapping the implementation thereof, *upfront* … these loaded objections and the pink mist spattered politicos or god-bothering cancellers … *behind them* … may be nipped in the bud and disarmed.

Something I'm cool with, no matter how thunderous the flack intensifies getting there.

You can expect to make enemies for rocking the pro-status quo. That is a foregone conclusion. Where the *Idea* has legs … is when a few of those erstwhile enemies become the *Initiative's* lifelong friends.
Then, we are in … *Here be miracles territory.*

Turning ostensible adversaries into championing strings of Pearls.

Yes …?

‡§‡

<u>Part Four – The Thorny Vine of the Knowledge of Good and Tap Roots of all Evil</u>

So, moving forward – the so-called *Caretakers* need to provide a titanium armored trust and will also oversee the *Financial Engine.*

This is about money like everything else is about money - how do you keep the funding for something like this from being stolen?
And while we are on the subject, isn't this *Idea* yet another form of … *Orphan Pimping?*

Charities and charity organizations are, in effect, financial black holes.

The same charities seek the same donations year after year – tax season after tax season. Many of them are money laundering operations or tax shelters – or scams.
Yet, some are legit.

Some do *actual* Good. As in … *The Gates Foundation.*

All of them disburse more to sustaining the organization and promoting the charity than reaching the target beneficiary … *if at all.*

That is just basic Economics 101.

‡§‡

Simply … no value is exchanged, nothing of Tangible Value is produced, and for all intents and purposes, the vulnerable and needy are merely the sad matériel *grease* to keep the money pump chugging smoothly for the … *Fundraisers*.

The problem is never actually resolved adequately. Just old gutshot Hegel rolling about in his grave.

Go into a grimy city in any third-world country … Or nip downtown quickly in someplace like Baltimore, Detroit, or Seattle.

In and around public thoroughfares, like train stations, taxi ranks, and bus terminuses – you might find a little gang of street urchins begging money or selling drugs, and probably mugging the weak and pick-pocketing the unwary as a sideline.

They are not midget entrepreneurs … *they Work for someone.*
Usually, *Someone* that lurks deep in the *shadows* but whom they work for just the same.
This is an example of a working principle that applies to way too many charities.

Orphan Pimping.

This initiative is not a charity. We do not pimp. We do not mug. We do not pick-pocket.

We will be dealing with and serving the financial affairs of Empresses.
Mothers of the Future.
Living Gods.
Star Princesses …

They don't owe anyone a damn thing.

The same must apply to the Initiative.
This needs an independent *Engine* to run an Empire, not a *dollar-pump gushing faux gilt* for a greedy ailing Republic utterly overrun by a self-centered *"democratic"* mob promoting social insanities and synthesized madness.

How much money?

Let's suck up a ballpark figure – make it ten billion in USD.

How should this fund be raised?

It doesn't need to be raised…
… the funds need to be redirected.

If the Christian Church worldwide repurposed the cash they blithely hand over to their so-called leaders – and instead, diverted those monies into this secular project … *Locally* … it could be funded and be on its way … *Everywhere* … by the time they celebrate their God's next symbolic crucifixion, or at any random time, they *Choose.*

See, that's the thing … the Money, resources, *intelligence* – everything needed to pull this Initiative off completely, is ALL out there … their *leaders* just flatly refuse to do what their own Bible ordered them to, and the sheeple Roleplay along – instead of confronting, dealing with and solving the problem.

Loud, proud, smug … *useless* … and all grimly waiting for the fucking Rapture.

Rather than giving the *Unwanted* a cup of water like Jesus ordered his disciples … *"The Faithful in Christ"* prefer to *buy* … a non-dividend bearing, non-disbursal shareholding … in a fundamentalist leader's Gulfstream VI luxury private jet … that they will never ever fly in …

… entirely like the unseen Heaven … they will also never See.

Imaginary people, do imaginary things … for no useful purpose.

Maybe … it may prove possible … that none of them have ever *looked* at it like this?

Maybe, just maybe … some might choose to come to their senses and redirect those redundant energies. And not just with a bullshit religious cash buyout all over again.

Become Pearls of Wisdom … to *Function* in an *unseen* Empire, they choose to *serve and build*

… but will never belong to … as an equal, *future*, stakeholding citizen. Actually DO what Jesus, the Buddha, Socrates, Confucious, Plato, and *Others Suggested.*

Make all these cool ideas they left behind … *happen.*

For once.

Maybe?

Until then, *or never for them* – Pearls of Wisdom will Make a Plan.

If we treat just One generation of children right, we will rewrite all of our common futures at the full expense of contradicting reoccurring history. And in the process … we will Heal our planet.

A number in the region of Ten Billion Dollars was mentioned. Deliberately.

Isn't it truly miraculous and utterly amazing how three silly little words, a mere seventeen alphabetic characters, in Total, can affect the human mind so speciously?

When those craven words are just *imaginary* … and, invariably translate into *Greed Castles* and *Kingdoms of Lust* with a *fancier-than-thou* … Mansion in the Sky.

Caveat emptor …?

Watch out.

See, a knee-jerk reaction would be to go hunt down one of the Big-Five Billboard Billionaires and ask for a philanthropic handout.

Kickstart the party … *if the mendacious religious freaks won't.*

But I would be seriously cautious with that.

Let us see … the currently trending favorites are Boy Bezos, Sinister Soros, Yukky Zukky, Sir Virgin Dick, and not forgetting, the ever *not-faithful* Dirty-Billy at Epstein's Pearly-thighed Gates.

A short while ago, Yukky Zukky's engineers broke his network while he was off fishing.
He shat gold bricks and wept diamonds while his site bled blood money, yet the victims of the humanitarian horrors organized with his software … *wept in short-lived joy and rejoiced.*
Right there that little fiasco cost him 70% of that seventeen character Big B-Word in only seven hours!

Sinister George rains sunshine onto umbrellas, onto umbrellas … until the rain drips into the open mouths of cunning bad men with guns and evil in their pockets. Wicked men who want nothing more than to keep their pockets full and slake stuffed bellies full of smoldering fire and hate.
Should we go on?

Don't go near Gates, not even his ex-wife will go there anymore. And Jeff, well he seems to be in the same sinking moral morass, while his cheaper paid staff apply for welfare benefits.

But wait!! I hear you cry …
… what about that other fella?

Tony Musk or *Elon Stark* or something?

Enjoys playing with electric cars and rockets and robots and stuff. Totally a Marvel Renaissance Man …
… So totally not … *the flying rat D.C. wonk.*

He, and Sir Dick, drag race into space for shits and giggles every other Saturday night.

Isn't Mr. Musk the very richest of them all by now?

Ah, yes indeed ... and apparently, he has pledged x amount towards slapping yet another Band-Aid on World Hunger ... *after the inevitable Begging Bowl landed on his lap.*

But keep in mind, this guy is a far forward-looking businessman.
Why in the hell is World Hunger ... *suddenly his problem?*
His business policies and practices didn't cause mass starvation in the slightest. His products aren't remotely at fault.
Is his role on the world stage that of yet another *boutique*, photo-op, *co-opted philanthropist,* being used and manipulated by the very same people who are at the root cause of these problems in the first place? Pushed up onto a virtuous pedestal he did not design or call for.
Simply because he is ostensibly the guy with the most stylishly desirable moolah?
Why should World Hunger even remotely be ... *His Baby?*

Why not Corporate Coke? Or McDonald's? Maybe KFC? Or even the bankers, shareholders, and bakers of Twinkies? Why *him*?

And subsequently ... why on earth would any of these morbidly obese, diabetic food and beverage manufacturers remotely care about a hundred and fifty million *Unwanted* children if they don't give a shit about healthier global nutrition? Or throw their hard-earned money from selling flavored sugar water and dodgy synthetic junk food down that bottomless stinky piehole?

That's like expecting Disney to give two goofy yucks about pedophiles. Not going to happen.
This is the financial legacy of an Empire of Empresses, with a dual string of precious natural Pearls of Wisdom hung around their sacred necks.

Value them a little higher than *Pity Prostitutes* to be sold to the cheapest guilt peddlers.

World Hunger will only be solved when living seeds get planted, fertilized, and *watered* by a determined group of responsible people.
That is a no-brainer.

Just do it ...

‡§‡

‡§‡

Part Five – Mr. Tesla's Electric Phone Call from another Planet

If I were hypothetical mates with Elon Musk, I wouldn't insult him by begging for his money…
… *that I did not Earn a cent of …*
I would prefer to fake challenge him instead.

This during an utterly fictitious telephone conversation, in a fairy tale tête-à-tête with the Dude. The chat would be something completely made up, all in my *medless*-head … *and along the lines of:*

Hey Elon, so here's the thing … you are a technocrat who deeply contemplates the transhuman future of mankind, and ponders whether we will overcome our current global crises to attain this goal realistically.

But on the other hand, you are also a forward thinker who foresees our positive common future logically, including humans permanently living on another planet – probably Mars. And, you invest heavily in this idea personally. From where I'm standing, I don't see a problem with landing exploratory boomerang boots on the frozen waste up there, that's just around the proverbial corner in any event.

It is the establishment of a permanent "colony" that is going to be a truly tricky bit.

See mate, what exactly are we going to pack into deep-space vehicles and send up there?
A carbon copy of what is going on down here?
Religion? Terrorism? Crime? Gang Violence? Rape? Child Abuse? Drug abuse? Murder?
War? Nuclear weapons?

Establishing a permanent colony on the moon will probably be based on a partisan agreement shared by all of earth's Sovereign stakeholders and would cover mining and other exploratory rights. Something along the lines of Antarctica. It's practical and would serve world leaders and their respective countries' best long-term interests.

Not so Mars.

Once a closed and permanent biological system has been established by neo-humans residing on Mars … Martians will cease to be Earthlings. At least that's how sci-fi foresees it.

The truth is, once that does occur … Mars becomes another World.
A unique, independent, utterly Autonomous World.

Are we going to infect that world as we did the Imperial Colonies?

Export Civilization in the form of Law, Order, Guns, Whiskey, God, Slaves, Smallpox, Orphans, Opium, and Syphilis? Then add some 21ˢᵗ Century social viruses like BLM, AIDS, Fentanyl, Morbid Obesity, Political Rentseeking, Pedo-porn Rings, Jihads, Crack, Religious Gaslighting, School shootings, Virtue Lovebombing, Parasite Televangelists, Militant LGBTQIA++ Othering, Food Cults, Animal Cults, Climate Cults, Communist Cults, Cult Cults … wharrawharra … along with all the other infernal Internet political religions, hard lethal narcotics, and other sordid flavors of social excrement banging about …?

Rather obviously Not … one would think.

And how exactly are We, who are infected with all this … and by this mentally … whether we want to be or not … going to be able to quarantine ourselves from psychologically contaminating the minds of those who will eventually take the Ultimate Journey? Never to return.

Mars will have a close relationship with us, it has to, simply to survive initially, and for Us, our relationship with our Sister Planet could prove to be the awakening catalyst that begins Healing our own. What is crucial is how we approach cultivating that specious relationship before it begins to form.

And right there is where we get to the kneejerk nuts and bolts of the matter. Who gets to go? What is the selection process? Who will fill the given criteria and be given a seat in the space can?

Long before that happens, Mars will need to have an independent Voice on Earth.

A Martian off-world Global Ambassadorship that will need to reside within a physical place on Earth, like any sovereign embassy of any country. And this is where the serious fun starts Elon.

We need to stake out a place to develop and manufacture Martian tech and raise Martians, who from birth, are focused entirely on Martian Proto-Tribal Affairs.

So here's my idea. You do your thing, make the money, but don't spend it on band-aids for world problems you did not cause. Buy a country Elon. I'm pretty sure there is an uninhabited and inhospitable part of Africa that nobody wants. Make a deal that purchases a territory big enough to be considered a viable country Marswise. Put the purchase funds into a UN monitored Trust that for instance may only be spent on regional education dedicated to permanent Agronomy and STEM by the political participants in the neighboring region. Or try Central Australia. The Ozzies might sell at give-it-away prices.
Whatever.
This new sovereign territory will be a Protectorate and completely autonomous in perpetuity. The entire economy and pre-designed sociological model will be wholly based on space, off-world survival, planetary exploration, and managing Martian Proto-Tribal Affairs.

Starting with raising Proto-Martians as full-fledged Martians.

Think of a next-generation Silicon Valley a bit bigger than say … Belgium, where the entire paid, very carefully screened, and volunteer temporary populace is engaged in advanced permaculture development, and are this world's leading experts in hydrology, solar energy, and developmental biology … among many other cutting-edge space age techs. But these folks may not own land there, and for all intents and purposes … are just visitors constructing the Protectorate, on a working visa, valid for say fifty years.

Something exactly like Dubai, but instead of basing the "country" on selling luxury global consumerism – base it on developing STEM, green planetary science, neo-human advancement, and the transhuman like.

As a "country", you will have total control over the economy – so you design the Central Bank, you design the future form of Martian interplanetary currency, you make up the stock exchange rules, and you decide what the rules are for participating companies who wish to invest and do trade with Mars in the Protectorate. You decide who is allowed through the border, under what social compact, into what biologically segregated zones, and what rules to apply when working or doing business inside the Protectorate.

See where I am going with this?

For instance, any company aligned with Martian interests may do business within the Protectorate, tax-free, but will relinquish a 51% shareholding to Mars and will be subject to Martian Law as well as Martian labor rules and social practices. This would include compulsory farmwork and social reconditioning to adapt to and uphold Martian norms of community cohesion before being allowed into strictly Martian Zones. The Martian calendar will be different from Earth's. The Martian encoding of circadian time will be different from Earth. Martians will rely on a different and closed bio-ecosystem first simulated here on Earth. And so the list goes on.

Martians will be dedicated to one thing only – scientifically sustaining and developing Life for Martians on Mars … by proxy, and continue on this quest until they land feet home permanently. They will always live to embrace designing their unique destiny in the stars. Starting here.

If it works in theory, it must be seen to work inside the Protectorate in a Simulated Mars Environment, and if it works in the Protectorate, it will eventually work on the red home planet. That's why it's a good idea to pick a completely uninhabited and very inhospitable place and build the Protectorate in every technical way, from scratch … starting right there.

Then Near Earth Orbit, then the Moon … then Home!

Being Martian should be almost like a Scientific Religion in and of itself.

So then, time for the Ten Billion Dollar Answer to the question …

Who are the Future Martians going to be?

And the answer is!!

Former orphans, Unwanted … from all over the world … under the age of Twelve months[15].

Remember my proto-Plan?

- *Mass adopt Unwanted babies globally into a common extended "family".*
- *Raise them scientifically as politically neutral, socio-independent, proto-Tribal networks.*
- *Seclude them safely in profitable high-tech very large-scale commercialized permaculture settlements they live upon.*
- *Create a recyclic financial engine of which they are the sole joint controlling beneficiaries.*
- *Create a legal framework in which they collectively own all corporate assets in perpetuity.*
- *Institutionalize their inherited joint Adult responsibility for continuing to drive the Initiative, and managing the Trust which rescued them, then brought them Home … by going back to Step One.*

This is the reason … why. This is both theirs, and too … our most Sacred Purpose.

One that we will very carefully design with the best minds we can gather, and then fulfill by constructing it on their behalf. And once successful … cut the Umbilical to send them off on their long journey …

Once they grow up, the kids will be the only legal citizens of the Martian Protectorate and will form its utterly unique society, government, and highly planned interplanetary future. They will be classified as Martian off-world citizens residing on Earth, Near Earth Orbit, or on the Moon and ought to take full legal control after fifty years or less if we work quickly. Thirty would be better.

But that's all easily doable. Mashup a ton of brains in a chain gang of think tanks and boom! Liftoff …

See Elon, the entire philosophy of this mass adoption should be an exact equivalent of the legal framework Gaius Julius Caesar employed when he adopted Octavian as his financial and political heir.
The same man who became Augustus Caesar and the First Imperator of Rome, and under whose rule the failed regressing Republic … became an Empire!

The point being, as the old Roman political dispensation began collapsing, and recollapsing politically, exactly like our world is now … a seasoned warrior and very cunning statesman crossed the Rubicon, then placed all his political power and wealth into the hands of his chosen teenage successor – to retain His Legacy and then went on to face the long knives he more than likely expected in his back.
He chose what he considered an infinitely positive future, for Rome, when faced with the threat of inevitable personal demise.

---

[15] Christians can have, or … *CONTINUE TO IGNORE* … all the rest of the older *Unwanted* … while endlessly twiddling thumbs waiting for The Rapture … *your Choice.*

Considering exactly how many of Octavian's decisions still affect the entire world to this day – it is probably the best place to start mentally and thus ratify the immortal edicts carved into the Third Cornerstone of Truth.

For first-generation Martians at the very least.

This brings us to … Payloads …

Elon you of all people understand the complex scientific concepts and the extremely high price of putting live payloads into space … you've been one yourself.

And for the Great Martian Journey … the most crucial biological payload to make the historic one-way jump will be a healthy human female uterus … along with a lot of presexed, DNA designer frozen embryos.

Think about that.

Martians in the Protectorate will secretly choose who these special women are to be from among themselves, and critically, how many of them will be trained and prepared to make the sacred journey. Martians will also determine what spectrum of engineered embryos the living Empresses of their planet will escort Home to maximize the Martian gene pool spread and how many children each Mother will be medically prepped to carry to a full term in subsequent surrogate pregnancies, once they land …
… to initially populate Mars with Mars-born … Designer Martians.

Star Princesses.
Rulers of a new form of humanity.
Mortal living Gods … far, far away.

But hey Elon, sorry mate, I'm about to run out of airtime … would love to brainstorm further, hell maybe we even do one day … I have a ton of ideas … but until then, thanks for the cool chat Bro … cheers.

‡§‡

Part Six – Travails of a Freshwater Ikigai Monk Armed with a Bristle Broom

Great talking to Elon, but the reality is different. If this Idea evolves into a working Initiative and *actually happens* … and *happen* in some way … it *must*. A million questions will immediately assail practical planning and among them will be perfectly rational queries like … *Where is:*

Statistical data?
Psychosocial data?
Sociological data?

‡§‡

What data drives foreseen facets of this proto familial/Tribal structure?
What is its social makeup?
How will education be applied?
Where is the proof that there is even a small likelihood that this will work?
How will abuse be prevented?
Who will police the Carers?
What safeguards will be put into place?
How will they be enforced?
What is the legislative framework?
Are there any reliable studies?
Has anyone made any possible prior attempts … etc., etc.?

These deeply serious questions, and many, many others to come – need to be asked unflinchingly and then answered *Wisely* – but Pearls of Wisdom should commit to implementing those answers regardless. If data does not exist, it is because this Idea is so out of the box that it needs to be approached by the very best minds that may be assembled and then mustered together in a room with a Plan.

Crucially, sex should also equally segregate the children into a symbolic binary grouping that must be the vehicle for healthy academic and other types of vigorous competition between them as they grow up. This should also ultimately serve as a bi-partisan democratic vote in all their internal affairs as adults. The model is derived from certain native American Indian Tribes that used to segregate each male at birth into one of two teams, regardless of the child's parents and clan affiliations. The braves in each team kept score - from children's games to hunting, to war. Their whole lives revolved around bolstering their team and its accomplishments in close competition with each other. It drove and strengthened them for thousands of years.

As toddlers, we should take extreme care to facilitate their bonding together. Well-trained caregivers ought to begin by teaching the children to care for each other and to comfort each other. For this reason, it would need to rotate caregivers often to minimize bonding with them directly. The toddlers should house in fairly large groups with a high caregiver interaction of say one to two. The best-known early childhood development practices should apply to them and as much data collected as possible for ongoing research.

This is a unique, socially engineered pro-active anthropological project and its data will prove invaluable.

It should house the kids in an inner sanctuary focusing primely on pediatric medicine and child psychology. When they reach primary school-going age, the children transfer to an outer sanctuary where they house in co-ed groups of twelve, segregated into rooms of four occupants, two girls and two boys. Wherever possible, children who have developed close bonds must house together or as near to each other as possible. We must not separate them into their competition groups. Those will remain completely mixed.

They should then be persuaded to gradually take on baby-sitting and play-dating with their younger siblings in the inner sanctuary as part of their daily activities. When this occurs, the Initiative must slowly reduce the high number of outsourced caregivers until, eventually, the older children take over the bulk of their non-medical care and play with them as much as possible.

We must encourage this model throughout their formative years.

The older kids monitor, take care of and tutor the younger kids who play with the toddlers until they are all grownups and take care of everyone and everything the same way and by their own rules.

I took the rooming and grouping system from the kibbutzim model employed by the Israelis on their desert farms because it is the most effective model for kids who have to grow up together as a sort of inadvertently extended family. Israel was born out of orphan survivors fleeing the aftermath of The Holocaust. We can learn worlds from them.

The kid's education curve is to be founded in STEM and Earth Sciences using the Singaporean education model as a baseline - with a large hands-on practical and competitive component to their activities. This, - so that they become completely immersed in the natural environment and the permaculture operation they live upon as part of their life education.
The same applies to the rest of their curriculum.

We should encourage them to learn other major languages and teach the history of politics and religion … *yet without indoctrination.*

Sports, Art, Music, and other extra-mural activities are to be vigorously encouraged, developed, and competed in.

Each child should receive a monthly allowance, to teach them the value of money and basic economics so that they can understand how finance works from a young age while also providing them financial autonomy and freedom of choice for acquiring things like personal possessions and clothing.

From early on, they need to be taught Who they are, how special they are, what their collective responsibilities are, and then be skillfully guided into understanding what they need to do among themselves to take over their entire Empire from within and continue its work in perpetuity.

Here are some of the hard-nosed questions that will dog and faceoff against the Initiative:

How does this model – without a nuclear family and attending Mother and Father roles – offer these children more stable social norms and the feeling of an inclusive home?

How do child-headed households do it living in tin shanties and urban holes? We cannot be asked a question that no one else wants to answer, except us.

Why would the Singaporean model seem preferential, given the best universities in the world are based in the West - Cambridge, Oxford, Harvard, Stanford, MIT, etc.?
Why would the American or UK educational system not be preferable?

The Singaporean model is based entirely on developing the child's abilities and natural talents to become what the child is *Good At*, not trying to conform the learner to a specific curriculum.
Very Platonic.
And, the top western colleges are probably the best places to find the brightest minds. Put them together. Do something unique and cutting edge.

How will the children have a sense of right or wrong if it does not teach them to understand a clear set of morals – for example – the Ten Commandments?

Religions do not set the standards for morals or ethics – those are internal *human* choices and the kids need to be brought up to understand this, by people who understand this.

Us.

How will they, as children, be able to understand various religions and the contradictions of each religion claiming to be supernumerary to the rest?
Will this not confuse them and contribute to a fractured spiritual identity?

There is, in this question, a fallacy that history is less important than indoctrination.
This is certainly not the case.
There is nothing in the Four Cornerstones of Truth that could ever harm or cause psychological impairment to another human being – least of all an unindoctrinated, *innocent* child.
Any religion or political dispensation, which cannot be filtered through the Four Cornerstones of Truth, *unscathed*, and in applied *Purpose*, is an imaginary old scam for power and wealth.
They will be raised as Pearls of Wisdom.

Then the seriously Tough Questions …

How will the children be taught about their origins – about being a "family" of the raped and abandoned? How will this Initiative benefit them as it might culture the identity of marginalization within them?

They will be known for belonging to a group of Unwanted throwaway products of violence and crime – how does this not stigmatize them?

Have you ever heard of a stigmatized Empress or living God? Their values come from each other and from within – not where they came from.

What background checks will be made on those adults that act as Caretakers / Carers / Teachers in the years that precede the children from taking over The Tribe themselves? What safeguards are in place to protect the children from financial, physical, emotional, and sexual abuse? How do these safeguards differ from those employed by any other orphanage, foster home, or place of safety?

Empresses need to be raised warriors – so cut to the chase.

I would employ 20-something-year-old Female Israeli Sabras or Swiss Army girls or any other young lady coming out of compulsory military service – a territorial army of them.

You try to mess with a politically pissed-off soldier, who is a female, and who knows that teaching anyone's kids to hate before they can speak is a truly cameldunged idea for the whole violently doorknobbed world.

If they speak English, train and filter them *before* contact according to a psycho-socio framework that you put them through, as a non-military aimed Bootcamp. Teach them English if they are truly keen.

Then pay them properly, house them in a beautiful place, and give them lots of babies to look after for a couple of years before rotating them out. Then try to prison doorknob with their *Protectees*. Israeli chicks are apparently the sweetest and most dangerous nannies in the world.

Pearls of Wisdom think smarter in a looming fight – it's not about punching harder.

How will the needs of the "Family", The Tribe, be integrated into the aims of the family and, subsequently – proscribe the education and the professional development of the members of said Family?

Will this be mandatory for these children?

How free will the children be to pursue ideals/norms/education/values/careers outside of The Tribe and its Goals?

If your destiny is to rule the solar system for starters, isn't highly possible that you already have a definitive career map and that others should seek a vocation with you? That you understand *who you are* and *what you are* better than most? That *you are happy*?

Don't look down … *Pearls of Wisdom look Up … Always up …*

The Unbearable Lightness of Smoking Dragonpipe

If the only thing you can do, to support this *Idea, for now* [don't quit your day job, this ain't Masterchef Down Under or a cool weird garage band in the making … *yet…*] … is to convince just two of your best friends to read this – you will have taken one active, very positive step to change two-thirds of the world's minds in the right direction. Pay it forward. Put this future story out there. Send this as a gift to someone you consider important. Especially those you love and trust. Those folks who care about *You*. Hell, present a copy to someone who badly needs a solid wake-up call in your discerning opinion. Sign a book, wrap it in sappy neon paper and post it to your worst enemy. Just for fun and kindness warfare. Wam bam Instagram or Twitter and tweet if you like. Use your imagination. Entirely up to you.

This is not a wannabe cult. Remember, we don't pimp. We don't mug. We do not pick-pocket. And we don't put some dumb schmuck on a religious pedestal to toast marshmallows in our heads and then hand over money to the grifter like drooling buffoons.

We Co-operate. We *Share* …

However, this idea will only ever happen if the little people like us *all get involved hands-on …* and *Do* something real. Exchange tangible human value by taking an infinitely positive step toward realizing this *Initiative* as a chosen reality.

In the same breath, if you or any future group of Pearls of Wisdom can bring light to the questions or rebuts, or add to them positively in any way … *we will have the next building block.*

And so on … brick by *precious brick.*

Now that you have heard and studied this very ad hoc *proto-Plan* and thought about all the challenges and inevitable tough questions … *that have already arisen,* including the expected howling objections, it will be up to you to move onward, *and … well … certainly exercise the Choice to do nothing …* or step up and *use* the power of Six Degrees of Separation to *recruit, activate and vocalize the Idea.* Even if that is all you can do. *For now.* You have no idea how powerful you are or how connected you are – *unless you stick your neck out and try.*

Always your absolute choice. Don't let other people make those choices for you. Least of all me. And, incidentally, it means utterly nothing if you choose to do nothing or are convinced you cannot do anything. Yes, People live. People die.

Kids get raped, beaten, and starve to death. They are indiscriminately bombed, shot, stabbed, die of ODs, and sometimes murdered for nothing. It's not your fault unless you did that to a kid.

And it is a part of the natural cycle of life.

However senseless, *evil*, or sad.

In fact, life itself is barren empty meaninglessness until we decide to attach common meaning to this chaotic existence.

I have.

I wrote "*Unwanted*" based entirely on my understanding of the Four Cornerstones of Truth. It was how I discovered *They* are what is driving me deep down.

Why I feel so involuntarily compelled to stick my own neck out and articulate this social *defense*, along with roughly designing a thumbnail permanent intervention for the *Unwanted* in writing.

Follow the Voices, pass the priceless message on …

Pen down this very captivating *proto-Plan* on behalf of the entire world.

This book is my expression of the Fourth Cornerstone. My Truth about tough as nails *Love*. A physical contribution, *an exchange of sincere Human Values*, which I am adding to the invisible Foundation to see this *Idea* built into a concrete reality.

You need to choose, *should you accept this critical mission* - What is Yours?

I am an orphan, but I am also a loving father and I need to *know* my lost siblings as much as they need me to try to bring them *Home*. Even if they are not aware of the terrible lifelong burden I carry for them. This book, *for now,* is the only tangible means I have to reach out and rile up a like-minded posse of butt-kickers, in an attempt to rescue the *Unwanted* and bring to them eternal value as an expression of chosen living gods.

Like many others before me, I have wrestled with and fought hard against my lack of genius. Ignored my lack of access to higher degrees of structured education, and completely discounted as utterly worthless the pursuit of my inherited lack of so-called "*Privilege*" and access to wealth.

Regardless … this work, *this ongoing labor of Love* … is the very best my mind and talents can offer. It is not and cannot be an immersive academic treatise … *not by me at least*.

But it is the Whole Truth as I know it.

Exactly like that stubborn old leery Hemlock Swiller exclaimed:

Think a great deal less of Me … Doorknobbers … and a great deal more about … The Truth!!

However, this *Initiative* is way too massive for one small insignificant man *or a steadfastly loyal Hobbit* to contemplate as a whole. Consider adding yourself as a Pearl of Wisdom to help to build the wall of coming resistance, *in your own unique way too* … then this *Idea* might become an imaginary vehicle to launch the greatest leap of all for mankind, a giant jump in forward thinking … *so far* … that someday soon, we sentient naked Apes will land feet-first on another planet. *Permanently.*

This part isn't rocket science … simply redirecting common Purpose for advancing the uncommon Confucian adventure I have labeled - Four Cornerstones of Truth.

People who claim to be *Spiritual* … are pretty much all motivated by either … morbid fear, the covetous adulation of naked great Apes they envy, despise, yet aspire to be like … or wistfully expend meaningless energy longing for an unclaimed hidden promise that they will never receive.

Primeval *Choice* … motivates a Pearl of Wisdom.
Driven to Life Purpose by *actualized* empathy.
Pearls find a Life Path to *Function* through being *Love* and demonstrating *Human Compassion* in this world. A minkey, who is also a Pearl of Wisdom, and … *just loves sharing tasty bananas.*

I have done my job and now deserve the exact measure of salt I shall duly receive after my personal hypocrisies and thin wisdom have been measured together … *against that Recompense.*

Hopefully, your judgment of my writ concerning these human Truths weighs in the positive balance, and you join me and many others so that this treasured message goes out very far and wide, and I get to realize my other secret dream and adopt at least one baby daughter …

If only there were "Gods" … that would be my singular yearning Prayer unto Them.

Please give me at least one daughter to Love.

I will plant Her a garden …

Yes, behind these words is a simple gardener, a fervid farmer, and …
… a *Water-managing Ikigai Monk.*

A reconstructive analyst and an old-school engineer.
A fallback theologian. Greasy-fingered garage-philosopher.
A reluctant poet … pencil chewing scrivener.
A limping warrior.
A Man and …
… *a grieving, lifelong … unrequited Sibling.*

A deeply loving Father.

Those are my inner *functions*. My callings. *My* … inside me.
This book, every last word … *is my Life's Purpose.*

I will return to my gardens, back to growing food & medicine. Having fun and engaging in the senseless mutterings I sometimes call inexpedient prayer to bastardized truant gods too embarrassed to show their inglorious holy countenances around this neck of the woods.

Since I have now completed writing *Unwanted* …

… deep into the whispering vagaries of this space-time continuum We miraculously Share …

It is time to return to Minkeyboy and dearly beloved Minkeymomma.

Doodle away at other weird-assed scribblings and enjoy taking care of those who love me.

My entire life's dream is simple.

Should the Four Cornerstones of Truth become a loving, living, insanely joyful reality in our short lifetimes, I should dearly like the honor of being granted the extraordinary privilege of planting a Sacred Garden in the first free soil my bare feet will ever walk on.

I would certainly ask for permission to seat a plinth for The Third Cornerstone of Truth, carved into stone tablets, and then set down as a monument in that Venerable Place.

Build a *Bonsai En* … and a *Zen Garden* … with a perfectly serene *Koi Pond* …

… and work in that blessed Sanctuary's fields, cherish the orchards, and fuss over the animals along with my tiny little brothers and sisters.

Rise with the sun … to the sound of bird's sacred hymns … accompanied by the wonderous music of my sibling's holy laughter … with *Love* and *Joy* – for all the rest of my days.

Smoke *Dragonpipe* …
… and sip Auspicious Tea.

Yes?

THE BEGINNING … 😊

‡§‡

Bedtime!!

More Daddy, more!
Yes, Daddy, tell us more!

It's sleepy time my little princesses. Time for Mr. Sandman to come and sail you off to dreamies.

Pleeezzz Daddy? Mr. Sandman can wait a little bit … can't he?
Please, Daddy, please? Tell us what happened to Socrates the wise old Stonemason's ideas? And what happened after his Four Confusing Cornerstones?

Confucius my luvvy … not Confusing

No, Daddy, the other one, the long one about Mother … tell us that one!
Yes, Daddy tell us about Mother and the Star Empresses again … Pleeezzz
Pleeeezzzz Daddy …. Pleeezzz

The whole story Daddy!
And how they came to Mars first Daddy!!
And tell us about Mother's wise plan for us all to live here in the Sacred Gardens on Mars!
And how all the animals and plants came too Daddy!!
Yes, Daddy, tell Mother's whole story about everything!!
Please, Daddy, pleeeezzz?

Alright, my luvvies, but this is the very last story … and it's a long story, so it must be the last, last … last one … then it's Mr. Sandman's turn …
… Are we all agreed?

Yes, Daddy!!

Okay then …
… Once upon a Time … Far away into the distant Future …

Printed in Great Britain
by Amazon

86708999R00147